# COINS
## IN THE
# ASHES

### A FAMILY STORY OF GRIEF, GRATITUDE, AND GRACE

### JOE MCHUGH

Calling Crane Publishing
www.callingcrane.com

© 2015  Joe McHugh

Cover Design: Paula McHugh
Front Cover Photo L - Beverly Quinn McHugh, R - Helen Spriggs
Rear Cover Photo L to R - Paula McHugh, Estella Belt, Joe McHugh

Printed in the United States of America

*To Lucy,*

*Spare me those tired mother-in-law jokes;*

*you're the tops*

# ACKNOWLEDGEMENTS

I wish to thank the many individuals and institutions who aided this pilgrim along his way. My special thanks go to the wonderful members and staff of First Christian Church in Olympia, Washington, my wife Paula, my daughters Anna, Emily, and Clara, my son Patrick, my brother Ed, my cousins Chris, Janna, and Michael, our dear friend Kathy Peck, my brother-in-law John Blasius, Carol Piening, Estella Elizabeth Belt, George Scott, Lydia Mallory, Joe Jackson, Alice Graham, Helen Jackson, James (Timmy) Jackson, Vivian Jackson, Gail Lee Thomas, Connie and Al Koenig, Thomas (Ty) Freyvogel, Bert Barnes, Ed Smyk, Giacoma (Jack) Stefano, June Johnson Dobson, Dr. Linda James, Evelyn Quinn, Sister Edwarda Barry, Sister Maria Cordis, Jimmy McManus, Roland Sainz, Roseann Berube, Jeff Kumar, Donald and Gay Reigel, Judy Bushell, Skip Houser, Denise Graham, Brian Walter, Dr. Louis Bloomfield, Bill Evans, Dr. Daniel Siegel, Dr. Bruce Perry, Dr. Stephen Bezruchka, Paddy Bowman, Morris Kosman, Dr. Rebecca Boehling, Robin Bowers, Bill Shrewbridge, Angelica Santomauro, Jackie and Clair Ebersole, Chris Haley, William Wenner, Kerin Shellenbarger, Dr. Laurence Glasco, David Bukovan, Liz Nelson, Fr. James Garvey, Mary Lynne Pitz, David Grinell, Dr. Eva Simms, Elsa von Eckartsberg, Dr. Arwin Smallwood, Bryna Kaplon, the Loudoun County Black History Committee, Wynne Saffer, Bruce Conklin, and Christine Moon.

# CONTENTS

# P R O L O G U E

On a cold winter night in 1931, a lone motorist driving along an isolated stretch of two-lane highway in Sussex County, New Jersey, was alarmed to see hungry tongues of yellow flame licking out from under the eaves of a small building next to the road. The building was a hamburger stand called Aunt Kate's, and the motorist, seeing no house nearby, raced down the road until he found a telephone booth where he called in the blaze. By the time the fire engines arrived, however, it was too late; Aunt Kate's was engulfed in flames.

The owners of the ill-fated restaurant were Al and Anna Quinn. When they arrived at the scene of the conflagration, what they found was nothing short of heartbreak: glowing sparks swirling upward in the fire's vortex, the roof caving in, the walls falling away, the despondent firemen in their three-quarter boots rolling up hoses and stowing axes, nothing more to be done.

Nine months earlier, Al and Anna lost their life savings when the bank in the nearby town of Netcong failed. Since then, they had stashed their hard-earned money inside a cigar box tucked behind a sack of Gold Medal baking flour on the bottom shelf of the storeroom at Aunt Kate's. Now the money was burned up, along with the building.

They returned later that morning to survey the wreckage with their daughters: Ruth who was fifteen and Beverly who was nine. The sky was overcast and the forecast called for snow later that evening. Al handed his younger daughter Beverly an empty coffee can and told her to sift through the ashes to see if she could find any coins. The ashes were still warm and the acrid stench made her eyes smart as she felt about with her little fingers for the hard, round objects. When she found one—the coins were so blackened, she couldn't tell a penny from a dime—she dropped it into the can, where it made a hollow, plinking sound. It was a moment she would remember for the rest of her life: picking through the warm ashes for the meager gathering of coins that was all the money her family had left in the world.

Beverly Quinn was my mother. In 1996, I recorded her stories. I was particularly interested in her memories of her grandparents and her parents and what it was like for her growing up during the Great Depression. Seventy-four and a lifelong smoker, she was recovering from a bout of throat cancer. I had just received funding to produce and host a public radio series called *The Telling Takes Us Home, a Celebration of American Family Stories.* Part of the project required that I travel around the country recording people telling their family stories, not comprehensive family histories, but the anecdotal stories we like to tell at weddings and funerals and family reunions, or perhaps share with close friends or a sweetheart. I had made my living as a traditional oral storyteller for more than twenty-five years, but this was my first public radio project and I hoped recording my mother would help me master the use of the high-end recorder and the digital editing software I would be using.

My mother was a delightful woman: witty, well read, and quick to laugh. She was also, like her father, a natural born storyteller, and I thought it likely that I had already heard most of her stories. I was wrong. For two hours and change she regaled me with one engaging tale after another, painting upon the canvas of my imagination a vivid and detailed picture of what life was like for my family in America during the first half of the twentieth century.

*   *   *

Born in Paterson, New Jersey, in 1922, her father, Al Quinn, was an auto mechanic and part-time driving instructor. He owned his own garage and supplemented that income with a contract with the Ford Motor Company that paid him to pick up newly manufactured cars at the railroad station in Paterson and deliver them to dealerships in the area. Early in 1929, however, the volume of cars being shipped dropped from dozens per shipment to only a few, and this spooked my grandfather. He saw trouble was on the horizon for the automobile industry, so he sold his garage and convinced my grandmother to purchase a small roadside restaurant in northwestern New Jersey, an area of woods, small farms, and lakes popular with summer vacationers seeking to escape the heat and congestion of the cities. Aunt Kate's customers included these vacationers, along with hunters, road construction crews, timber hicks, and perhaps a local or two looking for a cup of coffee and a newsy chat. Sadly, however, my grandparents' bright dream of financial success turned into a nightmare when the stock market collapsed that October and credit dried up across the country. Banks failed, businesses closed, and people were thrown out of work. It got so bad, in fact, that my grandfather resorted to selling hard apple cider out of a shack behind Aunt Kate's despite the fact that Prohibition was the law of the land.

Then came the fire in 1931, and that really knocked the props out from under my grandparents. Aunt Kate's was uninsured and they had no money to rebuild. But, as my mother liked to brag, her parents were survivors, the kind of people who were dogged in their belief that better times were bound to return. And sure enough, after several desperate months trying to find capital to fix and reopen Aunt Kate's, an old friend from Paterson offered to put up the money in exchange for becoming a silent partner and owning the mortgage. By the time I was born in 1950, Aunt Kate's had expanded into a highly successful restaurant and bar, the pride of Sussex County.

As for my mother, she coped with these worrisome times by escaping into the world of books. Behind their rented house there grew an old evergreen whose boughs hung to the ground, like a giant's cloak, creating within a room carpeted with a thick layer of pine needles. It was in this magical hideaway that my mother spent her days reading the novels of Charles Dickens, Jane Austen, and the Brontë sisters, familiarizing herself with the attitudes and customs of the wealthy and powerful, as well as the destitute and vulnerable. This love of reading assured her success in school. She graduated at the top of her class at Stanhope Grammar School and later at the Benedictine Academy in Paterson. She went on to college, the first in her Irish/English immigrant family to do so. After a semester at Wilson College in Pennsylvania, she transferred to Georgian Court College in Lakewood, New Jersey. Originally the 155-acre estate of the son of the railroad robber baron Jay Gould, Georgian Court was the school where many elite Catholic families sent their daughters to be educated and made suitable for marriage. As a student at the Court, my mother served as associate editor of the college newspaper and president of the thespian society. She also became friends with a fellow student named Nancy McHugh, whose family owned several woolen mills in Pittsburgh. Nancy's maternal grandfather, Patrick McGraw, founded the business soon after emigrating from Ireland, and it had grown over the years to become one of the city's top manufacturing concerns. The McHughs lived in a large Tudor-style house with servants in an exclusive section of Pittsburgh called Shadyside. Nancy's older brother Edward studied at Notre Dame.

When the war came in 1941, Ed McHugh joined up, received a commission, and went off to fight with the First Army under Omar Bradley. As a lieutenant and later captain of infantry in an armored battalion, he served in France, Belgium, and Germany. He was wounded three times and received three Purple Hearts. He was awarded the Silver Star for exceptional bravery under fire and the Bronze Star with three clusters. He returned home soon after VE day and promptly asked for my mother's hand in marriage. They settled down to a comfortable life on a small street called Shady Lane in a hilly wooded suburb of Pittsburgh called Fox Chapel.

In 1947, a year after their first child, Edward Jr., was born, my parents hired an elderly black woman to serve as a live-in cook and maid and someone to look after young Teddy. Her name was Helen. I was born two and a half years later in 1950, and Helen cared for me as well. This was at a time when formula feeding was in vogue among middle class families and neither Ted nor I were breast-fed. Instead, Helen prepared our bottles for us by heating them on the stove and testing the temperature by sprinkling a drop or two on her wrist. She then cradled us in the crook of her arm as we suckled and she sang to us as we drifted off to sleep. My mother shared in the warming of bottles and cradling as well. She also cooed to us, changed our diapers, and fretted when we were colicky. But as the wife of a successful businessman, she had a slew of other responsibilities. She was expected to attend charity balls and dances at the University Club, play in golf tournaments at the Field Club, and go on fishing trips to Canada with my father, who was an avid outdoorsman. What is more, she entertained a steady parade of friends, family, and business acquaintances at her home. It was a busy life, full of unfamiliar demands on my mother's time and energies, but a life free from the financial anxieties she had known all too well as a child.

In the fall of 1951, when I was a year and a half old, tragedy struck our family. Being the sole male heir, my father was in the process of taking over the family business but, soon after returning home from a trip to Boston to inspect and purchase a shipment of sheep skins from Scotland, he fell ill and was taken to the hospital. Two days later he was pronounced dead from polio. My mother was four months pregnant with her third child, and she was overpowered by grief and terror that my brother and I had been exposed to the highly infectious virus. My father was buried on the morning of his thirty-third birthday.

Four months later, my mother gave birth to my brother Patrick, but he was a month premature and only lived for forty-eight hours. This second blow, coming so close on the heels of the first, very nearly destroyed my mother, and she fled to the only safe haven she knew, her books, shutting herself away in her bedroom, reading and trying to make sense of what fate had decreed.

Fortunately for my brother and me, Helen was there. She continued to bathe and clothe us, to prepare our carrots and peas as we slapped our palms on the trays of our highchairs. She played referee when we fought over toys and tucked us in at night with a story or a song. There was deep sadness in our home, but there was also light and love.

Time, it is said, is the great healer and, after years of wandering amongst the shadows, my mother took up the business of living again. In the aftermath of my father's death, the McGraw Wool Company mills were sold and the money put aside for my grandparents to live on. My mother received a life insurance annuity, but she knew that inflation would devour much of it over time. She had to find a job to support us, or another husband.

My mother never remarried. In 1953 when I was three, she moved us from Pittsburgh to New Jersey so she could be near her parents and her sister Ruth. She begged Helen to come with us and Helen agreed. My mother sold the house on Shady Lane and we moved to Andover, a small village in Sussex County not far from Aunt Kate's. My mother found a job teaching at a Catholic elementary school and Helen took care of Ted and me. When I was five, we moved again, this time to a house on East 40th Street in Paterson, and soon after that Helen left us.

Helen was rarely mentioned in the years that followed. There were no letters or visits. It is both sad and true that the Irish handle separation poorly; our history is marked by the suffering of too many forced partings. As for my family, I do not remember anyone ever explaining to me why Helen left or where she went. One day she was there at the kitchen table with a glass of milk and Oreos when I got home from school, and the next she had vanished without discussion or goodbyes.

I assume the social norms of the time informed our relationship with Helen: she was hired help, fairly paid and sincerely appreciated, but everyone was expected to get on with their lives.

"Do you have any regrets?" I asked mother after we finished our interview and I was packing up the recording gear. This wasn't a question I had planned to ask, it just sort of popped out, and it felt a bit awkward. Regrets are a funny business. There are the relatively small, unavoidable regrets that come with living, a phone call not returned or a hurtful remark made in the heat of an argument. We may feel their sting for a day or a week, but over time they recede into the mists of forgetfulness. Then there are those regrets that pierce us to the core, perhaps not immediately, but in the years that follow. Rather than diminish, these regrets grow in strength with the passage of time and come back to visit us, often in the lonely, still hours of the night. We might recall a smaller regret and be willing to share it with others, but the other kind of regret we prefer to keep locked up in some out-of-the-way chamber of our hearts. I know I do.

So what was I asking? My mother stubbed out her cigarette and I could see through the haze of blue tobacco smoke that her expression had grown uncharacteristically serious.

"I have two regrets," she said. "One has to do with Joe Walls and the other is about Helen."

This was far from any answer I might have predicted. Had she said she wished she had remarried or sent me to a military academy when I started to go off the rails in high school, I would have understood. Instead, her regrets centered on Joe Walls and Helen.

\*   \*   \*

Joe Walls was a black musician who worked at Aunt Kate's for many years. After Prohibition was repealed, my grandparents added a bar to the restaurant, and Joe played piano while my grandfather sang songs to entertain the patrons. My childhood recollection of Joe is of a quiet, kindly man with sorrowful eyes. In 1960, my grandparents decided to retire, and they sold Aunt Kate's and moved to Paterson to live with us in the house on East 40<sup>th</sup> Street.

"There was a lot of discussion about what would happen to Joe," my mother said, "because he was getting old and had no place to go. The new owners didn't really want him, but after some haggling they agreed to keep him on. But I never felt that was the right decision. Joe was devoted to my parents; they were all the family he had. I wanted him to move in with us so we could take care of him. But Mother and Daddy were against the idea. They said Joe would be fine. I was working full time and had you kids to take care of, so I didn't push it. A couple of months later Joe was killed when his cottage behind Aunt Kate's caught fire. I've always felt responsible for what happened."

My mother then talked about Helen.

"I remember Helen standing at the door when I got back from the hospital after your father passed away. She knew what had happened, and I was so desperate that I threw myself into her arms and said, 'Please Helen, don't leave me now.' And Helen said, 'I won't leave you, Mrs. McHugh, until you want me to.'

"Helen was true to her word. She remained with us even after we moved to Andover where she didn't know a soul. But after we moved to Paterson, she went to visit her family and didn't come back. I was kind of angry with her, to tell you the truth, because I really needed the help. But she sent a letter and then another saying she had things to take care of, and I stopped writing back. I didn't send her any money or go to her funeral or anything. Helen had done a great deal for us, but I let my frustration get the better of me. That was wrong. I should have stayed in touch with her."

"Do you know how she died? Or when?" I asked.

"No. I lost touch with her."

I too loved Helen and, even though I have only a few distinct memories of her, I have always had a feeling that she is nearby, like a wise and kind guardian angel, watching over me and giving me encouragement as I faced my own challenges in life. But when I interviewed my mother, I never thought to ask for Helen's last name or where she came from. I accepted as fact that Helen had passed away because she was already a grandmother when I was a child, and that was over fifty years ago. So my mother and I reminisced about Helen and that was that.

Three years later in 1999 my mother passed away. We knew the end was near, but the loss, when it came, was hard to bear. She was always interested in my projects and dreams. Perhaps because she had successfully weathered the storms of life, she was the one in the family everyone turned to for advice and to regain their confidence and optimism.

During 2000, I attended several juvenile justice conferences where I gave speeches on how popular culture and the entertainment industry influence young people. Soon after arriving home from one of these conferences, I was in the kitchen doing dishes or making a cup of tea, I can't remember, but the radio was on. It was tuned to our local public radio station and the host of the program was interviewing an expert on brain development in young children. Given my interest in troubled young people, I found myself paying close attention to what the expert was saying, especially when he mentioned a condition called "sad brain syndrome." He claimed that a young child develops sad brain syndrome when the mother falls into a prolonged state of melancholy during the first three years of the child's life.

The developing neural pathways of the child's brain, in effect, "mirror" the emotional state of the mother, so that for the rest of that person's life, he or she will be prone to depression.

That moment was an epiphany for me. If the expert was correct, I reasoned, then the conditions for sad brain syndrome were present in my own life: I was only a year and a half old when my father and brother died and my mother fell into a severe depression that lasted several years.

The interview continued but I was miles and years away. Was I temperamentally prone to depression? Did I have a sad brain? I remember my childhood as a happy time. The nuns at St. Therese's Elementary School taught me my lessons and I spent my afternoons and weekends playing with friends. We were the last generation of "free range" children, roaming the backyards and alleyways of our neighborhood without restraint, ours a world apart from the adults with their cigarettes and jokes and alien concerns—until, that is, dinner or darkness drove us inside.

My Uncle George was fond of taking eight-millimeter home movies, and whenever the camera falls on me I am smiling. So I guess I was a happy kid.

However, everything changed during my adolescence. It was as if an invisible hand threw a switch. I lost interest in school and turned my attention instead to folk music, which in the 1960s was finding a new audience among young urbanites like myself. I bought an acoustic guitar and spent my weekends trying to bluff my way past the bouncers at the clubs along Bleecker Street in Greenwich Village, so I could listen to the likes of Dave Van Ronk and Richie Havens. I did graduate high school, but just barely, and the family packed me off to a small Catholic college in New Hampshire hoping that the good fathers would turn this fatherless youth around.

I liked college and was drawn to the natural beauty of New England. Best of all, I was given the opportunity to host a weekly evening show on the college radio station, where I could share the music I loved with my fellow students: artists such as Blood Sweat and Tears, The Jefferson Airplane, and Bob Dylan. And I might have stayed, but the year was 1968 and the world beyond the college's walls was being turned upside down by political assassinations, antiwar rallies, and race riots. There were also outdoor rock concerts, communes with teepees, roving troupes of actors and musicians, and my youthful, restless soul was powerless to resist these siren calls. So I packed my bags, bid the priests goodbye, and set out to hitchhike around the country, wintering first in Florida and then wandering back and forth across the Midwest. I eventually returned home to Paterson and worked through a summer selling ice cream from the back of a truck with the words Frosty Maid painted on the side. With the money I earned, I purchased a used VW van and drove it across the country to California where I learned how to make custom leather belts, purses, and sandals and sell them on the sidewalk in front of Cody's Bookstore on Telegraph Avenue in Berkeley.

Six months later, I moved up the coast to Oregon and traded my van to a farmer for a vintage school bus he once used to transport raspberry pickers. I converted the bus into a traveling leather shop with an old-fashioned wood cook stove and living quarters in the rear. I then drove the bus across the country, stopping for a day or a week in college towns along the way to peddle my leather goods. After some months of this pleasant vagabonding, I wound up in the mountains of West Virginia where, with a loan from the Kanawha Union Bank, I purchased an eighty-acre farm with a house and three barns for the princely sum of six thousand dollars. I also took over the recently closed shoe repair shop in the nearby town of Glenville. The previous owner, an elderly Italian man named Camelo Nocida, sold me his shoe repair equipment and the business for no money down and taught me the trade for free. He became a second father to me.

Next I got into a tussle with the Monongahela Power Company over a twenty-five dollar deposit, and they turned off the electricity to my farm. Thus for the next four and a half years I lived without electricity, although I did have power in my shop in town.

Understandably, my mother was seriously distressed by what was happening to her youngest child. It must have seemed to her as if I had been taken over by aliens, like one of those movies that scared me when I was a youngster: Invasion of the Body Snatchers, or maybe Invaders from Mars.

Yet despite this, my mother never lost faith in me. She was sure I would come around in the end and she even braved the lengthy drive to West Virginia through countless steep hairpin turns just to see how her son was faring.

My brother, by comparison, made his way successfully through college and went on to earn a law degree. All my first cousins graduated from college as well, and each found steady, well-paid jobs. Like my brother, each got married and settled down to the joys and challenges of a middle-class existence.

As for me, from age seventeen until my mid-twenties, I was a long-haired, self-styled mystic, perpetually broke, one of a small group of back-to-the-land urban refugees hiding out in the hollers of the Appalachian Mountains, growing organic vegetables and waiting for society to collapse under the weight of its mindless consumerism, war mongering, and disregard for the environment.

I learned to play the fiddle and the banjo. By luck or the decree of fate, the town of Glenville hosted one of the best old-time music festivals in the country. It took place in June and young folk musicians from all over the country traveled to Glenville to learn the old tunes from a handful of elderly men and women who had received their music, not from the radio or recordings, but from their mothers and fathers, their uncles and aunts. It was authentic American roots music, simple and unadorned, but imbued with a unique and potent mythical energy that reached back to the days when Europeans first made their way up into those ancient, trackless mountains.

I have many fond memories from that period in my life in West Virginia. But there were bad times, too: a pair of romantic disasters, the suicide of a friend and fellow back-to-the-lander, and the tragic murder of another friend. I was also separated from two children I dearly loved.

I have never been suicidal, which is perhaps interesting given my candidacy for having a sad brain, but those stretches of pain, confusion, and self-doubt wrought a profound change in me that helped me see what was truly important in life. One of those things was traditional music because it gave me the strength and joy to persevere. I was so taken with the music, in fact, that I eventually sold my farm and moved to Scotland, so I could study the fiddle music of the Highlands, while working at a home for mentally disabled adults.

After a time my mother was diagnosed with cervical cancer and I returned to the United States to be near her as she underwent months of treatment until she was cured.

So these were some of my thoughts that day in 2000 after listening to the brain development expert on the radio. And all mixed up with these reflections was the reality of Helen and the possibility that, during those early, formative years when my mother was emotionally unavailable, she had stepped in to make sure I would have the psychological and spiritual capacity to handle whatever challenges fate threw my way. Helen had, in other words, saved me from having a sad brain. I used the word "possibility," because I understood very little about the mind, the brain, and the formation of neural pathways in response to cues from one's caregivers.

All the same, a plan took shape in my mind: I would try to find Helen's family and thank them for everything that Helen did for my family and me. During the interview, my mother mentioned that Helen raised children of her own before coming to work for us. Where were they now, I wondered? Where were the grandchildren, the nephews and nieces? Would it be possible to locate them? I imagined myself knocking on their door one day and saying something like: "Hi, I'm Joe McHugh. You don't know me, but your grandmother Helen saved my life."

How would they respond? Would they welcome me into their home? Would they tell me stories about Helen, show me pictures of her?

I had only one photograph of Helen. It was glued to a page inside my baby book and showed Helen in a starched white uniform sitting on a couch watching me play with toy cowboys and Indians that are spread out on a coffee table. Underneath, written in my mother's hand, is "Christmas 1951," which means I am not quite a year old and my father is still with us. (On the next page under the headings for First discovered his own hands, First sat up, and First dressed alone, my mother wrote, "His nickname, given by Helen, is 'Pretty Eyed Baby.'")

There was, however, a problem with my plan. I never asked my mother for Helen's surname, or where she came from. She had always been just "Helen."

So I called my brother on the phone later that evening and asked him if he knew Helen's last name.

"No," he said. "We just called her Helen. Why do you ask?"

I told him about sad brain syndrome and explained that I wanted to find Helen's family.

"Do you know if she was from Pittsburgh?"

"I don't think so. She might have come from Maryland, but I don't know why I think that."

"I thought I heard she was from South Carolina," I said.

"Your guess is as good as mine."

"Would anyone else in the family know her last name?"

"Try Aunt Nancy. She'll know if anyone does."

My father's sister lives in a retirement community just north of Chicago. Her husband died some years ago, and she is the last of her generation in the family. I got Aunt Nancy on the telephone.

"Aunt Nancy, do you remember Helen who used to work for us in Pittsburgh?"

"Oh yes, I remember her."

"Do you know her last name?"

She thought for a moment:

"No, I don't. We had a black woman who worked for us for years. Her name was Lucille."

"Was Helen from Pittsburgh?"

"I don't know."

"Do you think my parents used an agency to hire her?"

"I don't think so. It was done mostly through friends. They knew someone who knew someone. I don't remember how we got Lucille, but I'm sure that's how we found her."

"What happened to Lucille?" I realized Aunt Nancy had not mentioned Lucille's last name either. When Ted and I visited our grandparents in Pittsburgh as children, an elderly white lady would come to the house on Devonshire Street to look after us when the adults went out. Her name was Mrs. Kuhns and she sat quietly in the living room reading a book, her hair tied back in a tight bun, while we watched TV upstairs or tore around the basement on tricycles. We always addressed her as "Mrs. Kuhns." Black servants, on the other hand, were just called "Helen" or "Lucille."

"We gave Lucille a pension after the children were grown and she was too old to cook and clean," Aunt Nancy said. "But I can't tell you anything about Helen."

I was no more successful in my conversations with my cousins Mike and Janna, two of Aunt Ruth's children. Mike is seven years older than me, and he remembered Helen quite well because he and Janna often stayed at our house in Andover. Janna, three years my senior, also remembered Helen, but neither cousin could shed light on Helen's identity or place of origin.

So I reluctantly gave up the idea of finding Helen's family and turned my attention to other projects, and the years passed.

Then late one night in 2008, my cousin Chris, the youngest of Aunt Ruth's three children, called me on the telephone from his home in Connecticut. He had come across a box of letters among his late mother's belongings. Many of the letters were written by my mother and mailed to Ruth or my grandmother, Nanny. Chris picked a letter out of the bundle at random and read it to me over the phone. We had never discussed my desire to find Helen's family because he was too young to have remembered her. I am also quite sure Mike and Janna never mentioned it to him, nor did my brother.

The letter began with news about a snowstorm in Pittsburgh and a party my mother attended. Then my cousin read this paragraph:

> *"On Sunday Helen got a message that her grandson burned to death down in Maryland. He was only nineteen and had a child himself under a year old. She left immediately for home and I got a message later that he burned in her house, so she is staying down there for a week to ten days to collect her insurance."*

I was shocked and elated at the same time. I asked if there was an envelope with the letter and he said there was. Could he make out the postmark?

"It's faded," he said. "It's either April 25th or the 28th, 1952. It's hard to tell."

My thoughts raced. Would it be possible to find Helen's family with just this scrap of information? I still didn't know her last name and, if the young man who died in the fire was her daughter's son, then he would have had a different last name. There was, however, one thing in my favor: Maryland is a small state.

The next morning I spoke with an archivist at the Maryland State Archive, and he told me I had too little information for them to be of any help. He suggested I consult newspapers from 1952 to see if I could find an obituary or a news article about a house fire that might lead me to Helen's family. He recommended I visit the Library of Congress because the library had microfiche copies of all the Maryland newspapers.

Then a friend who is a college professor suggested I hire an historian in Washington, DC, to conduct the initial research. An academic, he assured me, would have the proper training and, if he or she came up empty-handed, I would have saved myself the cost of the trip and a great deal of time. Failure was, I had to admit, a real possibility given the subject of my inquiry: a poor, young black man who met his end in some unknown town in Maryland in 1952. All the same, I was loath to outsource the work. As a boy I devoured many of the Hardy Boys detective novels, and now fate had handed me a real mystery. It was up to me to solve it.

However, I couldn't do anything for several months because I had two audio projects to complete and, as the weeks passed, a desire grew within me to expand the scope of my quest. I wanted very much to find Helen's family, if that was possible, but I also wanted to learn more about my mother's early life, to walk in her footsteps and experience the world, if only slightly, as she did. She had provided me with a wealth of stories the day I interviewed her, which taken together constituted a kind of map. I would begin my journey by visiting Hell's Kitchen in New York City, the rough and tumble neighborhood where my maternal grandfather was born and raised. Then I would visit Paterson, where my mother and grandmother were born, and Sussex County where my mother fell in love with books and picked through the warm ashes of a fire to find blackened coins. From there, I would travel to Georgian Court, now a university and, if possible, talk to some of the elderly nuns who still lived on the campus. It was a long shot, but perhaps a nun would remember my mother. I would then head south to Washington, D.C., to see what I could learn at the Library of Congress.

I also wanted to visit Pittsburgh and learn about my father's life before it was cut short by polio. I wanted to visit Shady Lane, the street where we lived in Fox Chapel, and the Field Club where my father and paternal grandfather played golf and hobnobbed with the upper crust of Pittsburgh society. I also wished to see if the woolen mills were still standing and talk to some of the descendants of the men and women who once worked in the mills and whose sweat and toil enabled an Irish immigrant family to succeed in America.

I knew remarkably little about the Pittsburgh side of my family, even though we visited my grandparents in that smoke-shrouded city at least twice a year up throughout my youth. But no one ever told me stories about my father or the McGraw Wool Company. Perhaps those memories were too painful to share, even decades later.

Of one thing I was sure: I wanted more than raw information—birth certificates, census records, data of that sort. I hungered for the stories that would give meaning to the information, to gather and weave the disparate narrative threads from my family's past into a cloth from which I might make a garment of understanding, like my namesake's coat of many colors. What was it all about, the struggle and yearning, the grand dreams and bitter disappointments? How did my mother and Helen fit into all of it?

I once read that the primary purpose of a legacy is to provide the person who receives it the means to properly say goodbye. This sounds simple, saying goodbye, but of course it seldom is. Sometimes we need to take time off from work to grieve or to visit old haunts or to patch up a disagreement with a sibling. We might spread ashes on a mountaintop or the surface of a cherished lake. One way or another, our task is to bring the universe back into balance so that each ending leads to a new beginning. A legacy can give us the time and space we need for reflection and the rituals of leave-taking and commemoration. And there was the unfinished business of my mother's regret regarding Helen. With luck, I might be able to complete that circle for her as well.

I decided to trust my intuition and follow the story both physically and psychologically from beginning to end, like the proper reading of a novel, no cheating by jumping to the last pages to see how it all works out. Maybe the end needs to be unresolved, a cautionary tale about how culture, class, and race will separate us if we allow them to.

But my heart told me that I would find Helen. And not just her descendants, but in some essential way, I would find her, my other mother.

I also hoped I would learn something about myself and how families—perplexing and unpredictable as they often are—can serve as crucibles in which our personalities and very souls are fashioned. I owe these two remarkable women, these two mothers, a great debt. The journey and the writing of this book are but partial payment.

Joe McHugh, 2009, Olympia, Washington

# CHAPTER 1

## THE TEN O'CLOCK DUNNIGAN

*"So it goes like it goes and the river flows,*
*And time it rolls right on,*
*And maybe what's good gets a little bit better,*
*And maybe what's bad gets gone."*

—Lyrics by David Shire & Norman Gimbel

My mother's hazel eyes shone with pleasure and pride whenever she talked about Hell's Kitchen, the neighborhood in New York City where her father, Al Quinn, the man I called Poppy, was born and raised. She could have just as easily felt shame, because for much of its history Hell's Kitchen was synonymous with poverty and crime. Roughly speaking, it is a district on the west side of Manhattan between 34th and 59th Streets, and between Eighth Avenue and the Hudson River. Early Dutch settlers called it the Vale of Flowers because of the wild blossoms that blanketed its meadows in summer. The Vale was home to mostly small farms until the building of the Hudson River Railroad in 1851, which brought in industry and legions of workers with families in tow, fresh off the boat from Ireland and Germany. By the time Poppy was born in 1892, the neighborhood was a jumble of tenement buildings, slaughterhouses, glue factories, lumberyards, distilleries, and stables, flanked by a procession of wharves that combed the waters of the Hudson River for passengers and freight like the teeth of a giant rake.

I decided the best way to begin my quest to recover the past is to do a walkabout in Hell's Kitchen. I also decided to interview Jimmy McManus, the director of one of the oldest funeral homes in the neighborhood. I contacted Mr. McManus because my great-grandfather, John Quinn, was a funeral director in Hell's Kitchen at the turn of the twentieth century. Perhaps Mr. McManus can shed some light on the funeral business and living conditions back then.

After catching a flight from Seattle to Newark and spending the night at my brother's house in Montclair, New Jersey, I ride the bus into Manhattan. I push through the doors of the Port Authority Building onto 8th Avenue, my jet-lagged brain scrambling to process the intense aural stimulation that is New York City: the ever-present staccato of jack hammers, the squawking of car horns like so many excited birds, the squeal of bus brakes as they kiss the curb. Then there are the animated voices colliding and merging with each other: English, Spanish, Russian, Arabic, Mandarin. New York is a city of talkers. It is also a city pulsing with purpose: a salesman flagging a taxi for an important meeting uptown, a mother hurrying her children toward Radio City, a shy Korean couple climbing the steps of a double-decker sightseeing bus—even the street hustlers go about their business with a determination that would make their mothers proud.

On this particular spring day in 2009, my purpose urges me west on 43rd Street into the heart of Hell's Kitchen. Sometime in the 1970s, the city fathers renamed the drug and crime-ridden neighborhood Clinton in honor of a former mayor. This attempt at urban etymological rehabilitation, however, failed to win many converts in the neighborhood, and, as if to underscore this, I come upon a restaurant with the words HELL'S KITCHEN emblazoned above the door. I check out the menu but the hefty prices keep me from going inside. I pass more upscale restaurants and gastropubs, art galleries and antique stores. I am surrounded by young urbanites happily pushing three-wheeled baby strollers down the street, even though the city and the country are suffering through the worst economic depression since the 1930s. All the same, the sun is shining, businesses are open, and nobody has blown up a building in the city in the last eight years. Life goes on.

I eventually arrive at the McManus-Ahren funeral home at 445 W. 43rd Street. The proprietor, seventy-four-year-old Jimmy McManus, inherited the business from his father. And like his father, Jimmy is a district leader for the Democratic Party, one of the last genuine Tammany Hall bosses—the man to go to for a judgeship, to get your kid out of jail, or sort out your union troubles. Jimmy is an unapologetic it's-not-*what*-you-know-but-*who*-you-know kind of guy.

"I'll tell you a story about how reputations go," he begins in a voice cured by decades of tobacco smoke. "We had these boat rides from the schools. I went to Powell Memorial High School, an Irish Christian Brothers school, and we'd go on a boat ride up to Indian Point each year. One time, my friend Donald and I met these two girls on the boat. They were our age, seventeen, eighteen, and we're coming off the boat with them and they said, 'Where do you live?' And we said—Donald came from the same block as me—'49th Street and Tenth Avenue.' And they looked at us and cried, 'Hell's Kitchen' and they *ran!*"

Jimmy laughs. "They actually ran away from us. That's the kind of reputation Hell's Kitchen had."

We talk about the Irish gangs of Hell's Kitchen, and Jimmy mentions the Westies—the most notorious and latest reincarnation in a long line of street thugs. In Poppy's day, the Gorillas, Parlor Mob, Fashion Plates, Pearl Buttons, and Gophers prowled Hell's Kitchen making life miserable for the cops and one another. Individual gang members sported colorful monikers as well, handles like Stumpy Malarkey, Goo Goo Knox, Happy Jack Mulraney, and One-Lung Curran. Burglary, murder, and extortion were so commonplace that one newspaper labeled Hell's Kitchen, "the most lawless area on the North American continent." The police considered some blocks, such as the infamous Battle Row—West 39th Street between 10th and 11th Avenues—so dangerous that they refused to patrol them alone.

For the first time the thought comes to me that Poppy might have been a member of a gang when he was young. I had heard numerous stories about Poppy clearing out crowds of rowdy toughs from Aunt Kate's using his fists or a baseball bat, so he knew how to handle himself. But he never mentioned any of the Hell's Kitchen gangs. He also adored the police. One reason for this was that his father had a twin brother who served as one of New York's finest. We have a portrait of the man hanging in our house, a beefy Irishman sporting an impressive mustache and dressed in a double-breasted, brass-buttoned uniform with a string of medals across his chest. He looks like he would enjoy nothing better than cracking a drunken hooligan over the head with his nightstick.

Poppy's own father, John Quinn, was a mild-mannered fellow, a reassuring trait for an undertaker, and the polar opposite of his law-and-order twin. He loved reading and once arranged a funeral in exchange for a set of leather-bound books published in 1754 that my mother inherited when she was in her teens. He never raised his voice in anger or disciplined any of the children. And there were plenty of children: four girls and two boys of his own, and another two belonging to his sister-in-law. The Quinns took in an additional five when a couple in the neighboring apartment died, making a total of thirteen.

"When the nuns told my father I was playing hooky from school," Poppy once told me, "my father sat me down and said very calmly, 'Now you know, Albert, you're only hurting yourself.' Of course I was hurting myself but I was a kid, how would I know that? What he should have done was taken his belt to me; that would have straightened me out."

The result of this well-meaning, albeit ineffective, parenting was that Poppy dropped out of school after third grade, and for the rest of his life he went to great lengths to conceal the fact that he could barely read or write.

John Quinn was also an alcoholic waiting to happen. He dealt with this destructive proclivity—what the Irish call "the Curse"—by taking the pledge to the Sacred Heart, a solemn promise not to taste a drop of the "creature" for a period of seven years. The family maintains that John was true to his word. But as the months, then weeks, and finally days, wound down to the end of the term, his wife, Molly, began to fret and she instructed her children to keep a close eye on their father.

Alas, fourteen pairs of eyes were simply not enough for John always found his chance to steal away undetected and go on a bender. Three days later he reappeared: clothes disheveled, money spent, and his memory scoured clean of where he had been or what he had done. Then John Quinn would march straight down to the church and take the pledge again for another seven years. He went on like this until the day he died in his mid-eighties.

Molly, meanwhile, was not without her own idiosyncrasies. One was her compulsion to change all the furniture in the apartment every five years. It worked like this: at breakfast one morning she would announce to the family that she was going shopping. She donned her best hat, gathered up her purse, and strode off through the bustling streets of Hell's Kitchen with the pertinacity of a bull terrier. Later that afternoon a horse-drawn van would pull up in front of their building and a pair of stocky workmen would begin the arduous task of lugging every stick of the Quinns' "dated" furniture down the narrow stairs and out onto the sidewalk. They would then carry up the new, replacement furniture. It was an expensive bit of fancy, but John never protested—the wise know that marital harmony has its price—and life in the Quinn household went on the same as before, only now the furnishings were ever so new.

"People romanticize the cold water flat today," Jimmy tells me, "but back then it was rough living. When my father was young, there wasn't any indoor plumbing. Instead, there was an outhouse in the yard behind the tenement, along with a water tap. A washtub hung on the wall in the kitchen. That's what you took a bath in, and you heated the water on a potbelly stove, which meant you had to carry a large barrel of coal up four or five flights of stairs. When I was a kid, twenty cents worth of coal filled the barrel, and it was a real job carrying the barrel up that many stairs, I can tell you."

The photographer Jacob Riis comes to mind and the pictures he took of the tenements from that period. I try to imagine how difficult life must have been for the people of Hell's Kitchen: the crowding, disease, drunken brawls, prostitution, and political cronyism. But I never heard these stories growing up. Not even the "You-kids-today-have-it-so-easy, why-when-I-was-growing-up…" bromide. Instead, Poppy regaled us with funny stories, as if his childhood were one grand adventure, which perhaps in his memory it was. The Irish, by necessity, have learned how to conceal the soiled rags of hardship beneath the bright fabric of humor, and Poppy was no exception.

However, there was one story that Poppy told whenever his sisters came to visit that gave us a flavor of the conditions he knew as a child. I met my great aunts only a couple of times and remember them as very proper Irish ladies in dark, old-fashioned dresses above black shoes with thick heels. They held their teacups in their laps and stiffened whenever Poppy reminisced about their lives growing up in Hell's Kitchen. Each was understandably proud of having escaped the squalor and indignities of the "Old Neighborhood," as they called it, for nice, respectable homes in New Jersey and the Bronx. Therefore, they did not appreciate it when Poppy brought up the Ten O'Clock Dunnigan, which I suspect he did just to nettle them.

"Oh, Al, you know that's not true." Great-aunt Agnes would protest.

"There was no such thing as the Ten O'Clock Dunnigan," Great-aunt Nellie would exclaim, vexation knitting her brows. "You just want to shock everyone."

But Poppy was seldom hushed, and with his blue eyes sparkling, he would launch into the tale.

"When I was a kid, there were no indoor toilets, so everybody used chamber pots."

At this Great-aunt Agnes would retreat to the kitchen to wash out her cup, while Great-aunt Nellie rummaged in her purse looking for a handkerchief, now seemingly deaf to anything Poppy might say.

"We were supposed to carry the pots downstairs and dump them in the outhouse in the yard. Well, every night, at exactly ten o'clock, the streets of Hell's Kitchen would empty. There'd be nobody on the stoops or strolling down the sidewalks. Then people in the buildings up and down the street would push open their windows and fling out the contents of their chamber pots. In the neighborhood we called it the Ten O'Clock Dunnigan."

As a youngster, I was fascinated by this earthy intelligence and my mind's eye beheld cascading yellow streams splashing into gutters filled with horse manure and tobacco spittle. How different Poppy's world was from the one I knew in 1960, where sparkling porcelain toilets flushed every time I pushed the chrome handle, and mermaids and sea horses cavorted across the bottom of the plastic shower curtain.

"Funeral directors were respected," Jimmy says by way of helping me place the Quinns in the pecking order of Hell's Kitchen. "They were a level above the workers, the people who worked the docks, dug ditches, took in laundry, or worked in the slaughterhouses. They were businessmen and always walked around in shirts and ties. Back then, undertakers usually buried the people from their houses. Most had a little store but they'd lay out in the homes. They'd have to drag up all the chairs, the whole bit, and set up a funeral parlor in the living room. Then, of course, the wake went on for three nights and nobody slept. A big bouquet of flowers would be put on the front stoop of the apartment building to tell people in the neighborhood that somebody there had passed away, and that a wake was going on. The whole neighborhood would come. As I said, it was twenty-four hours a day for three days. Funeral homes like we have today in the city are really only fifty to sixty years old. Before that the undertaker did the embalming right in the bed, in the apartment."

Nearing the end of our conversation, I return to the subject of criminality in Hell's Kitchen and ask Jimmy how the community protected itself from the predatory impulses of some of its residents.

"The criminals were mostly in bookmaking. We did have hit men, but they were the best ones with the senior citizens. They'd go to the stores for them, you know, and bring their food up to their apartments."

"But what did you do when someone was just mean, if he had his wires crossed and didn't care about anybody?"

Jimmy lights a cigarette, and, after a couple of puffs, he replies, "I'll give you a good example. He's still alive. A guy named Lenny. Lenny was a terrible drunk. I remember his poor mother. Beautiful skin, I'll never forget it. A little chubby woman, but her skin was as white and pure, and she would say, 'My poor Lenny.'

"Well, poor Lenny, he started fights with everybody, robbed cars, did everything. And so they told him he couldn't do it in the neighborhood.

"'We don't care what you do outside the neighborhood,' they told him, 'but you don't do it here.'

"But you couldn't tell Lenny anything. Never won a fight in his life, but he never laid down. He always got up. So they took him up to the roof and threw him off."

Jimmy shakes his head before taking another drag on his cigarette.

"What happened is, they threw him in the back and he hit the clothes lines going down, so it didn't kill him, but it damaged his brain and his movements. And he's very crippled today. But that's what they did. They gave him warnings, you know, plenty of warnings, but eventually they got fed up. He was a nasty son-of-a-bitch, and they just threw him off the roof."

Packing up my recording gear and bidding Jimmy goodbye, I continue my circuit of the neighborhood. I walk past a number of theaters and restaurants until I come upon the Actor's Studio where Marlon Brando, Marilyn Monroe, and Robert De Niro cut their thespian teeth. I begin to see the connection between Hell's Kitchen and the theatrical world in Poppy's early life, and, by extension, perhaps my own. Poppy was gifted with a fine tenor voice and he always found an opportunity at family get-togethers to launch into a song. He didn't sing traditional Irish ballads—there was no "Mother Machree" or "Danny Boy," not even the Americanized "When Irish Eyes Are Smiling." Instead, he preferred the Tin-Pan Alley songs of his youth, songs such as "What Goes Up, Must Come Down" and "Life is Just a Bowl of Cherries."

My mother's favorite story about Poppy took place when he was fifteen years old. He had no interest in his father's undertaking business, so he took a job with a wigmaker who plied his trade among the leading vaudevillians of the day. One evening Poppy was navigating his way through the crush of performers and stagehands backstage at a theater near Times Square. He was balancing several wig boxes, one on top of the other, and singing a popular ditty of the day.

At that moment, the actress Elsie Janis stepped out of her dressing room into the passageway. Miss Janis was a headliner on the vaudeville circuit who regularly performed on the Broadway and London stage. She would go on to entertain troops on the front lines during World War I and be immortalized as "the sweetheart of AEF" (American Expeditionary Force) and end her career as a film actress and screenwriter in Hollywood.

"Come in here, young man," she said to my grandfather. "I want to talk to you."

Poppy recognized the vaudeville star from the posters and dutifully obeyed the royal summons. He was a vigorous young man, straight of limb, with thick dark wavy hair, and fine Celtic features—the spitting image of James Cagney if early photographs are to be trusted. But Miss Janis was concerned only with his voice.

"Sing another song for me," she said.

"What kind of song?"

"Anything. I just want to hear you sing. Don't be shy."

So Poppy began a song, one I heard him sing many times over the years:

> *"Paddle your own canoe,*
> *After tonight we're through,*
> *If you think you're going to two-time me,*
> *This is one time I'm going to disagree.*
> *I've overlooked a lot.*
> *Loving you oh so what,*
> *So just forget, forget we ever met,*
> *And paddle your own canoe."*

He finished the verse and was pleased to see Miss Janis smiling.

"Young man, if you are interested, I want to offer you a job," she said.

A week later the new act premiered. After the jugglers and slapstick comedians had done their best and exited the stage, the headliner, Miss Elsie Janis, made her grand entrance. She moved like an angel in a bone-white satin evening gown adorned with rhinestones that sparkled in the glow of the footlights. The audience, most of them newly-arrived immigrants from Europe with hearts bruised by the sadness of separation, grew quiet with anticipation. They longed for the release of tears, and Elsie Janis, master of the sentimental song, knew how to coax them to the surface. Her signature piece was about a young lover who had gone away, never to return. Like Orpheus of old, he had won her heart with songs of love. But alas, an unkind fate intervened, dashing their hopes of wedded bliss. And her crowning despair was that she would never again thrill to hear his pure, sweet voice.

Suddenly, from high up in the third balcony, a second voice sang out, the voice of the lover singing to his sweetheart. The audience gasped in surprise as they swung about in their seats, craning their necks to see who was there. Then they smiled, some would laugh, and thunderous applause erupted as the rapturous duet came to an end.

The voice of the absent lover, as you might have guessed, belonged to my grandfather. In fact, the novelty piece proved so popular that Miss Janis offered to take her fifteen-year-old protégé on tour with her and give him his own start in show business.

"But Daddy turned her down," my mother sighed whenever she told this particular tale. "His mother thought theater people were disreputable and, besides, Daddy was in love with automobiles. He built and raced them. So that was that."

I step into Smith's Bar on the corner of 8th Avenue and 44th Street for a sandwich and a beer. Many of the older Irish bars are gone now, but in Poppy's day they were the heart of the neighborhood. Like funeral directors, bar owners were respected members of the community. They were independent of the working class hierarchy, answering to no boss, and they exercised complete authority over what happened inside their establishments. Even the cops respected them.

"You had to be a tough character to run a saloon," I recall Jimmy McManus's comment as I sip my beer, "because when they drink, five-foot-six people become six-foot-six people."

So maybe it is not that surprising that Poppy, ill-fitted by temperament for the role of undertaker, would, in the course of time, choose to own a bar.

I make my last stop of the day on 40th Street between the Croatian Church of St. Cyril and a Mercedes-Benz dealership. This is as close as I can get to the corner of 39th Street and 11th Avenue where the tenement in which Poppy was born and raised once stood. A victim to progress, it was torn down during the 1930s to make way for the entrance to the Lincoln Tunnel. Commuter buses from the Port Authority line up at the stop light, belching diesel fumes—the work-weary passengers lost in their newspapers or talking on their cell phones—each bus waiting its turn to pass underneath the Hudson River flanked by stretch limos, SUVs, and taxi cabs. A giant woman caressing a designer handbag smiles down at me from a billboard. Next to her is a second billboard, a suntanned colossus lounging about in Calvin Kline underwear.

My imagination shakes off these Madison Avenue wet dreams and the stupor of burning petroleum to savor impressions of an earlier time in the life of this great city: the rumble of iron-shod wheels over rough cobblestones, the cries of vegetable peddlers and fish mongers, the stench of manure and coal smoke, the pealing of church bells, and the cry of an infant issuing forth from some upper window.

According to my mother, Irish-Americans of her parents' generation came in two basic models—shanty Irish and lace-curtain Irish. Hell's Kitchen was decidedly shanty Irish: working class, tough as nails, and unpretentious. Another story my mother liked to tell that illustrated these differences was about her Aunt Emma, Poppy's sister, "the most lace curtain of the whole bunch."

When Molly Quinn, my mother's grandmother, died at age eighty-three, my mother was attending college, and she rode the bus into New York to attend the funeral, which was held at the Church of the Holy Cross on West 42nd Street in the old neighborhood. Poppy's sisters were all living in the suburbs of New York by this time, and they arrived at the funeral with their children and grandchildren. After the service, the family was sorted into several limousines for the trip to a cemetery in Brooklyn. As it happened, my mother rode in the limousine that was positioned behind the hearse. Aunt Emma, Uncle Jack, and their daughters Mildred and Edna Mae were also riding in the limousine. When Aunt Emma was young, everyone called her Emmie. When she reached adulthood, she became determined to rise above her humble immigrant roots, and so reverted to her real name—Emma—and all the children in the family knew better than to address her as Aunt Emmie.

So there was my mother on the jump seat, facing her very proper Aunt Emma in black dress and hat, as the procession inched away from the curb in front of the church. It was a sweltering day, but the windows of the limousine remained up to protect the mourners from the glances of the passersby. They had only gone a couple of blocks when the procession stopped at a red light at the corner of 44th Street and 11th Avenue. While waiting for the light to change, my mother noticed a garbage truck parked next to the curb, engulfed by flies. Suddenly, one of the garbage men flung open the passenger door of the limousine and stuck his head inside.

"Emmie Quinn!" he boomed. "My God, I thought it was you. Don't you remember me? I'm Tommy. Tommy Shea! We used to walk to school together when we were kids. Remember?"

The stench, my mother said, was overpowering and flies began buzzing around inside the car as Aunt Emma, nearly apoplectic with embarrassment, managed to force a smile.

"Oh yes, Tommy. That was a long time ago."

The man's features became sober.

"I heard about your mom, Emmie. I'm real sorry. She was a wonderful woman."

Then he brightened.

"Remember how we used to steal apples from Mr. Brown's cart when he wasn't looking? I'm telling you, Emmie, those were the days."

All Aunt Emma could muster was a nod. Meanwhile, my mother and her cousins were fit to burst, they so needed to laugh, but they had enough sense to know that Aunt Emma would kill them if they did. The older woman's mortification was complete as she made a feeble attempt to brush away a fly that had landed on her hat.

Then, thank God, the light changed and the procession began to move forward.

Tommy jumped back from the car and shut the door and yelled, "I hope to see you again, Emmie."

They turned onto 11th Avenue, the hearse in front, a long line of cars behind, while inside the limousine my mother said you could have cut the air with a knife, the younger women in agony to keep from laughing, while Aunt Emma stared out the window, her face a mask of wounded respectability.

# CHAPTER 2

## SILK CITY OF THE WORLD

In 1908, when Poppy was sixteen, he followed his doctor's orders and took the ferry across the Hudson River to New Jersey. He was suffering from "quinsy throat," a chronic inflammation of the tonsils that his doctor believed was exacerbated by the foul, coal contaminated air of Manhattan. The doctor hoped the fresh country air of New Jersey would do his patient good, and so Poppy moved in with his sister, Nellie, who was married and living in Paterson.

My grandmother, Anna Heathcote, who I called Nanny, was born in Paterson. Her father, William Heathcote, a silk dyer by trade, was from the Cheshire town of Macclesfield in northwest England, a city known throughout the United Kingdom as Silk Town because of its numerous silk mills.

In America, Paterson was positioning itself to become the premiere silk manufacturing center of the world. But the city's silk barons had a problem: they couldn't figure out how to dye their delicate product a true black. They were successful with other colors, but every time they tried to dye silk black it streaked, blotted, or turned gray, and they had to discard the entire run, a costly failure given that a bale of raw silk during the first quarter of the twentieth century was worth $1,000—a year's salary for a skilled blue-collar worker and twice the price of a new automobile.

The English, on the other hand, had mastered the technique. The textile industry revolutionized in the mid-nineteenth century, and manufacturers moved away from natural dyes that failed to produce bold, bright, long-lasting colors. Instead, they began using dyes synthesized from coal tar, a byproduct of carbonizing coal to make coke or coal gas. The chemical sophistication of these new processes was of a high order, and the English were not about to jeopardize their global advantage in the industry by sharing their secrets with manufacturers in the United States.

Determined to outmatch the competition, the Paterson silk crowd turned to a crude but effective form of industrial espionage, dispatching agents to England with pocketfuls of cash to lure away knowledgeable silk workers—in particular the dyers—from the mills in Macclesfield. The agents focused primarily on the young dyers, sixteen to nineteen-year-olds, who had recently completed their apprenticeships, but who were not yet bound by family obligations. Along with a generous hiring bonus, the agents paid each man's passage from England to Paterson, where the recruits were provided homes and installed as foremen and plant supervisors. That is how my great-grandfather William Heathcote came to America. He settled down, met and married Annellen Hutchinson, and raised a family.

Anna Heathcote was their first born of six children, and she was devoted to her mother, who suffered from migraines.

"She had long, beautiful hair," Nanny described her mother, "and I would sit with her for hours when she had her headaches, and I would brush her hair. That seemed to help ease the pain."

Nanny was also a dedicated reader who delighted in school, and she aspired to be the first in her family to attend college. This dream, however, was not to be, because when she was fourteen her mother died. The accepted story for years within the family was that Annellen died during childbirth. It wasn't until I was an adult that my mother revealed the truth to me.

"She died as a result of a botched abortion. She didn't want to have any more children, and abortions were illegal. So she went to someone, or maybe she did it herself. No one ever talked about it. It was considered shameful."

My grandmother was devastated by the loss. Then her father informed her that he was taking her out of school so she could run the household and look after her younger siblings.

"My mother was an excellent student," my mother told me, "but her father gave her no choice. His word was law. In fact, one evening her English teacher came to the house and begged my grandfather to let Anna continue with her education. The teacher claimed my mother was the brightest student she ever had. But my grandfather was adamant. As the oldest, her responsibility was to look after him and the other children. Case closed."

From everything I have heard, William Heathcote was as dour as they come and thought nothing of saddling his young daughter with all the household duties, including raising her younger brothers and sisters. It continued this way until the youngest entered high school, at which point William secured a job for Anna in the dye house of a silk mill in town.

Now and again Nanny talked about working in the mill and how she was forced to stand in dye-polluted water that came up over her ankles for ten hours a day. In her early thirties, she developed chronic arthritis in her legs. As a child, I was repulsed by how swollen and discolored her legs were. Now that I am older and understand her story, I wonder if standing in all that water caused her affliction.

I made Paterson the second leg of my journey because the city is where both my grandmother and mother were born. It is also where I was raised from the age of five. Alexander Hamilton and a consortium of investors who called themselves the Society for the Establishment of Useful Manufactures (S.U.M) founded Paterson in 1791 as the first planned industrial city in America. The founders' goal was to wean the fledgling republic away from the manufactured goods of England and Europe by developing the capacity to manufacture goods here at home. The investors chose for their city the land surrounding the Great Falls of the Passaic River, which at seventy-seven feet in height, is the second highest waterfall east of the Mississippi, dwarfed only by Niagara. The plan envisioned the falls providing the mechanical power to run the factories, but first the S.U.M. needed a capable urban designer to plan their new city. They settled on Major Pierre L'Enfant, a brilliant French architect and engineer, who came to America from France in 1777 at the age of twenty-three to serve as a military engineer under the commands of Lafayette and Washington during the Revolutionary War. A close friend of Hamilton's, L'Enfant threw himself into the project with great enthusiasm, employing an army of workers to cut down trees and pull stumps for a series of broad boulevards radiating outward from the city center like the spokes of a wheel. He simultaneously began laying foundations for a system of elevated aqueducts to carry water from the Passaic River to the factories.

But sadly, the members of the S.U.M. were, at heart, merchants, not artists, more sons of Hermes than Apollo, and they came to regard L'Enfant's proposed design as grandiose and ruinously expensive. So they sacked the visionary designer and handed the job over to a man named Peter Colt, a relative of the family that would become famous for its revolving pistols. Under his supervision, water raceways were built and streets put in, overall narrower and more cramped than those proposed by L'Enfant. (As for the discharged Frenchman, L'Enfant reworked the plans for Paterson when he laid out the District of Columbia.) In Paterson, factories of every shape and size sprouted up around the mighty falls, their trip hammers and looms toiling away day and night as wave after wave of immigrants from crowded city ghettos and the impoverished countrysides of Europe settled into neighborhoods with names like Little Dublin and Little Italy.

Paterson's industrialists manufactured more than just silk. One factory built railroad locomotives—a Paterson-made locomotive took part in the Golden Spike ceremony at Promontory Point, Utah, in 1869 for the joining of the Transcontinental Railroad, and another was put into service for the construction of the Panama Canal. One of the earliest submarines was also built and tested in Paterson. And thanks partly to Peter Colt, his great-nephew Samuel chose Paterson as the city where he would manufacture his iconic revolver.

Nonetheless, it was the textile industry that made Paterson one of the most successful industrial cities in the world. In celebration, the silk barons built huge mansions on the hills above town and sent their children across the Atlantic to be educated. Notable writers and theologians made sure to include Paterson on their speaking tours. The magnificence of the city's churches, theaters, and department stores rivaled those in New York and Philadelphia. Yet despite the gleam of Paterson's credentials, the working class, as is so often the case, struggled with exploitation and poverty.

Perhaps the most significant event in the city's history was the great industrial strike of 1913. Twenty-five thousand silk workers walked out of the mills demanding an eight-hour workday, a twelve-dollar minimum weekly wage, and an end to child labor. The strike organizers, the Industrial Workers of the World—nicknamed the "Wobblies" or the "I Won't Works"—brought in popular laborites such as Elizabeth Gurley Flynn and Big Bill Haywood to fire up the workers at huge rallies. The police arrested Elizabeth Gurley Flynn at one such demonstration, which triggered a riot. Mounted police went to work with their nightsticks, but the workers refused to disperse. Instead, they followed after Mrs. Flynn, a marching mass of solidarity and outrage, as she was transported to the police station in a paddy wagon. The mayor of Paterson was a doctor named Andrew McBride—his grandson Eugene was my best friend when I was growing up—and, at the urging of the mill owners, McBride forbade the striking workers from their holding meetings in the city. The strikers, however, remained undeterred, and simply shifted their operations to the adjoining town of Haledon where the mayor was a socialist and the lone policeman weighed a scant ninety pounds.

The bitter strike lasted through the spring and most of the summer of 1913. In the end, hunger compelled the coalition of strikers to capitulate. Reprisals were swift—some workers were blacklisted, and those who returned to the mills were subject to "stretching," the practice of increasing the number of looms each worker was responsible for. Worse, the strike contributed to the city's slow decline into industrial irrelevance as one textile mill after another moved its operations to eastern Pennsylvania where unemployed coal miners were willing to work for less. Other manufacturing interests soon followed suit.

The fortunes of the I.W.W. waned as well. The organization would never again wield as much influence in the American labor movement. Yet despite their decline, the Paterson silk strike is widely credited with significantly furthering the interests of labor around the world. What the Wobblies fought for, an eight-hour workday and a world without child labor, were in time realized in the United States and adopted by other developed nations.

I begin the day in Haledon so I can stand on the porch of the Botto House, where strike leaders addressed crowds of protesting workers and their supporters. It is now a labor museum, and the director, Angelica Santomauro, shows me a photograph of the home in 1913, the surrounding fields overflowing with men and women on strike with the I.W.W.

I first learned about the silk strike in the 1970s from a friend who was a labor organizer. My family never mentioned the strike when I was growing up, nor can I remember ever hearing about it in school.

My grandmother Anna was twenty-one when the strike began. I peered at the sea of bowler hats and women's shawls and wondered if she was one of the strikers, a young woman excited by the idea that power might be wrested away from the privileged few by those whose hard work helped create that privilege.

I leave the museum and drive along Mill Street in Paterson past a score of abandoned factories. I stop and take photographs of the narrow red brick structures, the glass windows mostly gone, silent relics of a vibrant industrial past. Walls that were once plastered with strike posters are now covered with spray-painted graffiti. Perhaps the strike was a painful experience for my grandmother, and that is why she never mentioned it. Although she herself was a factory floor worker, her father was management, and this must have tested her loyalties.

My mother told me that there was a moment when Nanny's mother was still alive when the Heathcotes believed they might make the leap from the industrial textile working class to the industrial textile ownership class, a leap my mother would make three decades later through marriage.

Silk manufacturing was ever a boom and bust endeavor, and one Friday afternoon several years before my great-grandmother Annellen died a mill owner visited the Heathcote home. He was a close friend of my great-grandfather William, the pair coming to the United States from Macclesfield years before as young dyers. The man had done quite well for himself in America and managed to build his own mill before the bottom fell out of the silk market.

"Will, I'm sorry to say I can't make payroll," he confided to my great-grandfather, "but I don't want the creditors to get the mill and throw everybody out of work. If over the weekend you can somehow come up with the cash to pay the wages, I'll sign the mill over to you, lock, stock, and barrel."

For William and Annellen, this was their big chance and they did everything they could to lay their hands on the money. They approached family members and business acquaintances, even a neighbor. They called in every favor and debt, counted and recounted their savings, but in the end they failed to come up with the money, and the mill was closed and the equipment sold off.

"Had they managed it," my mother reflected, "the Heathcotes would have been among the very top. Funny how those things go."

On my way to the headquarters of the Passaic County Historical Society, I turn onto Park Avenue and pull up in front of Eastside High School. I began my high school career at Seton Hall Prep in East Orange, New Jersey, where my brother was a senior. But I had trouble fitting in. Seton Hall was a school for aspiring young men, and I can remember only one African-American student, although there may have been others. His name was Henry, and we became friends because we were both members of the freshman cross-country team and discovered that neither one of us was all that competitive. So while the rest of the runners drove themselves to the limit of their endurance on race days, faces flush, muscles aching, eyes stonily fixed on the runner in front, we would hang back in the middle of the pack and lope along side by side. We commented on what a pleasant day it was, or how lovely the autumn leaves were. It was a new experience for me, this not needing, or even wanting, to win, an act of rebellion in some small way against a regime heartily committed to the Darwinian precept of survival of the fittest, despite their avowed belief in the teachings of Jesus.

A year later I acquired my folk guitar and when the weather was too inviting to stay indoors, I would cut class and spend the afternoon strumming away under the trees in a nearby park with a fellow folk musician. Sometimes two girls from another Catholic school would join us and we sang songs and held hands and were happy to be young. But there are other forces in the world, and this reckless behavior eventually came to the attention of the school's Dean of Men, Fr. Giblin, and he showed me the door during the autumn of my junior year. This presented my mother with a dilemma: should she find me another private school or enroll me in our local public high school?

The year was 1966, and, even though my mother was a former history teacher for the Paterson City School District, she knew that Eastside High was in a kind of educational and organizational free fall. Drug use and dealing were widespread, and violent confrontations occurred often, primarily between the black and Puerto Rican students. In 1989, Hollywood adapted a magazine story about Eastside High School into the film, *Lean on Me*. It stared Morgan Freeman as Joe Clark, a principal and former Marine Corps drill sergeant who was famous for patrolling the hallways of Eastside carrying a baseball bat.

I too was anxious about going to Eastside. What did I know about inner-city kids, other than the few I played basketball with during pick-up games on the weekends at the playground at St. Therese's? Would they give me a hard time? Would they beat me up? I really didn't know how to answer these questions.

My mother took me into New York City and had me tested by the wizards at Johnson-O'Connor, the world-renowned educational research institution. Their verdict: your son is bright but has far too many interests. Next we visited a military-style boarding school in New England where the students walked around in West Point knock-off uniforms, but neither of us warmed to that idea. So I opted to finish up high school at Eastside. The surprise, after a nervous day or two, was that I fit right in and made friends easily. I was particularly comfortable with the African-American students. I loved how they joked and jived and talked about things I never heard mentioned at Seton Hall Prep.

As I stand and look at the front of Eastside High, I believe it was Helen's early influence that prepared me for the year and a half I spent there. Had she not been part of my life, talking and singing to me, I think I would have found the environment at Eastside alien and frightening.

*   *   *

The home for the Passaic County Historical Society is Lambert Castle, a Norman-inspired structure of cut stone with battlements and gargoyles. It was built at great expense by a silk baron on the side of Garrett Mountain, overlooking the city. Ed Smyk, the county historian, has his office there.

When I first spoke to Mr. Smyk on the telephone and asked if I could interview him, he was rather curt. I explained my background in radio and how I preferred to record knowledgeable people whenever I had the chance, but he still would not commit to an interview. Hoping to bolster my bona fides, I mentioned that I grew up in Paterson and that my mother taught history at Central High School in Paterson.

This brought about a marked change in Mr. Smyk's manner and he asked, "What's your name again?"

"Joe McHugh."

"Was your mother Beverly McHugh?"

"Yes."

"You're kidding!" Ed said, his voice suddenly brimming with enthusiasm and good cheer. "I can't believe it. It's because of your mother that I became an historian. Really. When they published my book on the history of Passaic County, I wanted to invite your mother to the reception. I hoped to honor her, but I didn't know where she lived. Is she still alive?"

"No, she died in 1999. She was living in Clifton. Was she your teacher?"

"No," he said, "I'll explain. I was in high school in 1959, and one afternoon as I was walking home from school I heard the sound of breaking glass. It was coming from inside an abandoned factory building and I decided to investigate. What I discovered was a gang of young boys pulling squares of glass out of an old wooden crate and throwing them against a brick wall.

"They took off when they saw me, and I went and looked in

the box. It was filled with photographic glass plates with images of people and factories. There was also a typewritten manuscript. I carried the box and the manuscript home. I took them to school on Monday and showed them to my history teacher. He told me it was just a bunch of junk and that I should just throw them away. I was pretty disappointed, but I took them to another teacher and she said the same thing. Nobody was interested. Then I showed your mother what I'd found. She was younger than the other history teachers, and she got really excited. She believed I'd discovered something truly important. She was particularly interested in the manuscript."

Ed told me the manuscript was a transcript of an interview with John Colt, the son of Peter Colt who had overseen the design and construction of downtown Paterson. Together with the glass photographic plates, the manuscript provided a record of the Colt family's various manufacturing efforts in Paterson.

"We'll talk more when you get here," Ed said, and we scheduled a day and time for the interview.

The morning I arrive, the Castle is wreathed in a soft, ethereal fog as if, Brigadoon-style, I have been magically transported to the Highlands of Scotland. I park my car and tread the sidewalk toward a pair of stone lions guarding the entrance.

"Here's something you might find interesting," Mr. Smyk says as he hands me a piece of paper. We are seated in his comfortable office on the second floor of the Castle, a white mist the only thing visible through tall ornate windows. I examine the paper, which is a newspaper clipping. Above the article is a photograph of a woman seated at a desk with a teenage boy leaning over her and the caption: *"Edward Smyk is shown talking over his historical discoveries with Mrs. Beverly McHugh, social studies teacher."*

I am struck by how young my mother looks; in 1959 she would have been thirty-seven.

"Your mother convinced me to donate the materials to the historical society," Ed tells me, "and I wound up volunteering my time there. When I went off to college, I decided to major in history."

We talk for another hour about Paterson in its heyday and race relations in the city then and now. We part as friends.

That evening back at my brother's house in Montclair, Ted hands me a dusty cardboard box.

"I found this the other day," he says. "I didn't know we had it. It might contain something useful."

Inside the box is a small cache of documents, including copies of my father's military commendations, and a photo album of our parents' wedding. Then I come across a copy of the Colt manuscript with a note in my mother's hand clipped to the top.

*"In 1959 a senior in Central High School, Paterson, brought to his history teacher a twenty-five page typewritten account of a transcribed conversation with one of the earliest settlers of Paterson, John Colt. The author of the interviews—initials H.N.—had visited Mr. Colt in August 1873 when Mr. Colt was 87 years old and had taken down his reminiscences. The young student had found the papers and some early glass plate photographs in the loft of the abandoned S.U.M. building and had brought them to his teacher as a curiosity. In 1959 there was no plan to preserve the historic portion of Paterson and the Great Falls were neglected and inaccessible to any but daring children and homeless alcoholics. It was strange to read the recollections of this early Patersonian and to compare the daring optimism of Paterson's founders with the decaying industrial city it had become."*

Much of the charm of serendipity I find is in the timing. For years, I had sorted through snapshots, home movies, letters, and Mass cards, the flotsam and jetsam of our family saga, looking for anything that might help me better tell the story of my mother's life and her relationship with Helen. Then on the very day I interview Ed Smyk, I find a reference in my mother's own words to that happy meeting that gave direction to a young student's life. It makes you wonder.

# CHAPTER 3

*MEMORIES OF HELEN*

I set up my recording gear in the upstairs library of my brother's house. There are just the two of us and a fierce thunderstorm begins the moment I switch on the recorder, the wind-driven rain pelting the windowpanes with such force that I fear a power outage at any moment. Two and half years my senior, Ted was four when our father died and eight and a half when Helen left.

"I'm not exactly sure when she arrived in the family," Ted begins, "and she was certainly a member of the family. But I remember she was with us when we were living in Fox Chapel. So she was there through the death of our father and the death of Patrick, which, quite honestly, was completely a nonevent in my life. I'm not even sure the death of our father registered that much, given how old I was. I wouldn't use the word 'bemused,' but I was a sort of spectator of what seemed to be very serious events, which didn't make any sense to me. Life just rolled on, and the next day I got up and had breakfast and did whatever I was doing, because even by that stage of the game I wasn't in school.

"But talking about Helen, I don't remember anything particular about her other than her kindness, and the fact that I have no recollection of ever being disciplined by her, of ever thinking that she was going to tell either of my parents, or my mother after our father died, that I'd done something bad. She was just a loving and ongoing calm spirit in a household that, apparently, even though I was there and don't remember it particularly, was just destroyed by an unexpected and premature death of a very vigorous and active person, the only son of our grandparents, who was a major participant in the business, which was keeping up the family. And then life went on."

"No other specific memories?" I ask.

"Trying to prepare for this interview, looking for some reference point, it's terrible but the only thing I can think of is that Helen had lost a finger on one of her hands. It was one of those typical sort of prissy ways young people can be where a disfigurement registered further in my mind than anything else. I don't remember ever thinking she was a different color. I will say this: I don't remember there being racial references in the household in any fashion. Certainly we wouldn't have heard that from our mother, but neither from anyone else in the family, about black people and white people. Again we were young, and we weren't going to be involved in that. I just don't remember ever thinking of her as a different race or that somehow we were different. Other than the fact that she had this amputated finger."

I ask about his memories of Helen after we moved to New Jersey.

"She came with us from Pittsburgh and that seemed totally natural; she was part of the family. Then, I'm told, and I remember it vaguely, that some event occurred in her family, which always sort of surprised me because I couldn't figure out—well, we're her family, she doesn't have another family, and that's how naive and self-centered I was—but she had to go back and take care of that problem. And she did and never returned. That essentially is my memory of Helen."

"What do you recall about Mom during that time?"

"I do remember her going into her bedroom and not coming out. She had a suite of rooms upstairs in the house on Shady Lane. I'm sure she did come out, but I don't remember that. Of course, Helen was there, and I'm sure the rest of the family did what they could to help out."

"Do you remember hearing where Helen went?"

"No, not really."

"Did you feel loved by her?"

"I don't know if she loved us. That's an interesting proposition. I don't have any particular memories one way or the other. She certainly treated us as if she loved us. And she was an excellent cook who made ninety percent of our meals. I remember enjoying them as a kid.

"Then there was the fact that she really was, for long periods of my youth, *en loco parentis*, because Mom was either working up at the Stand or was away on her European tour. We were at that point living in Andover and Helen had been accepted by the family as being totally capable and responsible for taking care of us. I don't ever remember anyone coming in and even marginally suggesting that she wasn't doing an excellent job. In some bizarre sense, they basically turned over the keys to Helen, and, for whatever time that was, we did fine, and I didn't feel any sense of significant loss. Life just went on and you dealt with the things a young kid does, which is what toys can you have and what TV shows can you watch and all the selfish things young kids deal with. And there was always Helen taking care of us."

"Didn't she also take care of Mike and Janna in Andover when Aunt Ruth and Uncle George worked at the Stand?"

"She did and hopefully you'll get those stories and hear about their experiences with Helen. I'd be very surprised if they didn't have the exact same experience I had. I mean, she was a remarkable human being, and only now, when you look back and think what it must have been like for her in that environment, that's something we can think about, but we can't understand it."

"I don't remember her disciplining me either," I say, "although, like you said, she was taking care of us a lot of the time."

"After our father died, I'm sure we were spoiled. We may have been spoiled before that, but I'm sure I was spoiled after he died. I don't know whether that actually demonstrated itself in any sort of obnoxious behavior. I'm certainly capable of it. But I do know this: I don't remember Helen ever disciplining me in any significant way. I don't think it was because she couldn't, or didn't do it, but she must have done it in such a subtle way that it had its effect. So in that sense, she was, and still remains, one of the most remarkable people in our lives. It's a shame that when she left we were too young to appreciate her loss. But that's the way life is, and, most possibly, that's the way life will be in the future for people to whom we are important. But that's an aside."

Talking with my brother about living in Andover triggers a memory for me. For several months when I was between four and five years old, I suffered from a terrible case of athlete's foot. Everyday large flaps of white, dead skin peeled away from the soles and sides of my feet, exposing the red, infected tissue underneath. This meant my feet had to be constantly wrapped with sterilized gauze, and I will never forget the sickening stench of rotting flesh and the sour aroma of caked and yellowed Desinex ointment. Despite the best efforts of a host of doctors, my feet continued to deteriorate until they got so bad that I couldn't put weight on them and had to remain in bed most of the day listening to stories about Br'er Rabbit and the Lone Ranger on my little red record player. When I did go downstairs, it was often Helen who carried me in her arms. She would prop me up on the sofa in the living room so I could look out the large picture window at the front yard that sloped down to the road. She also carried me out to the car on the days I had to go to the doctor. She took turns with my mother dressing my damaged feet, gently removing the old gauze, stiff and stained brown by blood. This routine continued for months, which for me being that young, was an eternity. But through it all, Helen was there to help and comfort me.

Then one Saturday evening, Aunt Ruth and Uncle George came to visit and convince the fungus that it was high time to go off and torture some other poor sole. Uncle George was a traveling salesman. During a trip to Philadelphia to sell vinyl wall coverings to a hospital, he learned of an especially effective medicine for athlete's foot. With me in mind, he went to the pharmacy and bought a bottle, because anything was worth a try.

My memories of that fateful evening remain vivid. Helen carried me into the living room where my mother, aunt, and uncle were smoking cigarettes and having drinks. Helen placed me on the couch and left the room. My mother unwound the gauze from around my feet as Uncle George beamed a hearty, reassuring smile at me. On the carpet next to the couch stood a steel bowl filled with a green, slightly iridescent liquid.

"Don't worry, Joey," Uncle George said as he reached his footballer's hands under my armpits and lifted me in the air until I could smell the Canadian Club on his breath. He then dangled me over the bowl and said, "This won't hurt at all."

The next thing I knew my feet were on fire, a current of pain racing up my spinal column to explode as white flashes inside my brain. I tried to scream but no sound came forth, my youthful lungs in a state of paralysis from the pain and shock. Never before or since have I experienced anything to match the agony of that moment. I am told my face turned beet-red, and my mother thought I was having a seizure.

Meanwhile, a startled Uncle George yanked me out of the medicine and bawled, "What in Christ's sake is going on?"

Mom leapt from her chair and rescued me from my uncle's clutches. She raced me into the kitchen, where she put my beleaguered feet into the sink and ran cold water over them. Sometime during all this I recovered my voice and began to raise the roof—my screams alternating with wracking sobs as I fought to catch my breath so I could scream some more.

For poor Uncle George, it was a disaster. Instead of being the hero of the piece, he was suddenly the villain who deserved a brutal tongue-lashing, which Aunt Ruth was more than willing to deliver.

"What have you done to Joey!?" Aunt Ruth demanded as

George fumbled to put on his glasses so he could read the printed instructions on the side of the bottle, something he had, hitherto, not thought to do. He discovered much to his dismay that each dose of the medicine was to be diluted with ten parts water. In his enthusiasm to try out the heralded remedy, Uncle George had poured the entire contents of the bottle into the bowl and let her rip.

This revelation only added to the commotion and intensified Ruth's harangue. My mother carried me sniffling back to the safety of my bed.

For all the agony he had caused me, Uncle George managed to effect a miraculous cure, because from that night forward my feet began to heal. Within a week new healthy flesh had grown over the exposed subtissue, and soon after that I was able to go outside to run and play.

So I am grateful to Uncle George and even more grateful to Helen for helping me through the discomfort and confinement during that time. She urged me to be brave when I had to go see the doctors and comforted me when I screamed because the gauze stuck and tore my skin. I feel a special bond with her even to this day.

I cannot, however, leave the subject of Andover and Helen without relating another story, because it casts a shadow, small but distinct, over the recollections of my childhood.

I was five years old and attending kindergarten at the public school in Newton, which is the seat of Sussex County. In the 1950s, that part of New Jersey was overwhelmingly white, and racist attitudes were commonplace. Our house was a mile from the nearest town, Andover, which was little more than a wide spot in the road with a couple of stores, a doctor's office, a post office, and a summer stock theater housed in a converted old grist mill. The nearest black community of any size was in Morristown, twenty-five miles away. After living in Pittsburgh, the isolation of rural New Jersey must have weighed heavily on Helen.

One afternoon after the bus ride home from school, I was sitting at the kitchen table enjoying the snack Helen had set out for me.

We talked about school and then I asked her, "Are you a nigger, Helen?" I am sure I heard a fellow kindergartner use the word and realized it meant someone with dark skin.

Helen looked at me for a long moment. Then I saw her eyes well up and she turned and went upstairs to her room without a word. I knew I had done something terribly wrong; I felt sick inside. I desperately wanted to make things right, but didn't know how. So I just sat there at the kitchen table with my glass of milk half-drunk.

I do remember talking to my mother later that day, and she explained that the word "nigger" was insulting to black people and she made me promise never to use it again.

Even now, sixty years later, I harbor guilt for having wounded Helen in that way. From the day I was born until I was five, I saw no difference between her and the other people who loved and took care of me. How soon society would teach me differently.

# CHAPTER 4

## *THE DRUNK DOCTOR*

My mother was born at St. Joseph's Hospital in Paterson in 1922, the first in her family to be delivered in a hospital. (As fate would have it, my daughter Emily was born on my mother's birthday.) The attending doctor having been called away from a wedding arrived at the maternity ward dressed in a tuxedo. There were no problems during the birth, but after bringing her baby home my grandmother noticed that there was something wrong with my mother's left arm. It appeared weaker than the right, as if injured. Nanny immediately pinned the blame on the doctor, believing he was drunk and yanked the arm during the delivery. Poppy was so incensed, he threatened to go to the hospital and punch the careless physician in the nose.

Throughout the following year my grandmother rubbed my mother's arm with cocoa butter ten times a day. My mother's arm slowly improved, although it was never as strong as her right, and the elbow jutted out at a funny angle whenever she raised it. Like her parents, my mother grew up believing the inebriated doctor was to blame.

Years later, when my mother was in her fifties, a top orthopedic surgeon at New York-Presbyterian Hospital examined her for a pinched nerve in her right arm. As she shared her medical history with the surgeon, my mother mentioned the doctor who injured her left arm during delivery.

"It's wasn't the doctor's fault," the surgeon assured my mother. "It's a genetic condition. It's not serious; many people have it."

My mother welcomed this revelation, but she was also a little disappointed because for years she had enjoyed regaling friends and acquaintances with the yarn about the drunk doctor in his tuxedo. It was also too late to tell her parents, they were both gone, but perhaps that was for the best since they relished telling the tale themselves.

The Irish can make a habit of nursing resentment for wrongs done to them, real or imagined, and my grandparents were no exception. It is like the old joke: "What is Irish Alzheimer's? You forget everything but the grudge."

My mother spent her early years moving from here to there because Poppy found it difficult to settle on a career. Shortly after wedding my grandmother, he opened his own garage. He also became a new car dealer for the Ford Motor Company, giving driving lessons to well-heeled mill owners and superintendents who bought cars from him. After a while, however, he got bored and sold the garage. He then opened a bar in Paterson that became a favorite watering hole for local politicians, judges, and police detectives. But he was forced to close that business when Congress passed the Volstead Act in 1919, which made alcohol illegal. He then started a towing service and one of the country's first car rental companies. He often lamented, "Had I only stuck with the U-drive business, it would have been Quinn, not Hertz."

At some point my grandparents decided to take a whack at agriculture, and they bought a small farm in the nearby township of Preakness. The plan was to raise potatoes and chickens, but neither Poppy, born and bred in Hell's Kitchen, nor Nanny, the daughter of a silk dyer, knew the first thing about farming. Someone told them that they had to cut the eyes out of potatoes and plant them in the ground to grow more potatoes. Fair enough. So they invited a gang of their Paterson friends up to the farm one weekend to help cut out the eyes. Liquor was poured, cigarettes smoked, and jokes told, as my grandparents and their pals dutifully cut the eyes out of three bushels of potatoes—but only the eyes, mind you, not a smidgen more, so that each was no bigger than a pea. My grandparents planted the eyes the following week and were puzzled when their crop of potatoes failed to materialize. Soon after that, the old barn caught fire and burned down. Next the chickens got sick and died, and my grandparents sold the farm and moved back to the city. Poppy bought another garage and went back to work for the Ford Motor Company, this time picking up cars at the railroad station and delivering them to local dealerships.

Hands down the most popular story within the family from Poppy's formative years as an independent businessman was the day he chauffeured Andrew McBride, the former mayor of Paterson, to the Picatinny Arsenal for a meeting. The federal arsenal was located thirty miles west of Paterson near the town of Lake Denmark and encompassed 1,200 acres of buildings and bunkers connected by railroad tracks that were used for the manufacture and storage of military ordinance. The drive to the arsenal took a little over an hour and Poppy had to wait another hour for the mayor to complete his business. Then, just as they were passing through the gates of the arsenal on their way home, there was a terrific explosion. The force of the blast lifted their vehicle, a big, heavy Packard touring car with a cloth top, and dropped it upside down in a creek that ran next to the road. Somehow Mayor McBride was thrown clear of the wreck, but my grandfather was pinned underneath the car. The roll bar prevented the vehicle from crushing him but he couldn't get out and had to struggle to keep his head above water as the Packard slowly settled into the soft mud of the creek bed, pushing my grandfather down with it. He heard more explosions, men yelling, and feared no one would spot him before he drowned. Luckily, several men did come; perhaps Mayor McBride called them. They scrambled down the embankment and rocked the car back and forth until my grandfather was able to squeeze his way out to safety.

I fact-checked Poppy's story online and discovered that the Picatinny Arsenal did blow up on July 10, 1926 when a bolt of lightning from an afternoon thunderstorm set fire to a tree overhanging a powder magazine containing six hundred thousand pounds of TNT. The resulting explosion and those that followed demolished twenty buildings and rained a hail of debris and live shells over a fifteen-mile radius of the plant. Nineteen people were killed and thirty-eight injured and the damage was estimated at $80,000,000.

Digging further, I came across a website with photographs of the arsenal after the accident. The buildings were flattened, rail tracks pulled up and twisted, and scores of trees knocked down. One photograph shows the burned-out hulk of a car similar to the one Poppy was driving that frightful day.

Then in early 1929, as I mentioned, Poppy noticed that fewer and fewer cars were arriving from Detroit on the train. Sensing trouble, he decided it was time to get out of the automobile business altogether. Someone had told him about a roadside restaurant called Aunt Kate's that was up for sale in Sussex County, about as far back in the sticks as you could get in New Jersey at that time. Sandwiched between Upstate New York and Pennsylvania, it was a hilly area of lakes and woodlands where families vacationed in the summer, and where, each autumn, sportsmen went to hunt and live rough. The locals, often referred to as "hillbillies," were a mix of subsistence farmers, woodcutters, moonshiners, and descendants of Irish laborers who had been brought in to work on the Morris Canal in the 1820s and decided to stay.

It was not easy for Poppy to convince Nanny that they should use their savings to buy this small roadside restaurant. She eventually agreed, but only after Poppy promised that this was their final move, no more jumping from one business venture to another. They would sink or swim with Aunt Kate's.

Throughout the summer of 1929 business was good. Nanny proved to be a capable short-order cook, but it was her baking that made the difference. People drove miles out of their way to sample her Dutch apple, cherry, lemon meringue, and banana cream pies. Aunt Kate's was also the first restaurant in that part of New Jersey to offer the genuine Texas Weiner. Invented in Paterson, the Texas Weiner was a foot-long hot dog smothered in diced onions, mustard, and a special chili sauce.

Sadly, the contagion of failure Poppy sensed within the automotive industry was rapidly infecting other segments of the economy as well, and that October the stock market collapsed, drying up the country's money supply. The vacation and hunting sector was particularly hard hit, and it became a day-to-day fight for my grandparents just to stay in business. My mother was six, and her sister, Ruth, just twelve, looked after my mother while their parents worked.

Then the bank in the nearby town of Netcong went bust and took my grandparents' savings with it. This left them to soldier on as best they could, selling a dozen hamburgers on Monday so they could use the cash to buy just enough for a dozen more on Tuesday. It continued like this for eight long months. Then in 1931, Aunt Kate's burned to the ground. The family was devastated. Shortly afterward my grandparents sent Ruth to live with relatives in the Bronx while they rebuilt the business. This left my mother on her own. She went to the little grade school in the neighboring village of Stanhope but spent most of her time alone.

"I got used to being in the country," she said. "It was plain living. We had an outhouse and there wasn't much to do, but I grew to love it. My parents were always working and there was no one to play with, so I guess that's when I developed my solitary ways, living there after Ruth left."

For several years my grandparents rented and lived in a defunct vacation resort. The place had twenty-four bedrooms, and the only heat came from a massive stone fireplace that devoured a cord of wood every couple of days. My mother remembered the howling winter wind driving snow through the cracks in the walls and waking in the morning to discover her blanket was a field of white.

"That's when I started reading. I read everything I could get my hands on. *Lorna Doone* was one of my favorites, and of course I loved Dickens."

When my mother was ten, the family drove into New York City to purchase restaurant supplies. They walked through the Bowery district where men dressed in suits stood on street corners selling apples and pencils.

"I remember being confused by what I saw and asking my father 'Why are these men selling apples?' He said, 'Because they've lost their jobs, dear, and have to feed their families.' I'm sure we were on the edge of disaster ourselves, but my parents never said or did anything to make me afraid. Instead, my father would say things like, 'Everything will work out; just wait and see.' And I believed him."

They passed a store that had used furniture for sale on the sidewalk in front. One piece was a small bookcase packed with books, and my mother made beeline for it, pulled out a book, and started reading it. My grandparents were forced to stop, but instead of being annoyed, Poppy asked my mother if she wanted it.

"I thought he meant the book and I said, 'Oh yes, Daddy."

"Well, I'm going to buy you the *whole* thing," he announced and then went over and spoke to the shopkeeper.

"I think Daddy paid two dollars for the bookcase and all the books. He could have given me a chest of gold coins, I was that happy."

They carried their prize back to the car, and Nanny stacked the books in the back seat while Poppy tied the case to the roof. They then headed back to Sussex County.

"I can't remember now what the books were," my mother told me. "They were all hard cover, I know that; we didn't really have paperbacks back then. There was a Robert Louis Stevenson, but the rest were popular novels of that period. Most, I'm sure, were way over my head, but I read every one of them. I somehow felt I had to."

"Whatever happened to the bookcase?" I asked.

"I took it with me to college and then up to Pittsburgh when I married your father. When he died, I brought it back to New Jersey, and it was in our house on 40th Street in Paterson all the years when you were growing up. It's now in my bedroom in my apartment in Clifton. So what's that? Sixty some years I've had that case."

For me, this was a lesson about the importance of taking time to record someone's stories. The bookcase is a plain affair with four shelves and multiple coats of white paint. I may have pulled out a book now and again over the years, but the case certainly never made an impression on me. When my mother died, I was living on the other side of the country and my brother had a house full of furniture. I am sure, if not for that story, we would have included the case in the things we donated to Goodwill. Instead, the bookcase now sits in my living room filled with my own books—collections of folktales from around the world mostly. It is one of my most cherished possessions.

# CHAPTER 5

## WHEN DADDY WENT TO COLLEGE

Sometimes when the drinks and stories were flowing, my mother or Aunt Ruth would refer to the time "when Daddy went to college." I might have thought this curious, because I never saw my grandfather read a book or a newspaper. He never talked about history or offered to help with my weekly spelling words. But I was young and more interested in playing baseball or crawling through bushes to scout out enemy positions. So it wasn't until I was well into my teenage years that I learned the truth about the time Poppy went to college.

It began with the fire that destroyed Aunt Kate's. With no insurance settlement or savings to fall back on, my grandparents took on a partner who agreed to put up the money to rebuild the restaurant in exchange for holding the mortgage. He was an old friend of my grandfather's from Paterson and for a time the arrangement suited everyone. My grandparents ran the business and the partner shared in the modest profits. One day, however, he showed up at the Stand with bad news.

"Al, I've got myself into trouble and I need cash. I want to offer you a chance to buy me out."

My grandfather explained he couldn't hope to raise the money in the short term.

"Give me a year, maybe two, and I'll pay you back every cent, with interest."

The man began to cry. "I can't Al, as much as I'd love to. There's a lawyer in Paterson who's buying up mortgages. I have to sell him Aunt Kate's mortgage. I'm sorry."

My mother said the lawyer's name was Calwater—I am not sure of the spelling—but she assured me it is a name that lives in infamy within our family.

"What was so bad about Calwater?" I asked.

"Daddy never blamed his partner. The poor man had no choice. It was due to the times and Daddy hoped he could work something out with Mr. Calwater. But all Calwater wanted was to get control of the business."

"Was Calwater from Sussex County?"

"No, he was from Paterson. Cash was king back then, and Calwater had cash, so he set about buying up as many mortgages as he could. Then when the people couldn't pay them off, he'd foreclose and pick up the house or business for pennies on the dollar.

"One morning when Mother and Daddy arrived at Aunt Kate's, they found a padlock on the door and a notice saying the business was under a court order. Nothing could be removed from the property."

Poppy was beside himself, my mother said. The idea that some rich, scheming son-of-a-bitch was stealing what they had worked so hard to build galled him. So he hunted up a crowbar, busted the lock, and went inside.

When the 18th Amendment was repealed, my grandfather saw his chance to finally turn a profit. Poppy liked to say "you break even on the food and make money on the booze." With this in mind, he had just installed a brand-new set of gleaming brass beer taps that were connected to kegs in the cellar via a spider web of copper tubing. Poppy was inordinately proud of his beer taps and just as determined to keep Calwater from getting his greedy mitts on them. So he tore them out with his bare hands, twisting and stomping on the copper tubing until it was useless. He also removed six chairs, a couple of tables, and some cookware. He had no immediate use for these items, nor did the idea of selling them ever cross his mind. He did it out of spite and damn the consequences, which thanks to the attorney Calwater, were swift and certain. Poppy was promptly arrested and hauled before a judge.

Now, here is where the story takes an odd turn, because I never knew my maternal grandparents to be particularly racist or anti-Semitic. I cannot recall, for instance, Poppy or Nanny using words like nigger, kike, wop, or Polak, although I suspect Poppy did, given that such epitaphs were in daily use when he was growing up in Hell's Kitchen. So what came next in the story was to me a surprise.

"Daddy hired a lawyer named Nolan. During the trial, Nolan made a comment about Hitler having it right when it came to the Jews. Of course, he was alluding to the fact that Calwater was Jewish. This was in the early 1930s before anyone knew about the Holocaust. But the idea was in the air that the Jews were somehow responsible for the worldwide financial collapse and were using it to cheat people out of their money and property. Apparently, Nolan got Daddy excited, and he made some negative comments about Jews as well. What Nolan and Daddy didn't realize was that the judge was Jewish. He found both of them in contempt of court. Nolan got off with a fine, but the judge sentenced Daddy to six months in jail."

The impact of this upon the family was enormous. Not only were the Quinns in the process of losing their business again, now Poppy was behind bars.

Nanny decided to return to Paterson, where she rented a small apartment. Twice a week, she bundled my mother into the car and drove the two hours it took to reach the Sussex County jail in Newton to visit her husband.

"I don't know how mother found the money to pay for the gasoline, but we'd arrive and Daddy would be sitting on a bench in this little park that was near the jail. We'd sit and talk and he'd ask me how I was doing in school as if nothing in the world was wrong. Daddy's uncle was a cop in New York City and Daddy was very fond of the police. State troopers and county sheriff's deputies were always stopping by Aunt Kate's, and Mother would serve them huge three-decker club sandwiches, slices of pie, and coffee, all on the house. So I guess they returned the favor by making Daddy a trustee and he was free to roam the town during the day, sit in the park or go to a movie if he wanted to, but he had to go back inside the jail at night."

I asked my mother how old she was at the time.

"Ten, maybe eleven, and we would sit and talk and he'd tell us not to worry because he had a lawyer who was going to get the business back. Then we'd walk back to the jail and he'd go inside and come out with two huge bags of groceries. I'm sure he got the groceries from the jail kitchen and we'd take the bags home with us. That's what we lived on until we went to see him again."

My mother said this episode was very hard on her mother, because Nanny was a fiercely proud person whose first instinct was to protect her family's reputation. She was distressed in case word reached Paterson that Al Quinn, a well-known personality in the city, was a jailbird. So she went to Abe Greene, the editor of the *Paterson Evening News*, and he agreed to keep the story out of the paper. It also helped that my grandfather was released from jail after serving only a month due to "good behavior."

Thus the family adopted the practice of referring to Poppy's truncated incarceration as the time "Daddy went to college."

As for Aunt Kate's, it was saved by yet another Paterson lawyer who was also Jewish and very fond of my grandfather. My mother tried to remember his name but was embarrassed that she was unable to.

"He took the appeal pro bono and won. Aunt Kate's was restored to the family and Mr. Calwater was sent packing."

I commented on the fact that one Jewish lawyer tried to ruin the family and another came along and saved it.

"Funny how those things happen," my mother mused.

Did my grandfather take it as a lesson not to judge someone based on his nationality or creed? I never had the chance to ask him.

A final story about how life has a way of confounding us in the judge-not-lest-ye-be-judged department: My English grandmother was raised Episcopalian and had precious little affection for the Catholic Church. Father Dean McNulty certainly didn't help. They have a statue of the old boy in Paterson because he served as monsignor, and later bishop, of the city.

By all accounts, Fr. McNulty was a prelate of the muscular variety. When the Cathedral of Saint John the Baptist was under construction in Paterson, Fr. McNulty was famous for dragging his fellow Irishmen out of the bars and making them work as hod carriers and ditch diggers for the glory of the Kingdom. He also patrolled the neighborhoods at dusk, his black cassock flapping, a beret jammed on his head as he strode along the sidewalk. If he saw a young couple talking or kissing, he confronted them, whether they were Catholic or not, proclaiming, "We'll have none of that now. It's time for you to go home, young lady."

He did this to my grandparents at the gate in front of her parents' house when they were first courting. It made Nanny furious.

"She thought it was such a popish thing to do," my mother said, "and my mother saw to it that we never went inside a Catholic church."

But then came this:

"When Daddy was in jail, Mother was walking down the street in Paterson, and she ran into a different priest she knew. He asked her how things were going, and she broke down and told him what had happened and how she wasn't sure how she'd find the money to make ends meet. She wasn't looking for a handout, she was far too proud for that, but she must have literally been at the end of her rope. The priest pulled out his wallet, and even though he knew she wasn't a Catholic he gave her a fifty-dollar bill, an extraordinary sum back then. My mother often talked about that. She was truly grateful."

# CHAPTER 6

## *EDUCATION*

One day when my mother was in elementary school, her teacher took her aside and showed her a piece of writing paper that had been crumpled and flattened out again.

"Did you write this, Beverly?" she asked.

It was a poem my mother had written and thrown in the trash, as she had all of her poems, believing they weren't any good.

"It's really quite excellent," her teacher told her. "I think you should publish it."

This was as alien a concept for my mother as telling her Eleanor Roosevelt wanted her to drop by the White House for tea the next time she was in the neighborhood. My mother was speechless.

"The local newspaper publishes poems," the teacher continued, "and if you don't mind, I'd like to send this one in and see what happens."

Two weeks later, the poem appeared in the newspaper. Poppy and Nanny were over the moon. Poppy cut it out, stuck it in his wallet, and for months afterwards he showed it to every customer who came into Aunt Kate's.

"My daughter wrote that!" Poppy crowed as he pushed the well-worn scrap of newsprint under the poor man's nose before getting him a beer.

"It was as if I'd won a Pulitzer," my mother told me, "Daddy was that proud."

Sadly, I don't know whatever happened to that poem; I would give much to have it.

With her passion for reading, my mother naturally excelled in school. Even though she skipped grades twice during elementary school, she managed to graduate at the top of her class.

"But I'd have to say I learned more about life at Aunt Kate's than I ever did in school," she told me. "My mother was a great teacher. I called her the Philosopher of Sussex County because every evening, after working all day in the kitchen, she'd sit at her special booth across from the bar and people would come to her for advice."

A man who was having trouble with his wife would tell Nanny all about it, and she would say, "Well, you know, John, you spend entirely too much time in here drinking. Women like to get out once in awhile. You should go home and take her out dancing or to a movie."

"You're right, Mrs. Quinn," the repentant man would say as he gathered up his hat, wipe his bloodshot, watering eyes with a handkerchief, and head for the door, albeit weaving a bit from side to side.

My mother laughed when she recalled Nanny counseling such men.

"She'd make the poor guy feel so guilty for drinking, and here we were, the Quinns, in the business of selling liquor."

Sometimes a down-on-his-luck man would spill out his troubles to Nanny and she would lend him a few bucks. Then there were the young women who trusted Nanny to tell them whether they should marry Hank or Arlen.

They all came to Anna Quinn for advice, and so did my mother.

"Daddy was excitable and loads of fun to be around, but Mother was levelheaded and wise. She knew how to read people. It was very hard to fool her."

My mother also talked about Bob Ralbridge, another of her teachers at Aunt Kate's. Mr. Ralbridge fought as a soldier overseas during World War I and was gassed. Disabled, he fashioned flower

vases from spent brass artillery casings, which he sold to the
patrons of Aunt Kate's, while his wife Jeanne, a French woman he
met and married during the war, waited tables. He cut silhouettes
of flowers around the open end of the casings and then stamped
floral designs along the sides. My mother liked Mr. Ralbridge and
she often sat and talked to him about the war and what it was like
to return home and not be able to hold down a regular job. He
gave my mother one of his vases, which now sits on my mantle at
home. I assume Mr. Ralbridge learned his craft while recuperating
in the hospital; for him, there was more to it than an opportunity
to earn a few bucks. With his own lungs damaged and his skin
permanently discolored, perhaps he saw himself transforming an
object used to kill and maim people into a thing of beauty, a vase
to be filled, not with poison gas, but with flowers.

My mother also enjoyed talking to Joe Walls. They sat together
at the bar in the late afternoon; she would drink Coke while Joe
sipped his Four Roses. Soon after getting his license to sell liquor,
my grandfather decided to offer live music at Aunt Kate's on the
weekends. The challenge was finding good musicians, because the
only decent players were black and lived in Morristown, which was
thirty miles away. That meant Poppy had to drive to Morristown
on Friday and Saturday afternoons to pick up a combo and bring
them back to the Stand. Then around two in the morning, Poppy
drove the band home, and sometimes my mom tagged along
on these late night excursions. She said it was exciting to be out
on the empty roads at that hour, and she loved the company of
musicians. At some point, my grandfather hired Joe Walls, one
of the Morristown musicians, on a permanent basis. He paid a
contractor to build a one-room cabin behind Aunt Kate's for Joe
to live in.

Joe was a gifted piano player although he was addicted to
alcohol. He and Poppy made the perfect team: Joe played piano
on a small stage behind the bar and Poppy stood next to him,
entertaining the crowd in fine Irish fashion with songs.

\*    \*    \*

*"Life is just a bowl of cherries,*
*Don't take it serious,*
*Life's too mysterious.*
*You work,*
*You save,*
*You worry so,*
*But you can't take your dough,*
*When you go, go, go.*

*So keep repeating 'it's the berries,'*
*The strongest oak must fall,*
*The sweet things of life,*
*To you were just loaned,*
*So how can you lose,*
*What you never owned?*
*Life is just a bowl of cherries,*
*So live and laugh at it all."*

I have several photographs of Joe and my grandfather together. One shows Joe at the piano with Poppy standing next to him wearing a bowler hat, both of them grinning.

My mother remembered sitting with Joe at the bar when she got home from school and listening to him talk about being a black man and a musician in America. He used to tour with a band that was mostly white, but he was barred from staying in the same hotels as his band mates because he was colored. It was the same with some restaurants; they served him out the back door while the other guys went in, sat at a proper table, and enjoyed themselves. He also talked about having to step off the sidewalk to let white women pass, of strangers hurling insults at him for no reason, and the police giving him a hard time in many of the places they went.

These stories made a deep impression on my mother.

"I was eleven and I remember feeling how unfair it was, just because his skin was a different color. It changed the way I viewed the world."

Years later, in 1960, my grandparents sold Aunt Kate's and moved in with us in Paterson. That is when they decided to leave Joe behind. That is how my mother thought of it at any rate, although I never knew this until I asked for her stories more than thirty-five years later. She said she wasn't fond of the new owners, but she appreciated that they were willing to keep Joe on as the house musician. But then he was burned to death when the cottage he lived in behind Aunt Kate's caught fire. My mother suspected he was smoking in bed. The tragedy hit her hard, and she berated herself for not taking him in when she had the chance.

Regrets are like that: what troubles us the most is often not what we did, but what we failed to do.

In the spring of 1935, my mother was an eighth grader, and the family had to decide where to send her to high school. The nearest public high school was in Newton, but Nanny, despite her issues with the Catholic Church, believed the nuns would give her daughter a better education, so she enrolled my mother, who was only twelve at the time, at Benedictine Academy, a girl's high school in Paterson, run by Sisters of the Benedictine order. The school held classes in an elegant mansion, with carved stonework and expansive columned porches, that once belonged to a wealthy silk manufacturer. Perched on a hill overlooking the Passaic River and surrounded by lawns and mature maples and elms, the school afforded a panorama of the New York skyline in the distance, a setting far different from what my mother had known in rural Sussex County.

The decision to send my mother to Benedictine Academy required the family to make a significant sacrifice. First there was the cost of the tuition, which represented a substantial number of hamburgers, milk shakes, and whiskey sours. Paterson was also far from home, forty miles on two-lane highways that passed through a number of small towns. Poppy had to get up at four-thirty each morning to drive my mother to school. He then hung around in Paterson, visiting old friends, buying supplies, or delivering Nanny's pies to local restaurants, so he could drive her home in the afternoon. Then he worked the bar at night. He did this throughout her first year at the Academy, fixing flat tires when they happened—blowouts were a constant nuisance back then—and during winter storms, strapping on chains so he and my mother could make it through the snow. My mother said he was always there on time to pick her up from school, and since he had so little schooling himself, he always asked her to share her lessons from the day during the drive home, especially whatever she had learned of literature and history. My mother had fond memories of those drives, getting to know her father better, but it took a toll on the business. Instead of pulling her out of Benedictine Academy, the next year my mother stayed with a relative in Paterson during the week and came home only on weekends.

By this time, Aunt Kate's was beginning to make money despite the Depression. My grandparents built an additional dining room, and a year later they added another that was used for Rotary and Kiwanis Club meetings, wedding banquets, and other special parties. The key to Aunt Kate's success, however, was a propitious clause in their liquor license. Poppy was one of the first tavern owners in Sussex County to apply for a license after the repeal of Prohibition on December 5th, 1933, and Aunt Kate's was granted a license that permitted it to be open twenty-three hours a day. Shortly afterward, the licensing board tightened their restrictions so that most of the bars in the county were forced to close at midnight.

Developers, meanwhile, began building swanky resorts on the shores of Lake Hopatcong and Budd Lake that would cater to a more affluent, big city clientele. To enhance their draw, the resorts hired big name bands to entertain the guests. Still, the law required the resorts to shutter their drinking establishments at the stroke of midnight, and this left the musicians and many of the late-night revelers wondering what to do next. So they drove over to Aunt Kate's on Route 206. People also drove to Aunt Kate's from as far away as Paterson, Passaic, and Dover after the bars in those cities, under similar ordinances, were forced to close.

My mother liked to brag how musicians from the Dorsey Brothers, Glen Miller, and Benny Goodman bands regularly jammed at the Stand. They typically rolled in around one o'clock in the morning, and Nanny would go into the kitchen and make them all hefty sandwiches with french fries, coleslaw, and quartered dill pickles on the side. After eating, they vied with each other to see who would get up on the small stage to play. Arriving along with the musicians were tuxedoed gentlemen in top hats and women wearing elegant gowns and holding cigarette holders, the newcomers joining the crowd of locals to drink and laugh until the first gray light of morning. Parked cars often lined the state highway for a half mile in each direction and the bar got so crowded that patrons stood out in the parking lot because they physically couldn't shoulder their way inside.

Just before leaving on my trip, I called the Sussex County Historical Society Museum in Newton looking for information about Aunt Kate's. I spoke with June Dobson, a museum volunteer. June wouldn't divulge her age, although she admitted to being north of eighty. When I mentioned Aunt Kate's she grew animated.

"My mother was the mayor of Byram Township in Sussex County for many years and Aunt Kate's was in her township," she began and then laughed. "My mother got your grandfather out of jail a number of times."

I knew about Poppy "going to college" but that he had gone to jail more than once was news to me.

"A really rough crowd used to drive up from Passaic," June

said, "and sometimes fights broke out and your grandfather got involved. He was just trying to get them out of the joint. But the police would arrive and arrest everyone. Then my mother would get on the phone and tell the head of police that Al was all right, and they'd turn him loose."

I asked if it was true that musicians from well-established bands played at Aunt Kate's.

"Oh yes, they loved playing there. The music was great. Everybody loved going to Aunt Kate's. It was a lively place."

Then she told me something I had never heard from anyone in the family.

"Babe Ruth used to hang out at Aunt Kate's. He stayed with a rich guy who had a place on Lake Hopatcong, but Babe liked his fun and that's why he'd head down to Aunt Kate's. Like I said, it was a very popular hang-out."

Listening to June reminisce, I tried to imagine Aunt Kate's on a Saturday night in 1937. It is two in the morning and the place is packed. A wispy haze of blue cigarette smoke hangs in the air. On the stage behind the bar, Joe Walls bangs away on the piano accompanied by a guitar player, a clarinetist, and a guy on the trumpet, the music nearly drowned by the babble of well-oiled customers. Two bartenders, their white shirtsleeves rolled up, hustle back and forth mixing and serving drinks while Poppy tells a joke to a vacationing car salesman from Hoboken. In her place at her booth, Nanny is sorting bills and dispensing advice—everyone calls my grandfather Al, but they address my grandmother as Mrs. Quinn. Meanwhile, bells chime as a heavyset man playing the electric bowling machine scores a strike. At one end of the bar, a bunch of swells are bending their elbows. The tallest has a white silk scarf draped around his neck, his hair slicked back with Brylcreem, and he is talking horses:

"I've got two Cs riding on Seabiscuit to win," he brags, as his wife fumbles for the Zippo inside her alligator purse.

A little further down the bar is the Babe, the Sultan of Swat, the Colossus of Clout, holding court, his eyes shining, his arm around a brunette—little Georgie grew up in a bar in Baltimore so he feels right at home at Aunt Kate's. At the far end of the bar near the door, Bob Ralbridge peddles his artillery shell vases. Just another Saturday night at Aunt Kate's.

And where is my mother during all of this? July of 1937, she is fourteen years old. She is probably asleep in one of the three small bedrooms that are tacked onto the back of the bar. Or maybe she is awake listening to the music and voices coming through the thin walls. She might even slip unnoticed into the bar to see what is going on. She is not worried about the effects of secondhand smoke on her young lungs, neither are her parents—hell, doctors advertise competing cigarette brands in magazines and on the radio all the time. And her parents are not worried she will develop loose morals growing up around a bar. Not Beverly Jane. She reads books and writes poems. She gets straight As in school. She is going places.

"Your grandfather was a very friendly man," June says. "He loved practical jokes. Everybody liked him."

This reminds me how often when I was growing up I heard the story of "Oh Mae," an elaborate practical joke that started when one of the bar patrons at Aunt Kate's took my grandfather aside.

"Look Al, my wife's out of town visiting her sister," he would begin, "and I was wondering if you know any girls that might be looking for a good time."

Nanny ruled Aunt Kate's when it came to such things, and she made sure women of questionable character were promptly shown the door. All the same, my grandfather would whisper, "There are a couple of school teachers who've rented the abandoned house in the woods across the road, and I hear they like entertaining gentlemen friends."

The man's eyes would light up with anticipation.

"But you'd have to take them a bottle of booze," Poppy would be sure to add, "a quality brand."

"No problem, Al. I can buy a bottle from you, right?"

"You better leave and come back in an hour or so and I'll see what I can do."

So the man would leave, and with the speed of a wind-whipped grass fire the whispered phrase would spread through the bar from one regular to another, "We've got an 'Oh Mae'."

People would then begin filtering out of Aunt Kate's in ones and twos to hide themselves in the woods on both sides of the narrow lane that led to the vacant house.

"What's up, Al? Did you have any luck?" the man asked when he returned.

"The girls are at home and they're expecting you. Here's the booze. That'll be four dollars."

The guy would happily fork over the dough.

"Wait another ten minutes and then just follow the lane up through the woods. It's about a hundred yards to the house. But you don't want to scare them, so before you get there, call out 'Oh, Mae,' so they know you're coming. That's the name of one of the girls. Now, don't forget."

"I won't, and thanks, Al. Thanks a bunch."

Then Poppy would slip through the kitchen and out the back door and steal up to the house. He would stand behind the front door with a .22 caliber pistol loaded with blanks cocked and ready. A few minutes later the man would start up the lane, trying not to stumble in the dark, and when he got close he would call out in almost a whisper, "Oh, Mae."

When he didn't get a response, he would take another step or two and call again, louder this time. "Oh Mae."

That is when Poppy gave him the business. He would shove the door open and shout, "Who's out there!? Are you trying to fool around with my wife? Well, Buster, I'll show you!" And he would fire the pistol a couple of times into the air.

BANG! BANG!

The poor man would nearly jump out of his skin. Then he would wheel around and heel it for his life back down the lane toward the highway. And he wouldn't stop there but he would keep running until he had gone a mile or more, all the while frantically looking back over his shoulder in case the jealous husband was chasing him.

As often as not, there were several dozen bar patrons watching this animated performance from their vantage points among the trees, each with a hand clamped over his or her mouth to keep from laughing and spoiling the joke.

Later the man would show up at the Stand, his shirt soaked with sweat, the tail hanging out, his hair akimbo, and he would hunt up Poppy and draw him off into a corner of the bar.

"My God, Al, it was terrible. A man tried to kill me!" And my grandfather, the soul of sympathy, would pour him a drink to settle his nerves.

"Gee, I didn't know either of those gals was married."

One time Poppy waited in the kitchen for the victim to return with ketchup smeared all over his shirt.

"What happened, Al?" the still terrified man squawked when he saw my grandfather.

"Some guy I've never seen before burst in here looking for his wife's lover, and he shot me!"

"Oh Al, I'm sorry. I didn't know anything like that was going to happen. Swear to God."

Then the truth would come out, and the man, after a moment of extreme embarrassment, would allow it was a pretty good joke. And the next time there was an "Oh Mae," he would be in the woods with the rest watching the next poor sucker getting the crap scared out of him.

"Everybody who was in on the joke had had it pulled on him at one time or another," my mother told me. "Daddy pulled the 'Oh Mae' stunt for years, and only one guy got sore and threatened to hit my father. But even that blew over. One poor guy ran smack into the side of a white ice-cream truck that was parked alongside the highway and knocked himself out."

Most people today wouldn't even consider pulling such a prank; my guess is they would consider it cruel. But my grandfather was not a cruel man. My mother said she never knew him to drive past someone broken down by the side of the road with a flat tire or engine trouble without stopping to offer help. She said he was a "soft touch" when it came to money, too.

"Almost anyone could come into Aunt Kate's with a sad story and Daddy would help him out. He'd act like it was a loan but he knew he'd never see the money again."

What impressed my mother most about this aspect of her father's nature was how he made individuals of people.

"He always tried to have a story or anecdote about them. One that stuck in my mind—it's still here with me—we'd be driving along and we'd see what we called in those days a bum. These were the down-and-outers, the hobos, usually camped out in Paterson under the Eire Railroad trestle next to downtown. They had these dirty, old, long coats on and broken shoes and really looked terrible. And there usually was an empty wine bottle right next to them. And I'd say, 'Oh Daddy, look at that man. Doesn't he look awful.' And Daddy would say, 'You know, Bev, that man was once somebody's baby. He was a little baby and his mother and father loved him and they took all the care they could to find out what would be the right name for him.' And suddenly I realized that this was another human being. He'd been a baby once and very lovable. And it's been with me ever since. It flashes through my mind and I think, this was a valued human being. And you feel sorry it turned out that way and you wonder what might have happened. Maybe the mother died. But that person didn't become a bum. He became sort of a lost soul."

So in Poppy's world, the "Oh Mae" joke was just a harmless bit of fun, a way to make the drudgery and tragedies of life a mite more bearable. My mother's own dark days were yet to come, and would do their best to destroy her. But she had her memories of Aunt Kate's to fall back on. And all that great music, and trips in the car with her father to Morristown and Paterson. And her conversations with her mother, and Bob Ralbridge, and Joe Walls.

# CHAPTER 7

## THE COURT

On the eve of Hitler's march into Poland, my mother packed her trunk, kissed her parents goodbye, and headed off to college. She was seventeen and determined to conquer the world, including all those wonderful and mysterious places she had read about in books: London, Paris, Tangier, Singapore. For her staging area, she had chosen Wilson College, a small Presbyterian school for women located in south-central Pennsylvania that was originally founded to educate the daughters of missionaries serving in China. One reason for picking Wilson was that a high school friend was going there. Another was that she had an aunt who lived nearby, and that, she hoped, would lessen the homesickness.

Even though the national economy remained more or less in tatters, Aunt Kate's had improved her own family's fortunes sufficiently so that Nanny and Poppy could afford the tuition. This earned my mother the distinction of being the first in the family to go to college, an achievement her mother had longed for but been denied.

The first months at Wilson, however, turned out to be a bigger challenge than my mother expected. The course work, particularly chemistry, was far more advanced than anything she knew in high school.

"We received very poor science training at Benedictine Academy. In fact, all we had was going upstairs to the ballroom in this old mansion where the school was, and the teacher would do an experiment and we'd watch. We never did experiments on our own. There were only eighteen girls in my class, and we were the biggest class the nuns had graduated in a long time. Then my father said to me, 'Be a chemist, that's the coming thing.' So I signed up for chemistry at Wilson but I also had had four years of Latin and I wanted another year of Latin. That meant I had a very mixed-up curriculum. But it was the science that really knocked me for a loop. I broke everything. I was hopeless."

She also thought the food was terrible, and this, combined with staying up late studying, resulted in her losing a great deal of weight. Then there were her new friends.

"I had become very radical politically while I was at Wilson that first year, and there was a very small Communist Party, which is hard to imagine at a college for the daughters of missionaries. But of course, Wilson had changed over the years. So I joined the Party, which wasn't active. We really didn't know what we were doing. We just knew we didn't like the way things were."

I was curious what prompted my mother to become a communist.

"I read an influential book about the Panama Canal and how successful it was because it was run on socialist principles. I remember that was a big changing point for me."

I had known for years that my mother joined the Communist Party when she was in college; it was regarded as something of a joke within the family. But how bought in was she?

I asked her what she thought of Russia and Stalin at the time?

"I didn't think of Russia in that sense too much. I was more or less concerned with our country and socialism. But the only thing we could find was communism, the Communist Party. I was really a socialist but I *did* join. So I guess I'm the only one in our family who is a card-carrying Communist Party member."

As Christmas approached, my mother looked forward to going home where she could put aside the bookwork, be with her beloved family, and get a good meal. One of the rituals at Wilson College, like the fictional Hogwarts in the Harry Potter novels, was to charter a special train that stopped at selected stations along the way where parents waited to either drop off or collect their offspring.

My mother said she enjoyed the train trip but then she came down with a nasty cold and had to spend the better part of her Christmas break in bed. This proved too much for my grandmother. Her daughter was a Communist and an atheist. She had lost weight and was sick. So Nanny decided to look to the nuns again. Sister Germaine at Benedictine Academy recommended Georgian Court College in Lakewood, New Jersey, assuring Nanny that there were no communists there. Sister Germaine also arranged a small scholarship for my mother so she could attend "The Court."

I guess I owe a debt of gratitude to the American Communist Party, because, if it wasn't for them, my mother might never have married my father. I also admire my mother's appreciation of socialist ideals. If nothing else, the Depression brought to light the deep-seated economic and social inequalities plaguing the country, a nation starkly divided by class and race. Something had to be done to make things right and if socialism could help, then why not give it a try? Even my brother, a lawyer for State Farm Insurance, brags to his friends about his mother's brief political sojourn among the communists, as if it were a badge of honor.

Speaking of my brother, I am driving south on the Garden State Parkway in his vintage BMW. The car is immaculate: there are gauges for everything, the leather seats are as soft as an undertaker's palms, the ride is smooth, the steering effortless, and the acceleration impressive. Ted hopes I find Helen's family, and lending me his car is his way of helping. But there is no hiding the fact that he is also nervous.

"Sue and I think of the BMW as our baby," he tells me as he hands me the keys. He then suggests I park the car in the remote, unoccupied section of parking lots so no one will ding the car when opening their doors. Right, I tell him; I can use the exercise.

I have an appointment at Georgian Court University to meet and interview the dean of the college of arts and sciences, Dr. Linda James, and the assistant provost, Evelyn Quinn—no relation. I will also interview two elderly nuns, Sister Edwarda Barry, the college historian, and Sister Maria Cordis. When I arrive, however, Linda tells me that one of the nuns at the college has passed away and Sister Barry and Sister Cordis will be attending the funeral. She is not sure if they will be able to meet with me.

Linda and Evelyn begin the interview by informing me that the school is celebrating its centennial.

In 1908, an order of nuns from Ireland called the Sisters of Mercy founded a college for women in North Plainfield, New Jersey. The college was named Mount Saint Mary's. Several years later, George Gould, son of Jay Gould, the railroad robber baron, decided to sell his beautiful 155-acre estate in Lakewood, New Jersey. There were two bidders for the estate. One was a movie company from Hollywood that wanted to use the property to make films, and the other, the Sisters of Mercy, who wanted to turn it into a college. The Goulds decided to let the sisters have it, believing they would be better stewards.

"I forget how much they paid," Linda tells me. "It wasn't a small sum. Looking at it today it would look small, but for the sisters it was a substantial amount. And there was a stipulation: they must retain the name of the estate. I think it was partly because of the Georgian architecture and partly because George Gould wanted his name in there too. So the sisters changed the name of their college from Mount Saint Mary's to Georgian Court."

Linda recounts the story of Catherine McAuley, who founded the Sisters of Mercy in Ireland in 1831. Catherine was born into a poor family in Dublin. Her father was a hedge schoolmaster. At the time, the penal laws in Ireland made it a punishable offense to educate Catholic children. So Mr. McAuley hid his class of neighborhood children "behind a hedge," out of view of the authorities, so he could teach them their letters, numbers, and catechism.

But then Mr. McAuley died, and not much later Catherine's mother passed away, forcing Catherine into domestic servitude. She secured a position with a wealthy Quaker couple and worked for them for many years. When they died, because they had no children of their own, they bequeathed their entire estate to her. With this legacy, Catherine decided to help other poor Catholic girls who had to struggle like she did. Thankfully, the penal laws had been repealed by this time, so she bought a house on Baggett Street in Dublin and turned it into a school for girls. An elderly priest assisted her in this idealistic endeavor, making sure to square her work with the powers in Rome. After he died, however, another priest was appointed in his place. This man, staunchly conservative, did not think it right or proper for an unmarried laywoman to involve herself in public work. He told her that she must either become a nun or give up her dream of educating young girls.

"Catherine had no interest in becoming a nun," Linda tells me, "but she understood that if she wanted to continue with what she was doing, she had no choice. So she donned the veil and later started her own order, called the Sisters of Mercy, who became known as the "walking nuns," because they were out and about in the world and not cloistered, like most nuns at that time. They opened a second school in Carlisle, Ireland, and then opened more schools around the country. One group of nuns led by Sister Frances Ward came over to America to start schools here."

At about the same time, the leadership of the Catholic Church in the United States was concerned that, although there were several top-tier colleges in the country for Catholic young men, such as Holy Cross and Notre Dame, there were few options for Catholic women who wished to pursue higher education. Catholic women could apply to public universities, but, given the prejudice against immigrants back then, they had trouble gaining admission. A bishop in New Jersey contacted the Sisters of Mercy and asked them to start a Catholic women's college. The nuns threw themselves into this task with determination and zeal, but they didn't stop with just one college. They successfully found seventeen institutions of higher learning for women throughout the East Coast and Midwest. Georgian Court is one of them.

Evelyn Quinn talks about attending reunions and enjoying alumni recollections of life at the Court in the early 1940s. From what she tells me I am able to paint a picture of my mother's student days. She arrived on campus little more than a girl, the younger daughter of a tavern owner from a decidedly less fashionable part of New Jersey. What is more, she isn't even Catholic. Yet despite this, she bloomed at the Court as both a person and a scholar.

She was a reporter for the college newspaper and got promoted to the position of associate editor, with a regular column titled, "As I Was Saying." She was elected president of the Dramatic Society. She got dressed up for formal teas with the nuns at "the mansion," which was the former Gould residence. Evelyn tells me that before students were allowed to go on dates they had to present themselves to the nuns for inspection. Too much cleavage and the nuns pinned a linen handkerchief across the neckline of the dress. At school dances, the nuns prowled the dance floor, making sure the young men and women were not getting too close. If they were, a nun gently pushed them apart with the admonition, "There needs to be enough room between you for the Holy Ghost."

Occasionally, the school hosted dances at the elegant Pierre Hotel in New York City, and my mother donned her best gown and rode the train into the city to attend these soirees, a far cry from the smoke-and-jazz filled tavern she called home.

Now and again, a classmate tried to sneak a boy into the dorm. She would dress the young man in a shower cap, robe, and fuzzy slippers and wait until the nuns and hall mother had all gone to bed. One of the girls got caught doing this, however, and, after two days of intense negotiations between the nuns, the student, the young man, and the couple's parents, it was agreed that the boy would marry the girl. They went on to celebrate their fiftieth anniversary together. This, Evelyn tells me with a laugh, is a story the nuns love to tell.

During my mother's career at Georgian Court, the nation went to war. With most of the young men off fighting the Germans and Japanese, there were few dances and even fewer dates. Instead, the students ran drives to collect tin, rubber, and paper. They gave blood, sewed bandages, and put together boxes of warm socks and chocolate bars and sent them overseas. They also wrote letters, lots and lots of letters, to the Special Ones who were so far away.

"Remember that night under the moon when you told me…" and "Your mother called this evening to see how I'm doing. She's such a sweet, dear woman…"

And always the words, invisible on the paper but persistently implied: "Have courage. Don't despair. I'm here waiting for you."

I know my mother wrote this kind of letter, because my brother has a box of replies from her young men. She had numerous paramours, and reading their words I can see they tried hard to impress her. They were also aching to get back to her, and the United States, as soon as they could.

As I think about my mother's college days, I recall her telling me how she came to marry my father. I knew she had become close friends with my father's sister Nancy, who was in the same year at the Court as my mother. I had just assumed that my parents met, fell in love, and got married. However, there was more to the story than that.

To begin with, my mother only went on a single date with my father before he left for the war. He arrived at the Court one weekend with a bunch of his buddies from Notre Dame, and they all went out on a group date with my mother, Aunt Nancy, and some other girls. By happenstance, my mother was paired with my father, but nothing happened. They had some laughs, smoked a pack of cigarettes between them, but there was no goodnight kiss at the college gate or any promise to exchange letters. Then the Japanese bombed Pearl Harbor, and my father finished up college and joined the army. The war progressed, and my father survived months of brutal combat pushing across Europe with the Second Armored Division. He was wounded three times and decorated for bravery, and soon after Germany surrendered he sailed for home aboard the Queen Mary, along with thousands of other war-weary servicemen.

A week after arriving back in Pittsburgh, he told his mother he was taking the train to New York to visit friends.

My mother graduated from the Court magna cum laude in 1943. When my father returned from the war, she was enrolled at a business school in Manhattan. My father called her up and asked her out to dinner.

She was surprised by the call, but she accepted the invitation, remembering my father as an agreeable and attractive man. They went to an Italian restaurant, and while they were waiting for their spaghetti and meatballs my father reached across the table, took my mother's hands in his, and regarded her intently. She wasn't sure what was happening and became uncomfortable and self-conscious.

"During the war," my father said, "during the worst of it, when I was being shot at and believed I was about to die, all I could think about was you, Bev. I saw your face in my mind as clearly as I see it now, and I knew that if somehow I made it through alive, then you were the woman I was to marry."

My mother said you could have knocked her over with a feather. Never in her wildest dreams had she expected such a thing. She had no idea what to say.

"I know this must come as a shock," my father went on, still holding her hands, "but I'm asking you to marry me. I'll be taking over the family business soon. They've already made me secretary and Dad's going to retire in a couple of years and then they'll appoint me president. I'm sure I'll be able to provide you with a comfortable life. I'll be faithful. We'll have children together. Will you marry me?"

My mother said it took several seconds to find her voice, and her mind was a jumble of confused thoughts and emotions. Meanwhile, the couple at the next table were getting up and putting on their coats.

"Ed, this is really very sudden," she finally said. "I'm flattered, I really am, but I have to think about it."

"I know this is sudden, but when can you give me an answer?"

"I've got to be honest. There's someone I've been dating since before the war. His name is Bob Murphy. I write him every day. He's still in Europe. I don't know when he'll get to come home."

"Are you engaged to him?"

"No, not officially, but everyone expects us to marry."

She told my father that it could be months before Bob returned home, and it wouldn't be fair if she suddenly decided to marry someone else, at least not before she had a chance to talk it over with him. She hoped my father understood.

Well, my father was not happy having to wait, but he agreed. He asked if my mother loved Bob.

"I like him. I like him very much. But I'm not sure I'm in love with him."

"Then I'll wait for as long as it takes." And my father meant it at the time, but eventually the uncertainty got the better of him. Two weeks later he called my mother person-to-person long distance from Pittsburgh.

"I know I said I'd wait, Bev, but I'm the kind of person who'd cut off his nose to spite his face. You've got to give me your answer, one way or the other. It's now or never. Will you marry me?"

My mother said yes.

"What about Bob?" I asked.

"I felt bad about that. I really did. But I knew I was making the right decision."

"When did you know that?" I asked. "I mean, how long did it take before you decided to marry him?"

"I knew the moment he asked me, sitting there in the restaurant. I suddenly knew he was the one."

I was still curious about the jilted Bob Murphy.

She shook her head. "That was hard. I wrote to him. He was very unhappy."

I have an album of my mother's wedding pictures. In the euphoria that followed the war, my grandparents spared no expense in marrying off their youngest daughter. My mother's wedding gown and train is all satin and silk, with a Spanish-inspired bridal veil of intricate, handmade lace. Poppy, my father, and my paternal grandfather are attired in tuxedos and top hats while the bridesmaids are turned out in matching chiffon dresses and large brimmed, floppy hats.

There is a photograph of my mother before the ceremony, looking in a mirror, with my Aunt Nancy at her shoulder smiling encouragement, another of my mother, father, and the priest in front of the altar, and a third of the newlyweds greeting the crowd of wedding guests at the church door following the ceremony. Everyone is smiling and having a whale of a time.

However, my mother told me that Mrs. Murphy, Bob's mother, showed up at the wedding and sat in the last pew of the church and audibly wept throughout the service.

When I heard this, I wondered if the disappointed Mrs. Murphy had cast a spell on my parents' marriage, cursing them with the deaths and sadness to come.

Given all the heartache my mother had to endure, I asked if she ever regretted marrying my father; they were together for only six years.

"No, not for a second," she told me without hesitation. "I'd do it again."

There is a postscript to this tale that involves a ring. A few days before my mother died, she asked me to get out her jewelry box so she could decide which pieces to leave her daughters-in-law and granddaughters. There was a silver ring inside the box. It was set with a large agate stone that was cracked down the center.

"Where did you get this ring?" I asked.

She looked at it a moment and replied, "That's the ring Bob Murphy gave me."

"Did you know the stone is cracked?" I asked.

"No," she said, with a look of surprise.

"So it wasn't cracked when he gave it to you?"

She shook her head.

"When did it crack like that?" I asked.

"I don't know. It's been in my jewelry box all these years."

With a shiver I returned the ring to the jewelry box.

As I wind up my interview with Linda James and Evelyn Quinn, the telephone rings. It is Sister Barry. She tells Linda that if I am willing to wait an hour, then she and Sister Cordis will meet with me after all. This is great news. I feel I would have missed something if I didn't get the opportunity to interview them.

To take up the time I decide to tour the campus. I am amazed at what I find. Far from being the traditional college campus I had imagined, with ivy-covered brick and stone buildings interconnected by tree-shaded sidewalks, I find great expanses of sun-soaked lawns, broad boulevards, and sunken gardens with a panoply of marble and bronze sculptures and freestanding Corinthian columns. It looks more like a playground for the ultra-rich of the Gilded Age than a college, which is exactly what it was in George Gould's day.

One impressive sculpture depicts a giant eagle perched atop a boulder. Another, three bronze satyrs holding up a sundial. There is a fountain with a naked man holding a dolphin carved out of marble, and another with the god Apollo standing tall in his sun-chariot, a long curved whip extended above his head. The bridled horses are snorting and rearing, eager to be on their way. There are carved stone lions everywhere—George's totem animal—and carved stone benches and lanes illuminated by art nouveau globe light fixtures on slender poles. Except for a statue of Mary encircled by white columns, I find little to suggest that Georgian Court is a Catholic institution.

I then check out the mansion and another large building called "the Casino," a beautiful structure built by the Goulds for horseback riding and hosting of lavish parties.

"A condition of sale set down by the Goulds," Sister Barry the historian tells me later, "is that we had to maintain all the statuary on the estate. Of course, we've grown very fond of them over the years."

The image of the nuns and students walking past the satyrs and the naked dolphin man each day on their way to class makes me chuckle.

I begin the interview with Sisters Cordis and Barry. They are pleasant women who smile often, but I can sense their sorrow having that morning said goodbye to one of their own. With so few young women taking the veil, their order is dying out, an era coming to an end.

"Many of the other Mercy colleges have been forced to go co-ed just to survive," Sister Cordis tells me. "We've been lucky. The sisters who came before us made wise decisions and we have a sizable endowment. So we don't have to go co-ed."

"Are there no male students?" I ask.

"Our graduate programs are co-ed, as are our evening and weekend studies program. But the undergraduate program is solely for women," says Sister Barry.

Sister Cordis talks passionately about what makes a women's college unique. She ends with the comment, "You men are distracting."

"The Court has always been a place where a young woman can

find her voice," Sister Barry chimes in. "That's why it's special."

I tell the Sisters that my mother wasn't raised Catholic, but that she fell in love with the nuns while attending Benedictine Academy and decided to convert to Catholicism. A priest was assigned to question her, but he told her she wasn't ready. She was surprised and disappointed by the priest's rejection. She forgot all about becoming Catholic while she attended Wilson College, but during her second year at the Court she again experienced "the call" and informed the nuns of her intention to convert. Again a priest was assigned to work with her and this time everything was fine, except that she wouldn't accept the prohibition against reading certain books. Each year the Church issued a list of banned titles and asserted that it was a sin to read any of them. My mother, a lover of books if ever there was one, disagreed with this rule and told the conversion priest she wouldn't obey it.

"But you have to," the priest shot back. "That's what being a Catholic is all about. Obedience."

"I'm willing to obey God, but this rule was made up by men who don't like certain books."

"No, Beverly, it's more than that."

"Well, I don't think so. I simply won't go along with it."

"But you have to."

My mother said this back-and-forth went on for several weeks, but she eventually wore the priest down.

"Look Bev," he told her one day, "if the only thing keeping you from becoming a Catholic is this, then read whatever books you like, but just don't tell anyone."

And that is how my mother became a Catholic and remained faithful to the Church to the day she died.

The last part of my interview with Sisters Barry and Cordis touches the topic of the school's relationship with African-Americans. I am not surprised to learn that there were no black students at the Court during the years my mother was enrolled there.

"There were black people who worked in the kitchen, and we were very fond of them," Sister Barry says. "There was one man named Wilbur who had lost an arm, and he worked the big Hobart automatic dishwasher, loading and unloading the dishes and silverware with his remaining arm. There was also a woman who had a young child but no place to leave him when she was working. So we told her to bring him to the college and we'd look after him. There were a hundred nuns here at that time and we just loved that little boy."

Sister Cordis then tells me she entered Georgian Court in 1946, the same year the college admitted its first black student. The student's name was Naomi Jones.

"Did this create friction with any of the white families who were sending their daughters to the Court?" I ask.

"As students, we didn't see any problems; Naomi was accepted by everyone. But I'm sure the Sisters back then thought long and hard about who should be the first black student. Now we have one of the largest percentages of black and Hispanic students of any Catholic college in the country."

Throughout my visit at Georgian Court, I have been mulling over the divide between rich and poor, white and black. From the day the Sisters of Mercy opened the college, I suspect they found themselves pulled in opposite directions. Having been prodded into purchasing the Gould estate by the bishop—and forced, most likely, to borrow a large sum to do so—they had to appeal to wealthy families who could afford to send their daughters to college. At the same time, they felt honor-bound to carry on the mission of their founder, Catherine McAuley, which was to serve the needs of poor women. How often the Church has found itself impaled on the horns of this dilemma. To survive, She must make common cause with the rich and powerful, and yet the gospel of Jesus is unambiguous: "That which you do for the least of these, you do for Me."

My mother was in a unique position to observe this opposition, and, as I head across campus toward the parking lot, I feel her presence. The campus is oddly quiet. School is in session and yet I see few students—no Frisbees being tossed on the lawns, no cluster of young women talking and laughing as they stroll down one of the many boulevards. Instead, there is a muted, surreal quality to the place. Just beyond the boundaries of the campus, I sense the hustle and bustle of the world, the endless buying and selling, the competing and desiring. The Court is an oasis away from all of that, and this brings to mind my mother's favorite reading tree, the ancient evergreen on the hill behind the rental house near Stanhope where she spent so much time as a child, its aura of hidden-awayness, where, in amongst the boughs, she found a safe place to grow into womanhood.

"I see why you liked it here," I say aloud as I reach the car.

# CHAPTER 8

## FORT MEADE

I am driving south through Maryland on my way to Alexandria, Virginia, and I decide to make a side trip to visit Fort Meade, the military facility where my father did his basic training for the Army in 1942. It is late in the day as I pull into the parking lot of the visitor center, which is located just outside the entrance to the base. I go inside and am told the base museum is closed. Back in the car I sit and think about my father. Two hundred yards away is the multi-lane security entrance, with a huge illuminated sign overhead reminding everyone of the dangers of using cell phones while driving. Beyond the entrance I see a couple of small buildings, but that is all.

I know as little about my father's military service as I do about what is inside Fort Meade. My brother gave me a copy of his discharge papers and they state that my father graduated from Officer Candidate School on February 19, 1943. He shipped out for Europe on July 5, 1944, and arrived in England on July 28, 1944. He was a platoon leader for Company D, 41st Armored Infantry Regiment, 2nd Armored Division. On October 13, 1944, he received a battlefield commission and became a company commander with the rank of captain. The list of battles and campaigns he fought in include northern France, Ardennes, Central Europe, and the Rhineland. He was wounded in Frelinberg, Germany on October 27, 1944, fourteen days after his promotion, and again in Lamon, Germany, on March 10, 1945. He arrived back home in the United States on October 11, 1945.

My mother told me he was offered a promotion to major if he would go and fight in the Pacific, but he turned the offer down.

I also have the citation for my father's Silver Star. The Silver Star is the Army's third highest decoration, just below the Distinguished Service Cross and the Medal of Honor. When I was growing up we kept my father's medals in a framed box on the wall of the TV room. The medals included the Silver Star, the Bronze Star with three clusters, and the Purple Heart with three clusters, which means he was wounded three times. There was also the Croix de Guerre awarded to my father by the Grand Duchy of Luxembourg. The citation for the Silver Star was written by my father's commanding officer, Major General John M. Devine. It reads:

> *"Capt. McHugh and the men under his command have performed brilliantly and in the manner of professional soldiers. Capt. McHugh was always at the head of his company and no amount of enemy fire kept him from being the company leader. When riding on tanks, he was among the lead tanks, and when on foot, he was with the platoon meeting the heaviest resistance. His aggressive leadership and ability to control his men have made his company one of the most aggressive and hardest fighting outfits that the undersigned has witnessed in action. At Broistedt, Germany, on April 10, 1945, the tanks on which company "D" were riding were halted by a blown bridge over the Fhuse Canal, which was blown as the tanks approached. Capt. McHugh, acting without order, immediately dismounted his men and personally led them under heavy artillery and ack-ack fire around and across the canal and quickly secured a section of the town."*

The citation also describes the attack upon the city of Magdeburg, Germany, on April 18, 1945. My father's battalion was halted by two roadblocks that were defended batteries of 88-millimeter guns. The Allied commanders ordered another battalion forward in support, but before they arrived my father led his men in an early morning attack and overran the roadblocks. They captured nearly four hundred German soldiers.

The citation ends with the comment: *"Capt. McHugh continuously demonstrated the type of ability, courage, and aggressiveness as indicated above. His type of leadership is an inspiration to all that observe."*

Hung above the sideboard in our dining room in Paterson was an enormous painting of the man in his captain's uniform, like a god watching over us. Whenever I failed to come up to the mark in Poppy's eyes, I was sure to hear the refrain: "Why, if your father were alive, what would he think of you now?" Good question.

I never got to see my father make mistakes, even little ones like breaking a vase with a tennis racket while trying to get a bat out of the house or discovering by the side of the road during a rain storm that he forgot to get the spare tire fixed the last time we had a flat. These are the all too human screw-ups that reveal character. Instead, my father was held up as a paragon of manly virtue by which my behavior was judged. My mother, bless her heart, did precious little of this, but my other relatives seemed to delight in comparing me to my father—not often favorably.

All I have regarding my father's military experience, besides a few government-issued documents, are two stories that came down through the family. The first told how my father, as a college graduate, was eligible for an officer's commission, but that he turned it down so he could enlist as an ordinary soldier. His mother opposed the idea and urged him to take advantage of his social position and family connections. Apparently, however, this was the last thing my father wanted; he longed for the chance to succeed or fail on the basis of his own merit. So he boarded a bus to Fort Meade, suffered through six grueling weeks of boot camp, and achieved the rank of corporal by the time he graduated. The day he finished boot camp, however, he was on the phone with his mother in Pittsburgh.

"Do whatever you have to, but get me into Officer Candidate School," he begged her. He had learned a difficult but important lesson: being at the bottom of the heap is a misery, especially in an organization as crazy and unpredictable as the Army.

So my grandmother made some calls, and he was promptly enrolled in Officer Candidate School. He graduated as a second lieutenant. He was then assigned to an infantry support regiment in the Second Armored Division, an outfit whose epithet is "Hell on Wheels."

My mother often talked about the nightmares that plagued my father because of the war. His screams often jolted her out of sleep. The first time it happened, she tried to wake him with a gentle touch, but he grabbed her arm and flung her to the floor. It happened in a flash and she was terrified.

"It was all nerves. He was still dreaming. He didn't mean to hurt me. I kept calling his name and he finally came to. He was shaking and covered in sweat. He kept telling me how sorry he was. After that, I never touched him when he was having a nightmare. In fact, I never tried to wake him up by touching him because I wasn't sure what he might do."

Before bed, my mother used tweezers to remove tiny slivers of shrapnel from his back that had worked their way to the surface of his skin. She dropped the metal fragments into a glass jar she kept in the drawer of the nightstand and then dabbed the bleeding wound with a cotton ball dipped in Mercurochrome. Over time this became something of a ritual for them.

And yet my father wouldn't tell her the stories behind his wounds. In fact, he didn't share any of his war experiences with her, and she found this both frustrating and painful because she was the kind of person who constructed her understanding of the world through stories. Whether reading Charles Dickens to comprehend poverty and oppression, feeling beauty and longing in the arias of an opera by Puccini, or sitting behind third base at a Mets game, she was always looking for the mystical meaning hidden within the progression of seemingly ordinary events. From what I know about my father, he did not share her passion for stories. What he enjoyed was fishing and hunting, making model trains, and tinkering with equipment at the woolen mills. The only samples of his writing that I possess are letters he sent to his mother during the war, and these are so bereft of anecdotes as to be almost comical. It is painfully obvious that he was determined to avoid writing anything worrisome or frightening. There are no other letters, no essays from college, no diaries chronicling his life; just a void.

I suspect my parents were something of an odd couple, not just because they came from different social backgrounds, but also their differing appreciation for stories. They also viewed the conundrum of war quite differently. My father was a captain of infantry, a committed warrior. My mother was a peacemaker, the person in the family who made every effort to defuse a conflict and get warring parties to see eye-to-eye. So it is not surprising my father evaded my mother's invitations to discuss the war. He had a few standby excuses, but most of the time his comment was simple and to the point.

"Look, Bev, I just don't want to talk about it. Please understand."

But she didn't understand. She believed he should trust her with his most intimate feelings. She also believed there was the possibility that if he talked about the war, then his nightmares might end, and in this, she was not alone in hoping to exorcise the demons of wartime memories. All across America, young women were dealing with damaged husbands, brothers, and fathers whose incomprehensible experiences kept them apart from the simple joys and tranquility of peacetime.

One evening, my father gave in and agreed to tell my mother one story from the war if she promised to leave the subject alone in the future. She consented, and he prefaced his story by stating his firm belief that it is impossible for a person to take part in war and preserve his honor and inherent sense of human dignity.

He proceeded to tell her about a day when he led his company of soldiers through a German forest during the final months of the war. It was raining, and they pushed forward warily, fearing they might stumble into an enemy position at any moment. They had been fighting without a reprieve for months and were exhausted, physically and mentally. After some time, they reached the edge of the woods, and a large field spread out before them. Through the curtain of rain on the far side of the field, my father could just make out a camp or stockade surrounded by a tall wire fence and a series of guard towers. He led his men into the field expecting to come under fire from the towers, but nothing happened. His nerves were at a fever pitch. He felt exposed but he had to press on; turning back was not an option. Then, as he and his men drew near the camp, my father saw rows of people standing on the other side of the wire fence watching them approach. They were dressed in rags, their cheeks hollowed out, their eyes sunken, their shaved heads dripping with rain. He kept expecting to hear the rip of a German machine gun, but the only sound was the patter of water droplets on his helmet. The people, ghost-like, stood perfectly still and silent.

He realized they had come upon a civilian prison camp, one of the forced-labor outfits he had heard rumors about. He suspected the German guards had deserted, but he wasn't sure. Moving in teams of two and three through the wet grass, he and his men were at last stopped by a wide latrine ditch that ran parallel to the line of the fence for several hundred yards in both directions. The ditch was filled with human waste, and the stench was horrendous. My father noticed that someone had placed a board across the ditch. It was shiny and slick with rain. As he considered what to do next, he could feel the weight of the prisoners' eyes upon him, their faces pressed against the wire. His sergeant offered to cross the ditch first, but my father decided to go himself. He stepped onto the board and took a few steps, his finger on the trigger of his M-1 carbine, when suddenly the board tilted and he slipped, landing feet-first in the ditch, waist-deep in excrement. In that instant, he dropped his carbine, grabbed a grenade, pulled the pin, and threw it over the fence into the crowd of prisoners. He said he did it without conscious thought; it was pure instinct, the product of nerves and training. But by the grace of God, the grenade failed to explode; it was a dud. If it had exploded, he told my mother, he was certain it would have killed and maimed many of those wretched prisoners from whom the war had already taken so much.

My mother kept her word and gave up pestering him for more stories, so that is the only war story I have from my father.

The day before my mother passed away, she gave me a religious medal that had belonged to my father. It is a medal dedicated to Mary, the Mother of Jesus, and my father wore it throughout the war. I am fascinated by this expression of my father's nature. He had always been described to me as a real "man's man," someone who loved hunting and a round of golf with his buddies, and who was being groomed to take over a complex and demanding manufacturing concern. Yet in something as utterly masculine as modern-day warfare with its tanks and bombers and artillery cannons, he placed his trust in the feminine, in the primal protective power of the Great Mother.

Even though I never knew him, this is something we both share.

# CHAPTER 9

## FINDING HELEN

My son Patrick who lives in North Carolina drives up to D.C. to help me with my research at the Library of Congress before heading off to a conference in Chicago. He is working on his doctorate in political science at the University of North Carolina at Chapel Hill and hopes one day to be a teacher. I have ruled out finding Helen's death record because I don't know her last name, the month or year she died, or even if she died in the state of Maryland. That leaves searching through old newspapers for a reference to the house fire in 1952 that claimed the life of a nineteen-year-old man, Helen's grandson.

We spend the night with my friend Paddy in Alexandria and take the Metro into D.C. the next morning. It is a perfect spring day and cherry blossoms greet us as we emerge from the subway. Over the decades, the Library of Congress has expanded its collections to such an extent that it now occupies a cluster of buildings directly east of the Capitol Building. The original structure was Thomas Jefferson's library and is, far and away, the most enchanting building of the complex. From the street to the entrance, visitors climb a broad staircase that wraps itself around an impressive fountain starring Neptune and an entourage of aquatic creatures. On this spring day, there is also a vertical banner hanging next to the entrance advertising an exhibit celebrating the bicentennial of Abraham Lincoln's birth.

An archivist for the state of Maryland recommended that we begin by looking in past issues of the *Afro-American*, a Baltimore-based paper that is one of the oldest black newspapers in America. The Library of Congress has copies of the newspaper on microfiche dating back to 1892.

"Newspapers and periodicals are housed in the Madison Building," the guard at the Jefferson Building security desk informs us. "Go back out and turn left. It's across the street."

A half-hour later, after filling out forms, getting our photographs taken, and receiving official-looking badges, Patrick and I enter the newspaper room. Our spirits are buoyant as we thread the microfiche onto a reader and begin perusing issues of the *Afro-American* from April of 1952. We discover, however, that we are not going to find what we are looking for: a story about a house fire and the death of a young black man. The *Afro-American* is published in Baltimore, and that is most likely where the fire took place, but the newspaper's scope is national, not local, featuring stories about prominent black athletes, entertainers, statesmen, and scientists. We see numerous articles about legislation of particular interest to black Americans. There is also a smattering of international news. We scan hundreds of pages and read every obituary but find no mention of a nineteen-year-old black man dying in a fire.

We eventually give up and request back issues of the *Baltimore Sun* for April 1952, also on microfiche. After scrolling through weeks of obituaries without success, I decide to revisit my calculations regarding the exact date of the fire. I reread my mother's letter and consult a calendar for April 1952 that the librarian on duty graciously prints for us.

The faded postmark on the letter's envelope appears to be either the 25th or the 28th. I let my son hazard a guess with his young eyes.

"I go with the 28th," he says and that is fine with me.

"Okay then," I say, sounding like one of the Hardy Boys, "the 28th was a Monday. If that is correct and the letter says, 'last Sunday Helen heard...' Then my mother probably wrote the letter on a Sunday and mailed it on a Monday."

"Which means Helen heard about the fire on the 20th," Patrick completes the line of thought.

"Someone from Helen's family would have called her, not written," I conjecture, "which means the fire took place either late Saturday, the 19th, or early Sunday, the 20th."

I decide to check the *Baltimore Sun* for Monday, April 21st, counting on two unlikely scenarios: first, that when my mother wrote "Maryland" she meant Baltimore, and second, that the editors of the *Baltimore Sun* considered the accidental death of a young black man to be sufficiently newsworthy.

Seated at the microfiche reader, our faces bathed in the photons streaming through the ribbon of film, I rotate the knobs until the front page appears for Monday, April 21. A headline in banner type across the top of the page type reads:

5 CHILDREN PERISH, FOREST DESTROYED AS RASH OF FIRES HITS CITY AND STATE

Underneath, a photograph shows the charred ruins of a lumberyard. The article begins:

> *"An epidemic of fires in Baltimore and other parts of Maryland claimed the lives of five children and a man, burned through hundreds of acres of brush and woodland, caused $200,000 damage to a Washington Boulevard lumber yard, and seriously damaged two East Baltimore apartment houses.*
>
> *"In addition to the three multiple-alarm blazes in the city, there were at least eighteen forest fires throughout the State. One, believed caused by a firebug, burned over nearly 1,500 acres in Anne Arundel County. Five of the forest fire fighters were taken to hospitals."*

The article then divides into two columns that run side by side down the remainder of the page. One is titled URBAN and the other RURAL.

We read about the city fires first. Children were suspected of starting two of them: one consumed a lumberyard and another severely damaged an apartment house. There is nothing, however, about Helen's grandson.

We turn our attention to the rural fires. The first is tragic: five children burned to death in a one-room log cabin near Ellicott City after an oil stove exploded.

I scroll to page two and read about the forest fires. My hopes are slipping as I near the end of the article. But then I reach the last paragraph, which describes a fire in Brunswick, Maryland, that claimed the life of a twenty-year-old man named John Harold Thomas. My mother's letter said Helen's grandson was nineteen, not twenty, but this death is the only one that is even remotely close. The article says another young man named James Jackson was badly burned in the fire, but he survived by jumping from a third story window. There is, however, no mention of their race, which gives me pause. The paper identified the two children who were injured in a Baltimore apartment house fire as "Negro." If John Thomas was black, I feel certain a newspaper of that time would say so.

Also, I have never heard of Brunswick. We step over to the map rack, select one for the state of Maryland, and locate Brunswick. It appears to be a small town on the north bank of the Potomac River in the western part of the state. Part of Frederick County, it faces Loundon County, Virginia, to the south on the opposite side of the Potomac. Looking west, it is only a few miles from Harper's Ferry, West Virginia, where abolitionist John Brown raided the federal arsenal in 1859. This region, in the shadow of the Appalachian Mountains, is a far cry from where I had imagined finding Helen's family, and yet there is a chance, if only a slight chance, that John Harold Thomas of Brunswick is the young man I am looking for.

That evening, before heading out for supper, I call my wife Paula and tell her what we found. She calls back a couple hours later after researching an online newspaper archive. Their offerings are limited, but the site does include *The News*, a daily published in Frederick, Maryland. Using what Patrick and I discovered, Paula located a detailed account of the Brunswick fire, which does identify the two young men as being "colored." The article also states that John Harold Thomas was survived by a wife and daughter. It has lodged in my mind that Helen's grandson had a baby boy, not a daughter, and so I reread my mother's letter and discover that the word she wrote was "child" not "son." If John Thomas was only twenty, his daughter could easily be a year old, the age, coincidentally, I was when I lost my father in 1951.

With hope rekindled, I decide to drive to Brunswick and see if I can find someone who might know the Thomas family. I bid farewell to Patrick, and the next morning I set off for western Maryland. Even though I get an early start, I get trapped in the ravenous maw of D.C. traffic, and I don't reach the town of Brunswick until nearly four o'clock in the afternoon, seriously anxious because the day is slipping away.

To reach Brunswick from Loudoun County, Virginia, I have to cross a bridge that spans the Potomac River and an expanse of rail yards. I round a traffic circle and enter downtown where a large billboard greets me emblazoned with an American flag and the words WELCOME HOME in giant letters. I understand the sign is intended for soldiers returning from the wars in Iraq and Afghanistan, but the words strike an emotional chord in my own heart as well. When I was a young child, Helen was a vital part of that sacred space I called home. I loved her, and I miss her even now.

Much of Brunswick is built on a hillside that slopes down to the switching yards with the Potomac River flowing eastward just beyond. The buildings are modest but well maintained. There is only one traffic light, and the business section on West Potomac Street runs for four blocks. There are a handful of antique stores, a cafe called Mommers, a hardware store, a couple of secondhand stores, and an old church that has been converted into a coffeehouse, called Beans in the Belfry.

Brunswick is like many rural towns in America: unassuming, sleepy, and a touch ragged around the edges. It also exudes a melancholy air as if waiting for something, as if the hucksterism of Best Buy, The Shopping Channel, and Donald Trump will one day go away and the town can pick up where it left off as a commercial and cultural center of American life.

I park my car in front of the church-turned-coffee shop and head up the street. My plan is to hunt up the town hall and see if the clerk can put me in touch with the Thomas family. Fifty-seven years have passed since the night of the fire; many things can happen to a family in that span of time.

Looking across the street, however, I notice an impressive three-story red brick building with BRUNSWICK VOL. FIRE CO. spelled out in large letters above a pair of bay doors. The flat chrome grill of a modern fire engine glints proudly from its spot in one of the bays, and a group of men loaf in front of the building enjoying the late afternoon sunshine. One sits and polishes hose fittings and another sips a soda while the rest chat idly away; together they are a Norman Rockwell tableau with only one character missing—the faithful Dalmatian.

Who better to ask about John Harold Thomas and a house fire, I reason, than a crew of firefighters? So I pick out the oldest, a man I judge to be in his sixties, and introduce myself.

"I'm investigating a fire that took place here in Brunswick in 1952," I say. "A young black man named John Harold Thomas was killed in the fire, and I'm trying to locate his family."

The man rubs his chin before shrugging. "I wouldn't know anything about that. Sonny Cannon was the fire chief back then, but he passed away about ten years ago."

The Frederick newspaper quoted Sonny Cannon several times in the article Paula found, and I experience that special regret that comes when death steals away the keeper of a story.

I have a small recorder in a pouch on my belt. I ask the fireman, whose name is Ronnie Lowe, if I can record our conversation and he shrugs as if to say, "It don't bother me."

"Do you happen to know a black family named Thomas?" I ask him.

"I know some Thomases in the back of my head, but I don't know exactly where they are."

"There was another young man in the fire," I add, "a cousin who survived. His name was Jackson."

This brings Ronnie to life.

"There's a family of Jacksons—a couple of families of Jacksons around town. Black Jacksons. Now I hear at the edge of town, in what we call Petersville, there's a lot of blacks live out there, on Route 180. They're very nice people, very nice."

I mention that I left a message with the pastor of the African Methodist Episcopal Church in town, but he had not gotten back to me. I ask if there is anyone else I should talk to.

"There's a policeman working right now. His name is Andy Smothers. He's a black guy. I'm sure he would probably know. His family's been around here for years. His son and daughter both run with us. His son runs the ambulance."

He turns to one of the younger firemen.

"Go back in the office and give Andy Smothers a call. Tell him to come by the firehouse. I seen him over in town today. By God, I talked to him here this morning."

While we wait, I ask Ronnie if he has lived in Brunswick all his life.

"Sixty-five years. This is my roots. I've been with the fire company forty-eight years; started in high school."

I ask about the town, the railroad, and the dangers of fighting fires. Another fireman joins the conversation to say that extinguishing fires in newer homes is more dangerous because the construction materials are lighter and a fireman never knows when a floor will give way.

"I work in Washington and the houses there are older," he says. "But the wiring's older, too, and that causes fires."

He smiles and shrugs.

Meanwhile, there is no sign of Andy Smothers so I ask the firefighters to give me a tour of the firehouse and their "equipment," which is what they call the fire trucks. They are only too happy to oblige.

"Upstairs is a dance hall," Ronnie begins the tour. "Back in the fifties Jimmy Dean and his Texas Wildcats played here every Saturday night for about a year. Old Jimmy's not doing nothing now but selling sausages or something. And we had Guy Lombardo here and his Royal Canadians. Patsy Cline from Winchester, she was here. A lot of famous people played here over the years in this old building."

"The firehouse was built in 1948," a younger fireman chimes in. "The auditorium and kitchen take up the whole second floor. The building plans were drawn on the back of a carnival poster. At least that's what the old timers say."

"Yep, everyone got together and built it theirselves, all the old members," Ronnie adds.

"It cost one hundred thousand dollars, and some of the stuff was borrowed from the B & O Railroad."

"A lot of it, at that time," Ronnie says and everyone laughs. Then he becomes wistful.

"It's a good old building, but it seems like when they built it they didn't plan for the future. Right now we've got three pieces of equipment here, and out at our other building we've got three more pieces of equipment. We can't get 'em all here together. We're hoping we'll build us a new building at the edge of town, a nice building, everything on one floor. Maybe next year, if things work out for us."

"How often do you get called out?" I ask.

"We run five hundred some calls a year. A lot of 'em are mutual-aid over into Loudoun County. And we go into West Virginia, too, in this tri-state area. We keep busy. Good thing about it, we're all volunteers."

I glance at my watch as we work our way through an inventory of the gear on one of the fire trucks—the jaws of life, K-12 saw, backboard, air bags, cord reels, air struts, rams...

It is ten past five and I am tempted to bail on Smothers, break off the interview, and see who else in town can help me. But I am not sure where to go. The town hall is probably closed now and I don't know a soul in Brunswick.

"What do you think happened to Officer Smothers?" I ask Ronnie.

"I don't know where he is," he says and turns to one of the younger firemen. "Go call his cousin and tell him to ask Andy to come over here."

We continue the tour, which concludes with Ronnie digging out a stack of old photographs including one of the original firehouse and some engines from the early 1900s.

"A lot of freight comes through Brunswick," Ronnie says, "and the commuter trains that come out from Washington stay here overnight. They go back into the city each morning. We have a lot of people who work for the government living here now in housing developments just outside of town, and over in Virginia. Some of them houses cost five to six hundred thousand dollars. With the economy the way it is, there've been a lot of foreclosures. It's not been good."

Again I look at my watch; it is coming on five-thirty and the voice of my rational mind is growing more insistent: You are wasting time. You have a long trek back to Alexandria and you are tired. You will just have to come back again.

Yet I persist in this Godot-like waiting game because I have that distinct sensation I sometimes get that I am *inside* a story and stories can be like ships upon the ocean of time with the firemen, the missing Officer Smothers, and me as crew members hoisting the sails to catch the winds of destiny. I consider getting my fiddle out of the car and playing the boys a tune, but then Ronnie notices a man entering the building that houses the ambulance service across the street.

"That's Clair Ebersole," he tells me. "He's been around here forever. He might remember that fire."

One of the younger firemen escorts me across the street and introduces me to Clair who, when he hears my question, shakes his head.

"I was away in the Marines in 1952," he says. "But my wife's from Brunswick. She runs our little museum here in town and she knows everybody. I'll give her a call."

He picks up a telephone, dials a number, and speaks for a moment before handing the receiver to me.

"This is Jackie Ebersole," a voice says.

I tell her what I am doing.

"I'm sorry," she says, "I don't remember that fire. But there's a black woman who volunteers her time as a docent at the museum. Her name is Estella Belt. She'll be eighty-two this week and she's one of the nicest people you'll ever meet. She might be able to help you. She knows all the black families in the area. You can probably reach her at home now."

Jackie gives me Estella's number and Clair tells me to use the phone. "It's not the emergency line," he assures me. "Talk as long as you want."

I dial the number.

"Hello?" the voice on the other end is slow and pleasant.

"Hello. Is this Estella Belt?" I ask.

"Yes it is."

"My name is Joe McHugh. I'm from Olympia, Washington. I'm visiting Brunswick and Jackie Ebersole suggested I call you. She thought you might be able to help me find someone I'm looking for."

"Yes," she says.

I hope I am not interrupting her supper.

"I was born in Pittsburgh in 1950 and I'm looking for the family of a woman named Helen who worked for my family when I was young. In fact, she took care of me from the time I was born until I was five. Unfortunately, I don't know her last name."

I pause, but Estella doesn't say anything.

"There's the possibility that Helen was the grandmother of a young man who died in a fire here in Brunswick in 1952. His name was John Harold Thomas. I was wondering if you might know the family."

I wait the length of a heartbeat, maybe two, and then she speaks, again quite slowly.

"So you're looking for Miss Helen," she says. It's more a statement than a question.

"Yes," I tell her.

"Well, Helen was my mother-in-law. I married her son James, and I worked for your grandparents in Pittsburgh on Devonshire Street after Helen went with you to New Jersey."

I am speechless. My heart floods with gratitude and I struggle to find my voice. Estella invites me to her house so we can talk. I jot down the directions and hang up the telephone. At that moment, in walks Andy Smothers, his policeman's uniform pressed, his badge polished.

"I heard you were looking for me," he says.

Father and Joe

Joe and Helen - Christmas 1950

Beverly Jane Quinn

Quinn's Garage in Paterson, NJ - Al Quinn standing nearest the car

Aunt Kate's - Route 206, Stanhope, NJ - 1950

Joe Walls and Al Quinn

Beverly Quinn at Georgian Court College

Captain Edward McHugh

Dearest Mother —

Well, try as I may, I never seem to get seated down to write.

The trip back was uneventful except that I ran into snow in the mountains — just like winter, really. I sure can't seem to hit it when I'm travelling back here. I swear I'll run into a blizzard in July. Still, we made very good time and I made it to school that night.

Friday I went to that party. I'll write Ruth about it so check with her. On Sunday, Helen got a message that her grandson had burned to death down in Maryland. He was only 19 and had a child himself under a year old. She left immediately for home and I got a message later that he burned in her house, so she's staying down there for a week or ten days to collect her insurance.

Consequently I've been quite busy. I've done some house cleaning — I'd love to get it over with so I could relax.

Both boys have bad coughs, and I've never quite lost that sore throat I had down there. I guess it's the usual virus business — I'll be glad when the summer comes if only to cut these colds out.

Letter written by Mom in April, 1952

THE SUN FINAL

# 5 CHILDREN PERISH, FOREST DESTROYED AS RASH OF FIRES HITS CITY AND STATE

$200,000 BLAZE SWEEPS LUMBER COMPANY HERE; BRUNSWICK MAN KILLED

Oil Stove Explosion Sets Cabin Afire Near Ellicott City; Arsonist Blamed For Woodland Burning In Anne Arundel County

EISENHOWER FACES 21 VITAL QUESTIONS

Governor Fine To Head GOP Delegates From Pennsylvania

PARACHUTISTS GET A BOMB TEST ROLE

Four Killed As Racing Car Goes Into Dayton Grandstand

Front page of *Baltimore Sun*, April 21, 1952

# CHAPTER 10

## ESTELLA

*"I have great respect for that unsung army of black men and women who trudged down lanes and entered back doors, saying "Yes, Sir" and "No, Ma'am."… [These] Black men and women knew that the job had to be done, and they put their pride in their pockets in order to do it. It is hard to believe they were in any way inferior to the white men and women who opened those back doors."*

—James Baldwin, *The Fire Next Time* (1963)

The center of Petersville is a T-shaped intersection three miles north of Brunswick. There is a church, a private residence that looks as if it was once a general store, and a warehouse-style building surrounded by an acre of dated cars. The rest of unincorporated Petersville is rural with white clapboard houses tucked in among rolling fields and woodlands.

At the intersection I turn right onto Route 180 and drive a short distance to a white-columned mansion set back from the road. The mansion has seen brighter days. The top slab of one of the stone pillars guarding the entrance to the drive lies moldering on the ground like the severed head of a French aristocrat. As instructed, I ignore the drive to the mansion and turn onto a gravel lane just beyond that leads to a small single-story house. I park next to a row of slender poplars bordering a tilled field. There are no other houses in sight.

As I get out of the car, I am greeted by a flock of birds filling the upper branches of the poplars. The intensity of their riotous melody gives me an odd chill; it is as if they are telling me that Helen's spirit is glad I made it.

I walk up a narrow sidewalk to the back door and knock. In a moment Estella Belt appears and welcomes me in. She is a slight woman who seems younger than her eighty-two years, her lightly grayed hair tied back, her voice soft and melodious.

The house is largely packed up, moving boxes filled and stacked against the walls. Estella tells me she might have to move soon. She accompanies this statement with a chuckle and shake of the head as if to say, "If it's not one thing, it's another."

I follow her into the small kitchen and sit at the table. The room is circa 1960, with painted white cabinets and a linoleum floor worn thin by decades of sweeping and mopping. Whatever sharp edges there once were have been rounded and made comfortable by time. I wonder how many home-cooked meals have graced the small table between us, how many cups of coffee sipped over tidbits of gossip. It brings to mind some of the farm kitchens I knew during my time in West Virginia, serviceable and welcoming places with painted cabinets and plain furniture, where I often sat playing fiddle tunes and sharing jokes far into the night.

Estella and I talk for a moment, and I am so full of emotion I fear I will forget important details. We have only just met, and I don't want to be rude, but I ask if I can record our conversation. She agrees with a nod and a warm smile. In fact, she appears amused, and this works wonders to lessen my awkwardness; I feel at home in her presence.

"Miss Helen would be so pleased to know somebody remembers," Estella tells me. "She was truly a wonderful woman."

"What was Helen's last name?" I ask. "Was it Thomas?"

"No, it was Spriggs. Helen Spriggs."

"When did she die?"

"In 1964. She's buried in the cemetery at St. Mary.

"Is that a Catholic Church?"

"Yep, it's just up the road."

"So Helen was Catholic?" I ask. I don't generally associate African-Americans with the Catholic faith and it never crossed my mind that Helen might be one.

"Oh, yes," Estella smiles. "So am I."

"How did Helen die?" I ask.

"I think she was already sick when she came back home from working for you. She had an open sore on her side that wouldn't heal. She was taking a lot of aspirins. She must have been in a lot of pain, but she wouldn't tell anyone that something was wrong. I think it was some kind of cancer."

That means Helen lived only seven years after leaving Paterson in 1956, and during much of that time she was suffering.

I ask Estella about her own life and why she is moving. She explains that she was the housekeeper for a retired general named Delmar for many years. He owned the mansion and the house where Estella lives. However, he died recently and a woman bought the property. The new owner is in the process of restoring the mansion, but Estella doesn't think she needs a housekeeper. That means Estella will most likely have to move.

Her voice is wistful as she tells me this, but she doesn't appear worried or sad.

"Where will you go?" I ask.

"I'm not sure," she says. "I've filled out papers for a retirement place that the county runs. Maybe they'll take me in there."

Estella then goes back to talking about Helen.

"She was born Helen Laetitia Palmer in Loudoun County. That's across the river, in Virginia. Her father, I don't know what tribe of Indian, but he was pureblood Indian. And her mother was just an ordinary little black woman, a beautiful little thing. Her name was Mary. Mary Gaskin, I think it is. And she married Mr. Palmer. I have the marriage license somewhere but with all this packing up, you can't find what you really need."

She tells me the names of Helen's brothers and sisters:

"There was Douglas, who everybody called Big Doug, and Uncle Snowy. And there was Florence and Aunt Linda. There were a couple more, but I can't remember their names just now."

"When did Helen come to Maryland?" I ask.

"She was married when they [the Palmers] came to Brunswick. Her first husband was a Furr and he was from Virginia. His name was Richard Furr but he died—I don't know how soon or anything—but she had three children by him: Mary Elizabeth, Margaret, and Douglas who everybody called Little Doug. Then James, my husband, was born to Howard Belt who was Helen's second husband. Then he died. He had some kind of illness, I don't know exactly what it was, pneumonia, I guess, because in those days they seemed to get pneumonia a lot and, if they got it, they died. Most of the time, you know."

I mention this must have been before penicillin.

"Oh sure," Estella nods, "that was a long time ago."

I ask her how many children Helen had with Howard Belt, and Estella says her husband James was the only one.

"Then she married Theodore Spriggs who was a Maryland man, and they lived down in Brunswick. They had three children together. But then he died, too."

So Helen lost three husbands to illness and raised seven children pretty much on her own. I try to imagine my mother's situation in the wake of my father's death: she is twenty-nine years old—we seldom think of our parents as young—and she has two young children and is pregnant with a third. She is also living far from her parents and sister, which often makes her homesick. Then her husband dies. Perhaps this is why she spoke with such feeling about Helen. Helen was a widow who knew the twists and turns of that stony, desolate road as well as anyone could. My mother must have turned to Helen for emotional support as well as help holding the family together. A seasoned woman paired with an inexperienced younger woman, both living together under the same roof, my mother half crazy with grief. Helen, like Joe Walls, was someone my mother could relate to.

I recall my mother's description of the day she arrived home from the hospital after my father's death and how she threw herself into Helen's arms.

"Please Helen, please don't leave me now," she said.

And the simple answer from Helen that meant everything to her. "I won't leave until you want me to."

"Did you get to know Helen when you married James?" I ask and Estella laughs.

"Oh no, I knew Miss Helen since the day I was born. They all lived over in Shady Lane."

Shady Lane? I am confused. I ask Estella if she means the Shady Lane in Pittsburgh where we lived when my father and brother died.

But Estella gestures with her hand as if pointing and tells me Shady Lane is where the black families in Petersville lived.

"It's close, just up the road," she says. "That's where Miss Helen's daughter Margaret lived for many years. It's just a little place, and Margaret and them had a home there. Helen would be there a lot when she'd come home from Pittsburgh or something."

I am stunned to learn that there are two Shady Lanes and I say as much.

"I'll tell you, it is a coincidence," Estella says. "That's where Margaret lived, on Shady Lane, and the child that burned up [in Brunswick], John Harold. Margaret was his mother."

The name "Shady Lane" has exerted a kind of magical influence over me for as long as I can remember. When I was nineteen I lived for some months in Portland, Oregon. One weekend I visited Cannon Beach, a small town west of Portland on the coast. I was so charmed by the broad public beaches and the enormous rocks jutting out of the surf that I decided to move there. I began looking for a house to rent. One property was a gray-shingled bungalow set among towering Douglas firs on a high bluff overlooking the Pacific. The view from the living room picture window was breathtaking, but the house was quite a bit farther from town than the other places on my list. Also, the rent was on the high end of what I could afford, and I had to descend a steep, narrow trail to reach the beach. In the end, however, I decided to rent the bungalow, in large part because it was at the end of a street called Shady Lane.

Thirty-five years later, when I considered becoming a filmmaker, I named my fledgling production company Shady Lane Films.

Now, sitting in Estella's kitchen, I begin to consider the complexity of the name. Shady Lane can mean respite from the bright, oppressive heat of a summer's day, an avenue winding its lazy way under a canopy of leaves with shafts of sunshine piercing through and birds chirping in the high branches.

But "shade" is also an old word for a ghost, a restless spirit trapped between worlds. My father and brother both died while we were living on a street called Shady Lane, and that is where my mother was debilitated by depression. So it stands to reason that the name could have conjured up emotions of sorrow and loss in me, and yet it never did.

Now I have learned that here, in rural western Maryland, there is another Shady Lane, and it too is associated with tragedy and death. Helen's grandson John Harold grew up on Shady Lane and was living there when he died. And Helen, after returning from working for us in New Jersey, lived on Shady Lane as the cancer slowly drained her life away.

"I met you and your brother when James and I came up to Pittsburgh to work for your grandparents," Estella tells me. "That was just before Helen went with you all to New Jersey. We went to your house to pick up Miss Helen, and I remember it was at the top of a hill, and you children came out with your mother. She was a beautiful woman."

"Did Helen talk about working for my mother and father?" I ask.

"Well, she always thought they were very nice. She liked you all very much. I mean your family—especially your mother's brother-in-law. She talked about this man a lot. I have a picture of him because she would send pictures every now and then and I know I have that one."

I realize she is talking about my Uncle George, the football player turned traveling salesman. George enjoyed his Canadian Club and a good joke. Each shred of information helps me flesh out the kind of person Helen was.

I ask Estella if Helen convinced her to come to Pittsburgh.

"Yes. Miss Helen wanted us to come up there and work for your grandmother and grandfather. Her son James and I. I did the cooking and James did odd jobs and sometimes he drove the car. But he didn't like that kind of work and he came back here to Maryland after just a little while. I stayed on and worked another four or five months and then came back myself."

When I ask Estella what she thought of my grandparents, she responds with a smile. "They were very nice."

I am not surprised she would think my Papa was nice, but I suspect she is soft-pedaling her opinion of Nana.

Edward McHugh, my Papa, was one of the kindliest men I have ever known. He was gentle in speech and conduct, considerate of others, funny, and straightforward. He was also a master golfer and bowler who won many tournaments. Children were drawn to him because there was nothing to fear. My Aunt Nancy said she knew her father to raise his voice only once in anger, and that was when her younger sister, my Aunt Mary Ann, was a child and ran out into the street and was almost hit by a car. My brother describes Papa as just this side of being a saint. I know my father was devoted to my grandfather; he even asked Papa to be his best man when he married my mother. My grandfather never recovered from the shock and grief of my father's death. He went through the motions, but something vital went out of him.

Papa loved baseball, and I have such fond memories of watching Pittsburgh Pirates games with him in the upstairs TV room at the house on Devonshire Street. There was a small refrigerator just out in the hallway where Papa kept his stash of Coca-Cola. Papa would pop open a pair of green bottles so we would have something to sip on while we admired the skills of the great left-fielder Roberto Clemente and the fork-ball relief pitcher Elroy Face. At night, I often slept in the spare twin bed next to his, all safe and warm. He didn't tell me stories or take me fishing. Maybe if he had lived longer he would have taught me to play golf. But he died in 1963, when I was thirteen. My brother and I still miss him.

Nana, by comparison, was determinedly Victorian in her manner and values. She was greatly concerned with rules and tradition: proper and improper behavior were clearly delineated; there were "respectable" people who had "character," and then there was the rest of humanity, who often fell woefully short in these two crucial departments. Children were to be seen and not heard. I was lucky insofar as Nana doted on boys. My only female cousin, Alice Sexton, had endless trouble gaining Nana's approval.

Nana was not unkind; she was just a hard customer. And there was never any question as to who wielded authority in the McHugh household. We didn't talk about going to Papa's house. We loved to seeing Papa, but we *went* to Nana's house. Her father, Patrick McGraw, started the McGraw Wool Company in Pittsburgh shortly after stepping off the boat from Ireland. He had ten children, but only six survived and all were boys, except for my grandmother.

My Papa was born and raised in Connellsville in southwestern Pennsylvania and exhibited a genius for numbers from an early age. As a young man of twenty, he came to Pittsburgh and took a position as an accountant with the Johns Manville Company. He met my grandmother at a dance, and in the course of time they were married. Another kind of courtship soon followed; Patrick McGraw worked to persuade his gifted new son-in-law to leave Johns Manville and join the family firm. Papa resisted the elder McGraw's enticements for several years, but he at last made the move. A grateful Patrick McGraw rewarded him and his daughter by purchasing for them a house on Devonshire Street in the Shadyside neighborhood of Pittsburgh. But even though both names appeared on the deed, it was Nana who ruled the roost, and she routinely scolded and demeaned her husband in front of family, friends, and anyone else within earshot. My older brother remembers Nana's persona far better than I.

"Nana was one of the most decent persons I've ever known, and that's probably why she loved our grandfather as much as she did. And she did, although she treated him terribly in the sense that in our presence she castigated him; she belittled him. It really was a Virginia Woolf sort of situation. Every Saturday when we were kids and lived in Fox Chapel we had to go to Devonshire Street for dinner because that was what was required, which was fine, we didn't mind. We would have cold leg of lamb, because it would take forever to come out of the kitchen and be carved by our grandfather, with much ritual, and he would be at one end of the dining room table and Nana would be at the other end. And she would say, 'Will you please carve the roast?' and he would be talking and doing things, he wasn't a raconteur—he wouldn't have talked half as much as I'm talking now—but she would just tear into him. And I remember sitting there as a kid and thinking, My God, why are you doing this, Nana? Because in all other respects she was marvelous. But it seemed cruel. I don't know why; it just seemed cruel. And yet it just bounced off Papa. He'd turn the other cheek. I later learned that was the real fundamental quality of his personality."

My mother was convinced that Nana, despite her sharp tongue

and free criticism, was devoted to Papa and that she gave him absolutely anything he desired. Her shrewish ways were just a pretense that Papa understood and, in some odd way, may have even appreciated.

I say to Estella, "My grandmother could be a bit thorny. That's how I remember her."

Estella studies me a moment and then breaks into a hearty laugh, shaking her head. "Something I never did understand is why your grandmother gave her husband such a hard time. Your grandfather was such a gentle, nice man, but she was on him seems like all the time."

Now I am laughing, and I appreciate Estella's willingness to be honest with me.

"What did Helen do on her days off?" I ask.

"She went to church. She was Catholic, as I said, and I am, too."

"What about James? Was he Catholic?"

"James was going to be a Catholic, but when he was little Helen went up to the church and asked the priest to baptize her baby. But that priest was a sour, mean man—Helen said she didn't like him for nothing—and he said to her, 'Well, Helen, if you'll bring that *thing* over here, I'll baptize it.' And Helen thought to herself, If my baby is all that much of a *thing*, you'll never baptize him. So she never had James baptized. But when he got older, after he left me there in Pittsburgh, he married another woman. They had one child in that union, so he was baptized, him and his son, at the Methodist church. And that's how that was."

"Is that son still alive?"

"Oh yes, but James just died, this June past."

"Were you angry at him for leaving you and remarrying?"

"At first I was, you know, but then I got over that. I wasn't going to let him ruin my life, because he was already gone. Then later, in about 1980, after he'd left his second wife and got divorced, he come back here to live with his sister Margaret up in Shady

Lane. And so when she died in 1982, he didn't have no place to live, because them children didn't want him staying there in that house. So I just let him come back here and stay with me and he was here from '83 to this present time and died. I just took care of him and helped him all I could. But we never remarried, because I just wasn't going through that again. So that's when I took care of him, until he died."

"That was kind of you, to take care of him after what he put you through," I remark.

"Well, I don't look at it that way. I just think that's the way of life. I always say about things like that, I put all that stuff back here"—she touches the back of her head—"I don't let it keep running up here in the front, so it worries you, does something to you. If you put it back here and you just sort of…you don't forget really…but you just don't let it keep nagging at you. That's the way I live. I don't worry about things, because that's not going to help you any. I just live my life each day. I get up, I start off, and whatever comes, I try to face it. I laugh and tell my friends, I say, I'm ready for anything that happens. If you come to my house and say, 'Let's go to California today,' I'm not going to say, 'Oh I can't go because I got to get my hair done or I have to…' I say, 'I'm ready. All I got to do is get my coat and hat and I'm ready to go.'"

Estella chuckles. "Just whatever comes. And I go to bed at night, I go to sleep, and if I wake up in the morning, okay, and if I don't, I'm still okay. That's my motto, and that's the way I live every day."

"What about Helen?" I ask. "What was her philosophy of life? What was she like as a person?"

"She was really and truly a beautiful woman. Because as she had all these hardships way back, she learned how to cope with things. She didn't get excited. She wasn't an excitable person. But she didn't take a lot a guff off of people. She didn't let people run over top of her. That's the way she was. But she was a lovely, lovely woman."

"What do you think the hardest thing was for her in life?" I
ask.

"I guess her husbands dying and having these children to take care
of. And she had to work. She was a mother without a husband and
she had to get out there and find a job. And them children weren't
old enough to work until the boys got up in years, and the girls, and
then they could help her. She had a hard life, but she learned how
to cope with it. She got so she could get out and be free and didn't
have to worry about whether them children had something to eat
or whether they didn't, because they're married now, they can take
care of theyselves. Then she was free in that respect."

"Did she come to Pittsburgh after her third husband, Mr.
Spriggs, died?"

"Yes, that's when she went to Pittsburgh. A man took her up
there. He said he could find her work."

It is getting late and I ask if I can come back in a day or two
and record her memories of Helen and the fire and anything else
she can remember.

"I have a couple of pictures of Helen," she says. "Would you
like to see them?"

She goes into another part of the house and returns with a
small photo album that she opens up on the kitchen table.

"I only have three pictures of Miss Helen," she tells me and
I realize I have always taken for granted that families have lots
of photographs. But given what I have seen and heard, I suspect
there wasn't extra money to buy cameras and pay for developing
film, especially back when Helen was alive.

Estella removes a photograph from the album and hands it to
me. It looks like it was taken in a photo booth, the kind where
you drop a quarter in a slot and it spits out a strip of monochrome
images. This photograph shows a middle-aged Helen sporting a
broad-brimmed straw hat and a generous smile, light bouncing
off the edge of her spectacles. It is a delightful image, full of joy,
and my heart fills to the brim as I study her face.

The next photo shows a much older woman in a dark dress sitting in a straight-back chair next to a dresser. Her hands lie in her lap and her shoulders slump with fatigue. It takes me a second to realize I am looking at the same person, but I know it is Helen, because the dresser in the photo is now in our dining room. But where the picture was taken, in the house on Shady Lane, Andover, or Paterson, I cannot tell. Then Estella pulls out the last photograph and I have to catch my breath. The photograph, which is badly faded, shows Helen, a large, tall woman in a white uniform, standing next to my Uncle George, who is sitting in a chair next to his son Michael and my grandfather Poppy. Helen is smiling and handing Uncle George a cigarette. And there on Uncle George's lap is Joey, staring out of the photograph. I am five years old. What moves me so much is the knowledge that for over a half a century Helen's family has kept my likeness in their family album.

Estella and I walk outside together so I can get my camera from the car. It is very quiet, the greeting birds have flown off, and I feel a welcomed calmness inside me. There has been so much wondering, planning, and hoping, and now that I am finally here, all is right with the world.

I need to head back to Alexandria but I want to take Estella's picture first. I also want to visit Shady Lane and the cemetery where Helen is buried. I ask where I can find the grave.

"There's no marker," Estella tells me and there is sorrow in her tone. "There's a stone for Belt and I think they buried Miss Helen nearby."

"Is that Howard Belt's grave, your father-in-law?" I am still trying to work out who is who in my head.

"No, it's another Belt, but I don't know which one. I wish I could tell you more than that."

Estella lets me take several pictures of her, one on the walkway to her house and another by an old water pump in the backyard. A man comes out of the house to get something from his car. I don't know his relationship to Estella, but I ask him if he will take a picture of Estella and me together.

I get into the car and drive less than a quarter mile up the road to a street that goes off to the right. There is a street sign with the words SHADY LANE. I turn and follow the lane for two hundred yards, past six modest houses, until the street dead-ends. To my left, across an empty lot, is a large cemetery with a white-framed church at the far end. To my right is a second cemetery, smaller and slightly overgrown and without a church building. The larger cemetery belongs to Saint Mary Catholic Church. According to Estella, this is where Helen is buried. The two cemeteries are but a stone's throw apart from each other.

I am struck by another coincidence: my memories of the Shady Lane in Pittsburgh are of a dead-end street serving a half dozen houses with ours standing at the end.

I get out of the BMW and walk over to St. Mary Church in the gathering dusk. It is an old church, nineteenth century is my guess, and its cemetery encompasses several acres with a magnificent maple in the center. I meander among the gravestones looking for the name Belt. I find it near corner of the cemetery at the edge of the gravel parking lot, a simple headstone, no epitaph or carved figures, just the name, BELT. But at least this Belt, whoever he or she was, has a marker. Not Helen. She is buried somewhere nearby but I can't tell exactly where.

There is this thing about cemeteries; you can suddenly find yourself talking aloud to a loved one who is buried there.

"Well, Helen, it's been a long time. My mother was truly grateful for all that you did for us. I wish she were here to tell you herself. Maybe she is. I'd like to think so. You helped us when we really needed help, and I want to thank you and tell you that you are missed."

The air is soft with the coming of night. Peepers begin their spring serenade in the distance. Like many in my family, I can be a bit high-strung, and yet the calmness I felt as I left Estella's house persists and even deepens as I stand in the cemetery and soak in all that has happened today. If nothing else, I have reconnected my mother's life to Helen's and washed away in some spiritual, karmic sense, perhaps, a portion of the regret my mother carried for so many years.

I take out my fiddle and play Helen a tune before climbing back into the car and driving away.

# CHAPTER 11

## NIGHT THOUGHTS

It is twilight as I return to the car to begin my drive north to Frederick, then east on I-270 toward DC. I will return to Estella's home in a couple of days to fill in as many gaps as I can in Helen's story, but I realize there is much I will probably never know.

As the miles slip under the wheels of the car I think about Helen and how a child's brain is formed in the first five years of life. From what I understand, one of the first organs to develop inside the womb is the ear. This occurs at around eight weeks when the fetus is about the size of a grape, and from then on the baby can hear sounds coming from the outside world. The eye, by comparison, only begins to perceive the outside world in a meaningful way after birth, and even then it takes another six to eight months before the eye-brain circuitry is fully developed. Inside the womb we can hear our mother's voice, her unique tonality and cadences, and our brains use this information to start forming impressions of what the world will be like after we are born. The BBC reported on research done at the University of Wurzburg that found that newborns of French-speaking parents cry differently than babies with German-speaking parents. Studying sixty healthy babies that were only three to five days old, researchers discovered that the cry of the French newborns consistently had a rising inflection at the end of their cry, while the German babies had a falling inflection. This suggests that infants are influenced by the sound of the first language that penetrates the womb, and they learn to mimic that sound as a way to foster a stronger bond with the mother. And this intimate aural relationship between children and caregivers continues to shape the neural pathways inside the child's brain for years after the youngster comes into the world.

I recall an interview I did with the musician Peter Rowan at a bluegrass festival some years ago. Peter, whose father survived a bout of polio, toured and performed for many years with the legendary Bill Monroe. He also played with David Grisman and Jerry Garcia in the 1970s' band Old and In the Way. Besides being a gifted songwriter, vocalist, and guitarist, Peter also plays the mandola. The mandola is a larger version of the mandolin, in the same way that the viola is the larger sibling of the violin. Few bluegrass musicians play the mandola, preferring instead the brighter tones of the mandolin. Peter told me that it wasn't until he turned sixty that he began to consider seriously the influence his parents had upon his musical career. He also figured out why he chose to play the mandola. It was because his mother often sang lullabies to him when he was a young child and the pitch and tone of her voice closely matched the pitch and tone of that obscure instrument.

As I have mentioned, I too have a relationship with folk music, more particularly with a genre called "old-time" music, a rural style that predates bluegrass and country-western music. In fact, old-time music proved my salvation when I lived on the farm in West Virginia and was stumbling and lurching my way into manhood, the proverbial youthful fool making one questionable decision after another, slipping in and out of destructive romantic relationships, and struggling to find a clear sense of purpose. It is not that I didn't mean well; I just had a lot to learn about the world, myself, and the art of navigating through life's many trials and tribulations with some degree of grace and dignity. Fortunately for me, I attended the West Virginia State Folk Festival in the nearby town of Glenville, where I discovered a traditional style of music that continued to thrive in the mountains. For generations the people of Appalachia created and passed on this art form that stitched together fiddle tunes, humorous songs, dulcimer melodies, religious hymns, and haunting ballads like the squares of a quilt, adding a richness to life I found sustaining. Moreover, people learned to play this music by ear rather than from sheet music, and that appealed to me. So I traded a handmade leather purse for a secondhand fiddle and set myself the task of learning how to bow the old tunes. I got so caught up in this endeavor that I wound up spending an entire year living in the highlands of Scotland where I explored the Celtic contribution to old-time music. Along the way, I picked up other instruments—the banjo, lap dulcimer, hammered dulcimer, guitar, and pennywhistle. As I studied, I learned that traditional Appalachian music has deep roots in the African diaspora as well. The banjo, for one, is an African instrument, originally fashioned by stretching an animal skin over a hollowed gourd fitted with a wooden neck and strings. The men and women who were enslaved on the southern plantations brought the knowledge of this instrument with them from Africa, and eventually the banjo made its way up into the mountains, transforming American frontier music. Appalachian tunes often share the same name as the ones I heard in Scotland, but they had tonal and rhythmic differences that were the result of this unique cultural marriage between Celtic and African music.

As I drive and think about early neurological development, I cannot help but wonder if I was drawn to old-time Appalachian music because it is a blend of the two primary aural influences of my early childhood: the lilting voices and songs of Irish-Americans that filled the air around me and Helen's rhythmic voice as she bathed, fed, and lulled me to sleep. Estella told me Helen's family came to Maryland from Virginia. Were they a musical family? Did Helen sing to me? I have always had this strong feeling that she did, but no specific memory of it. Perhaps Estella can tell me.

It is eleven o'clock by the time I reach Alexandria, and I decide to stop in Old Town for a beer to celebrate the day's discoveries.

I wander into a crowded bar on King Street and a group of men on a pub-crawl draw me into their circle. Their mood is very hail-fellow-well-met, and they buy me a beer and encourage me to join them as they continue on to the next bar. Although I am tired, I decide to tag along for an hour or so. They tell me they are firemen in town for a convention. So again I find myself hanging out with firemen, the same tribe that welcomed me in Brunswick and pointed me in the right direction. I tell them about Helen and Estella and the fire in 1952. This earns me another beer, and we end the day toasting those happy fates that graciously led me to Helen's family.

# CHAPTER 12

## THE SECOND INTERVIEW

I return to Petersville two days later, after first stopping at a bakery to purchase a birthday cake for Estella. My brother and cousins remembered Helen as being an exceptional cook, especially when it came to desserts, a fact Estella confirmed during my first visit.

"If you remember how good she could cook. She was a beautiful cook. When you can go into a refrigerator and make a meal for your family and there's nothing in there in the beginning, you know you have to be a good cook. But that's the way she was; she just knew how to do things. She could make the nicest food. I just thought she was, as we always say, 'Top shelf'. She was a beautiful person to me."

I was too young to form strong memories of Helen's cooking, but I present the cake to Estella by way of showing my gratitude. This time we sit in her living room, surrounded by boxes packed with her belongings.

"Can you describe what Helen was like physically?" I ask after switching on the recorder.

"Helen was a large woman. I'd say she was six one or two. She was that tall. And big boned. To me, I thought she had a beautiful shape, as big as she was. But not sloppy big. Just very stately. That's the way I looked at her. I always said she was a handsome woman when she was dressed and everything.

"She was a hard working person, too, a regular person in the community. And she was a good mom, taking care of her children and minding her own business. She didn't do any great things or anything like that, but she was *nice* to people. Anybody needed a helping hand or whatever; she'd try to do that. Even though she was busy and she didn't have money, she would try to help any way she could. Her whole family was like that. They just took care of everybody, tried to help everybody."

I tell Estella how I found the letter my mother wrote in 1952 about the house fire in Brunswick. My mother mentioned that John Harold Thomas left a one-year-old child behind when he died.

"That is Gail Lee," Estella tells me. "She has a brother they call Bubby."

"Is she still alive?"

"As far as I know. I think she lives somewhere near Hagerstown, but I don't know how to get in touch with her. Her mother was Dorothy, and she died not that long ago."

"Did Dorothy remarry after John Harold died?" I ask.

"No, she didn't marry again."

When I ask Estella to tell me about the night the house caught fire in Brunswick, she reaches for the telephone and calls James "Timmy" Jackson. Timmy is John Harold's younger cousin, the fifteen-year-old who survived the fire by jumping out of a third-story window. He is now in his seventies and lives in Frederick. I hold the microphone up to the earpiece as he tells me the story of what happened that fateful night.

"At the time, I was living in Petersville with my grandmother. I used to like to shoot pool as a youngster, so I went down there to Brunswick on Saturday night to play pool, and couldn't get no ride back home. Everybody knew me because I grew up right down there with all of them [on Shady Lane], but I couldn't catch a ride back home. So John said to come over to Momma's—that's what he called Aunt Helen—and spend the night over there. So I went and they were all drinking and everything. I think it was in April, that time of year, and it might have been chilly that night. It was a three-story old house and they made a wood fire. The fire probably got away from them—I'm guessing they sat there and the heat from the fire put them to sleep—and when I woke up I was screaming and hollering and I heard little John screaming and hollering. I was up on the third floor and they were down on the second floor. And it was only the grace of God that got me out of there. They say that was an old house that was crooked, and it had windows up on the third floor that probably had never been opened in years. But somehow or other I managed to raise that window up and jump out the third floor. I hit the ground and didn't break any leg or bones or anything. I ran over to my uncle's house, who lived over back behind the Swing Inn, and that's when they called the ambulance and got me on up and carried me to the hospital.

"That's as much as I remember about it. I think I was in the hospital twenty-three days trying to heal from that, and I'm still carrying the heavy scars from it. I was young but I knew John had a kid. I knew his wife. I don't know where his daughter is or anything like that.

"As for Aunt Helen, you see, I had another grandmother that lived right there beside her. I'm sure Aunt Helen used to work for Dr. Watson out on Rosemont. When she used to come home in the evening, she had to walk across in back of the old house where my grandmother lived to get to her place. That's how we knew her so well.

"Aunt Helen was very pleasant, I guess that's why we where there, you know, because if she wouldn't have been, she wouldn't be letting people come in her house and stay there and things like that. I guess her home was a place for everybody. Back in them days, it was kind of like that."

I thank Timmy for his story and say goodbye, all the while thinking about how Helen's home was a place for everybody.

"How did the Brunswick fire affect the family?" I ask Estella.

"To me, it was a terrible thing to think this child had burned up in the house. He was my husband's nephew, his sister's son, and

James loved that boy very much. They worked together a lot and he [John Harold] was just a young man. But I never knew why John Harold was there, because he lived with his mother Margaret, who had a house in Shady Lane. And that's where Helen went to live after she come back from New Jersey. She lived with her daughter Margaret in Shady Lane. And that's where Helen died."

Brunswick was a roaring railroad town for most of its history, a community, as some locals like to quip, of "hills, whores, and liquor stores." Estella tells me the town once boasted the second-largest marshaling rail yard in the United States, stretching more than six miles along the Potomac River. All the freight coming east through the mountain gap at Harper's Ferry fetched up in the rail yard in Brunswick. From there it was redirected up and down the eastern seaboard of the United States.

"It wasn't this puny little two tracks you see down there now," Estella tells me, "a westbound and an eastbound track. That whole thing was just tracks, and they did everything. Cattle and coal and anything that needed to be transferred, that's where it would be made up, in Brunswick, when it come down [through the mountains]. So this was a big concern; you needed men to keep that thing really going. That's why they finally give the blacks a job. I know James worked on the railroad. They laid rail from Brunswick to Germantown. That was a long stretch. They had a large bunch of men do that with a foreman in charge. They all enjoyed it."

Estella confirms what Timmy said about Helen working for a dentist named Watson in Brunswick before moving to Pittsburgh.

"Mrs. Watson said it was just 'white slavery' taking Helen away," Estella laughs, remembering how upset the dentist's wife was when Helen left the household. "But Helen enjoyed being up there in Pittsburgh. She felt freer. It wasn't as hard as it was in Brunswick, slaving and working for Mrs. Watson all those years. She used to have to walk to work and walk back, not that downtown Brunswick was that far. Everybody had to walk wherever you went. You didn't have a car. You didn't have enough money to buy a car; where you going to get one? Sometimes Mrs. Watson would bring her home, and then in later years, she [Mrs. Watson] started to come and get her in the mornings."

"Can you tell me more about the house in Brunswick, the one that burned down?"

"It belonged to John Kaetzel. Helen worked for them some too. He was her landlord. When she'd get off working for Mrs. Watson, she'd go and work in their house. It was right up the hill there on Potomac Street. Rent wasn't very much and working for them [the Kaetzels] helped pay the rent. She lived there and raised her children, the younger bunch, the Spriggs children— that's Thelma, Virginia, and Charles. And of course James was with her a lot. But he mostly was out with his grandmother until he went into the Army. When he came out of the Army, he stayed with his mother then."

I ask about James' family, his father's people, the Belts.

"James' grandfather was from Alabama. He was a slave down there, and he often told James how he came to Maryland. He said he just got sick of this man telling him do this and that and beating him and carrying on. And so one day, they were in the field, and the man started this mess and James' grandfather took a singletree, and he struck the man in the head. Well, he knowed that if the man died or whatever, he wasn't going to be able to live, so he caught the first train. A freight come through and he just reached up and got the freight and kept going. So that's how he got to this part of the world from Alabama."

Howard Belt married Helen but later died. Estella couldn't remember how old James was when this happened. Helen then married Theodore Spriggs, who everyone called "Thee," and they had three children together. Estella tells me that James babysat the younger ones while Helen worked for the Watsons.

"He used to laugh and say how he had to watch them, these kids, and they want to be playing, doing something else themselves. And he got to watch these little ones because his mother's working, you know. And if she come home and they'd done anything, well, he said, 'She'd be whipping them good.'"

Estella laughs. "Well, she had to keep law and order to be able to raise her children and keep 'em from being in jail or being taken away from her or whatever, you know? And she worked hard. Yes, she had a hard life."

We talk more about Helen's children; all of them are gone now, and she mentions that Charles Spriggs died trapped in a fire in Philadelphia.

"They said this woman set the house on fire. He was up on the second or third floor and couldn't get out."

I realize I have heard a lot about fires and their victims. Aunt Kate's, Joe Walls, John Harold Thomas, and now Charles Spriggs. The lead article in the *Baltimore Sun* in April 1952 was about fires. We forget today how common fires once were. Many families used coal and wood for heat and their chimneys were unlined and often caught fire. People also used electrical fuses back then, not mechanical circuit breakers. When you blew a fuse and didn't have a spare, a regular practice was to insert a copper penny in its place. Poppy got the lights back on at our house using this trick more than once. Of course, that made the old-style knob and tube wiring heat up, and sometimes that caused the house to go up in flames. On top of this, more people smoked in bed, and smoke alarms and fire retardant fabrics and mattresses had yet to be invented.

I ask Estella if Helen was alive when her son Charles died; did she have to suffer that loss? Estella has to think for moment.

"No," she says, quite definite. "That fire was after Helen died, because we were living in Knoxville at the time." (Knoxville is a small settlement upriver from Brunswick.)

Estella then tells me about the man who took Helen to Pittsburgh.

"His name was Jack Robinson," she says with a laugh. "I don't know how Miss Helen got entangled with him. I still don't understand how she ever come on him, but it must have been a friend of hers in West Virginia because she was up there working for a man and I think that's where she met some lady named Sally, but don't ask me what Sally's last name was, I don't remember. Then this man, you know how men go from place to place, and he's showing off his big car and all. He had a Lincoln."

She pauses and then breaks into a big smile.

"No, he had an Edsel! You remember the Edsel? James' brother said this thing is so good, it'll run right up the side of the Empire State Building. We laughed about that. But it was an Edsel. And he was one of them, I call them a 'gigolo,' that's what he was like, and because she was kind of smitten with him, too. And then he's telling her about this job, and he took her up to Pittsburgh. That's how she got there. Mr. Spriggs was already dead; she was on her own again.

"He [Jack Robinson] had a woman here and a woman over there and a woman over here, you know, one of those things. That's the way he was. I don't know if he had a job or whether he didn't, but I guess them women, they were all taking care of him. That's why I say he was a gigolo."

So Helen came to work for my family because of a sharp-talking lady's man who skipped town and ended the love affair.

I am beginning to see Helen in a different light, as a real person with needs and passions. I see her kicking up her heels after a lifetime of raising children and scrubbing floors in Maryland.

Then I remember my thoughts while I was driving back to Alexandria, about how sounds can influence a child even when he is in the womb.

"Was Helen musically inclined?" I ask.

"Oh my, yes," Estella says, her face brightening with the memory. "Miss Helen was a large woman and she loved to dance. There was always music in their house. Black fiddlers and guitar players would come from all over to play there, and they'd have big parties."

"What were the parties like?" I ask.

"When everyone was still working, you'd go on Saturday evening and we'd all be over there at Miss Helen's house, and they'd be having a little *sit out*. They'd be drinking and dancing and eating, that's what they did to entertain themselves. You had to make your own entertainment, and they'd be singing and dancing and all that kind of stuff. And sometime her sister would come down; she just lived up the hill, because her sister's husband Willie ran this bar across the street called the Swing Inn. Her sister would come over to Miss Helen's house sometimes, and they'd be sitting there and everybody be drinking and having a good time, just laughing, lying, and telling all kinds of tales. But then they'd be playing these guitars, and somebody would have a fiddle and a mouth harp, and they'd be dancing and carrying on. And that was really fun. It was really nice."

"Was there much mingling between white and black people in the 1940s and 50s in and around Brunswick?" I ask.

"Not much. That's how the Swing Inn come to be. If you didn't have a place, you had to go downtown to buy beer and liquor. You could buy it, but then you couldn't drink it at the bar downtown. You had to bring it home. So that's one of the reasons Bill Winter, a white man in town, built that place for the blacks to have, and it had a beer license and everything and we'd go there. At that time, it had a jukebox and you could dance and have a good time. I guess that place was built in the late forties, and Willie was the manager."

"Do you think Helen ever sang to me?"

"Yes, Miss Helen would have sung to you. And she would have sung them *old* songs out of Virginia."

We have talked for some time and I don't want to overstay my welcome, but I do want to hear how Helen's life ended.

"Can you tell me about Helen's illness?"

"Well, she didn't complain, but you knew she wasn't well. Then when she got this thing on her side, we took her to a doctor and he opened it. It was like a little egg. It was here on her side—" Estella shows me by touching her side—"and he drained it, and it never healed. It never got better. She had started to work out for Mrs. Elva Feete, and the Feetes were the funeral directors. But Elva's daughter, Lorraine, she just loved my mother-in-law; she loved Helen and would do anything for her. So she came and helped take Helen to the doctor and helped to look after her, because Helen been down there helping them. And they took Helen to Baltimore to Johns Hopkins, and that's where she died, down there. She was down there two or three weeks. But it was from this thing on her side, which it had to be cancer. But that thing never healed."

"Do you know if Helen wrote my mother after she came back to Maryland?"

"I don't know. I guess it was because she was getting sick then. But I never paid a lot of attention. I sent a letter for her things."

It is time to pack up my gear. I have grown very fond of Estella. She has been gracious and generous with her time, stories, and laughter. We pass a few more minutes talking about her experiences in Pittsburgh, and then I begin the drive north to New Jersey. I return my brother's BMW without a scratch on it, much to my relief, and then it is home to Olympia. Estella couldn't tell me how to reach any of Helen's grandchildren. If the women are married, I wonder how I will discover their married names. I am back to playing history detective.

# CHAPTER 13

## *THE GRANDDAUGHTERS*

Upon my return to Washington State, I purchase subscriptions to an online genealogical service and several on-line newspaper archives. Even though I love history and am fascinated with family stories, I have never conducted genealogical research. According to the market research firm Global Industry Analysts, as reported recently in Bloomberg News, "Genealogy ranks second only to porn as the most searched topics online."

Sitting in front of the computer in my home office, I discover that mucking about in time, generational time that is, can be oddly seductive. First, there are the hard data: the U.S. Census, Social Security records, death certificates, marriage licenses, and military service records. These provide me with bits of information about Helen and members of my own family, but not enough to help me track down any of Helen's grandchildren. So I turn to newspapers and the obituaries. Mouse click, type a name, and hit the RETURN key. Nothing. Hold down BACKSPACE until the search terms vanish into the ethers and try again—with a date this time. Still nothing. Jump to another newspaper. Type in a name and hit the RETURN key. Tap the PAGE DOWN key. No luck. Try a different name. It is like playing a musical instrument, only the time signature covers decades. I do more searching before glancing at the clock. Two hours have passed. Impossible. Paula calls me on the intercom. It is time for supper. I tell her, "Start without me; I'll be there in a minute."

As I check census and death records again I realize I am only one of thousands of people using the Internet in this way. It is like chasing fairies through a dark, enchanted wood, a shimmering figure glimpsed and then gone, a mischievous laugh floating upon the air. Perhaps they are better fairy hunters than me.

Armed with a new name, Helen's daughter by her first husband James Furr, and the date of her death, I return to a newspaper archive and hit pay dirt: a two-paragraph obituary that includes the name of one of Helen's granddaughters, along with the state where she lives. Or used to live, when her mother passed away fifty years ago. It is a western state, far from Maryland. I wonder if the daughter still lives there.

Her name is Lydia, and I dig a little further and find a work email address for someone of that name. It is the only lead I come up with. I compose an email introducing myself and asking if she is related to Helen Spriggs. I hit the SEND button and my message whooshes off into cyberspace. I switch off the computer and go down to my cold chicken and mashed potatoes. I can see that too much Internet searching overheats the imagination, so after supper I fight off the urge to fire up the computer again, and instead grab my fiddle and play some tunes with Paula. I will wait to see if Lydia writes me back.

Two days pass, and I get no response to my email. But on the third day, the telephone rings and it is Lydia. Yes, she tells me, she is Helen's granddaughter. She seems pleased that I contacted her and talks freely about Helen and growing up in Shady Lane (I realize Estella and Lydia say "in" Shady Lane instead of "on" Shady Lane.) Lydia is quick to laugh, much like Estella, which puts me in mind of a quote by Mark Twain.

"Humor is the great thing—the saving thing after all. The minute it crops up all our harnesses yield, all our irritations and resentments slip away and a sunny spirit takes their place."

We set up a time the next day to do an interview over the telephone. She says she will give her younger sister a call. Her name is Helen, and she lives in a city not far from Lydia's home.

Helen works as the housekeeper and cook for a wealthy man who is often away traveling.

The next day I call Lydia and we begin the interview.

"Let's start with when were you born and your memories of Helen," I say.

"I was born in 1947. I don't remember a lot about my grandmother. But I remember she was a very tall, big-boned lady because I have an uncle, Aunt Estella's husband James—well, he's dead now—but he was tall, just like my grandmother. And I remember when she used to come home from Pittsburgh, she always tried to bring us something. Just a little something, not much, but something. She always brought my brother white shirts. I just remember this so well. And they were just the whitest shirts I have ever seen, just white, white, white. And to this day my brother is so meticulous about his clothing and how he looks. He really is."

"What about your grandfather?"

"I have no memory of him, or of Helen's other husbands. I think Nanny's [Helen's] family, a lot of them, came from Lucketts, Virginia, because I remember my mother talking about Lucketts, Virginia. I also remember Nanny's mother when I was young. She was dark. Real short and dark. We called her Grandma Palmer and she made rabbit stew. I remember that, and I know this sounds weird," Lydia laughs, "but she had whiskers coming out of her chin and we used to pull them out."

"Did Grandma Palmer live with your family in Shady Lane?" I ask.

"Shady Lane, that's exactly where it was. We lived right between two graveyards, the Catholic Church and the church we used to go to, which was an A.M.E. Church—I can't even think of the name right now. A lot of people from back there had died from cancer, and we just feel it's from living between those two graveyards with the tombstones and everything. It may have nothing to do with it, but that's what I feel. Both of my parents had cancer, and I really believe it's from living between those two graveyards and that water. I don't know, it may not have been, but that's what I feel."

I recall my visit to Shady Lane and how the two cemeteries dominated the landscape, a borderland of sorts where the joys and suffering of life end and the long sleep of death begins. I wonder if it is possible the ground water was polluted with embalming fluids, as Lydia seems to suggest.

I ask her to talk about growing up in Shady Lane, and Lydia replies in a light and youthful voice.

"We used to have the best times. We had baseball games in the summertime, and this one family, every 4th of July, they used to have a barbecue and everyone from Brunswick and Burkettsville would come out to this barbecue. Yes, we used to have the best time. We didn't have the things most kids had. I remember us rolling tires where the A.M.E. Church used to be. We used to roll tires up and down the road. That was fun for us." Lydia sighs and then laughs as the memories return.

"I think we had more than most people up in the Lane, but one thing about the people who lived up there, we were all very close. Very, very close. If I did something that I wasn't supposed to do, anybody up there could correct me. If I needed spanking, they could spank me." More laughter.

Lydia talks about her parents, how her mother worked as a domestic servant most of her life and how her father labored for the railroad.

"My parents, how can I put this but be nice about it? They were very uneducated. My dad was a self-taught person. He was very smart with numbers. He read the Bible. But they were uneducated in a lot of things, because they didn't read the newspaper or books. I don't think they could read. You know what I'm saying?

"But we never went without, that's one thing I can say coming up. We always had plenty of food and my mother was an excellent cook. Because I like coconut cake and coconut cream pie, my mother would make me a coconut cream pie and she would make my brother a chocolate pie and she would make my other sister a lemon pie and we always had those things because she knew we liked them. She was an excellent baker. I guess she learned to cook from Nanny and Grandma Palmer.

"And we had a stereo and my mother had all these old records. It was a phonograph with a needle and all that stuff and she would put on blues, like B. B. King, music like that, and tears would just be rolling down her face and we'd say, 'What's wrong, Mama?' And she'd say, 'Nothing honey, this is what the blues does for you. This is what the blues will make you do.' And she'd be crying and smoking a cigarette and drinking her coffee. Oh yeah, I remember that.

"I don't know anything about my dad's family because he always told us he was a hobo. He said he came from Cincinnati and he was the funniest person you'd ever want to meet, and he would tell us some of the funniest stories and we'd laugh. In the wintertime, we used to walk from our house to the filling station where you bought gas, and my dad had an account with the owner and we could go up there and get ice cream. I still like to eat ice cream in the wintertime. My dad always ate ice cream in the wintertime.

"And my dad used to like to see my sister and my brother and me dance. He thought that was the best thing going. He just loved to see us doing that. And he smoked cigars and smoked a pipe and today I love the smell of a pipe. I have one of my dad's pipes and I also have a thimble from when my mother used to sew. It could have been her mother's [Grandma Palmer].

"My dad wasn't a drinker, but at Christmastime he would take a little shot glass and take some whiskey or bourbon and put it in some coffee with a lot of sugar and that was his toast for the year. He did that every Christmas."

I am curious to know how her parents dealt with the racial

attitudes back in the 1950s and 60s when she was growing up.

"Well, for me, my parents were very prejudiced people. They were very, very prejudiced against white people. I remember once this guy who lived up in Shady Lane, he had brought this white lady home, and my parents just thought it was horrible! They would say blah, blah, blah, and I'm thinking, wow. And I remember when my mother worked for the mayor and she couldn't eat with them, she had to eat in the kitchen by herself. Things like that used to just bother me, and my mother used to always tell me, 'Just don't say nothing. Let it go. Just do what you have to do and be nice to these people. It's okay, it's okay, it's okay.' You know, because she needed that job. My mother worked very hard for white people for many, many years and making maybe five or ten dollars a day. We never owned a car. Never. And the clothes we had were all hand-me-down clothes from the people that my mother used to work for. My mother used to always tell me, 'You can kill a person with kindness.' And it's true." Lydia laughs.

"What were your experiences with prejudice?" I ask Lydia.

"Trust me, I was right there in the middle of it and I didn't like the way black people were treated either. At the time, I was very rebellious, and I didn't like that my mother had to work so hard for these white people. I remember walking down the street in Brunswick one time and this man literally spit as I walked past. He spit on the ground when I walked past.

"From the first to the sixth grade, I went to an all-black school. I went to a school where we had to go outside and ring a bell. And when I rode the school bus we couldn't sit in the front of the bus, and we couldn't go into establishments. If you went in there, they'd say, 'Whites Only.' We had to go to the back of the business to be served. I remember things like that. When we did go to a white school, it was very hard. We had to literally fight to get along with the kids. But through all of that for me, I had some of the best friends. Some of my best friends were the people that I used to fight in school."

As we talk about the civil rights movement, Lydia tells me a story.

"As I said, I didn't like how we had to sit in the back of the bus going to school. I remember once there were five of us and I said to these other kids, 'Today, when we get on this school bus, we are not sitting in the back of the bus. We're sitting in the front.' And because of that we had to walk to school, literally walk to school for ten days. They put us off the bus and the only way we got to school was if somebody picked us up or we had to walk. I was maybe eight or nine and I was the ringleader."

I ask if she did this because of Rosa Parks.

"You know, I didn't know anything about Rosa Parks but I had to say enough is enough.' And I remember going to school and if you did something wrong on the bus they would make us, the black kids, sit on the step where you get on the bus all the way to school. That's where we had to sit if they felt we were bad.

"And today, believe it or not, I can tell you when somebody is prejudiced. You don't even have to open your mouth to me, I can see it. Even now, and I'm almost sixty-two years old, you wouldn't believe the things I've gone through. Some of the things, even working for the city, I had to go through in order to get through. It's not a pretty thing, but for me I had to get past it. Because if I didn't get past it, I can tell you right now, I'd be a very angry, bitter person. And my parents didn't raise me to be like that."

We talk about Helen and how she lived in with my family. Lydia tells me that her parents always came home at night, which meant a great deal to her. But then she talks about other women, mothers with young children, who took jobs as live-in maids and how hard it was on their families.

"A lot of people back there, they worked like that. They had no choice. That was the only way they got income."

As we are finishing, I mention my mother's regret that she never stayed in touch with Helen.

"I can understand that," Lydia says. "I can truly understand that. Wow, that's interesting."

Three days later, Lydia's younger sister Helen Jackson calls me on the telephone. Born in 1954, she describes herself as a late child—"almost an accidental type of thing"—because her mother was forty and her father was sixty at the time. She never knew her brother John Harold, because he was killed in the fire in 1952, two years before she was born. As we talk, I tell her about the fire that destroyed Aunt Kate's, because I want her to know that my mother did not come from high society, but from ordinary, working class people.

"Well, you know our house burned down, don't you?" she says.

"You mean the house in Brunswick that burned down?" I am confused.

"No, our house in Shady Lane. My dad built it out of old railroad ties that were full of creosote, and the fire was horrible. I remember it was a sunny day, and we were in church for choir practice. I must have been five or six at the time, and it scared me so bad because I thought my father was in the fire. I tried to run in there and get him out, because he was my heart, you know, but they held me back."

"Was he inside the house?"

"No, he wasn't, and nobody got hurt. But I remember the flames, the fire was so, so hot, and the billowing smoke was black. It was like our whole little neighborhood was there watching it, and I was crying. I remember it took the fire department such a long time to get there and, by the time they did, our house was just in smolders."

Helen then says something remarkable.

"My mother was a saver of coins. She used to save silver dollars, and after the smoke settled we all started looking through the ashes for those silver dollars that never burned up in the fire. I remember that so vividly, and I remember we found a bunch of coins, I don't know how many, but it was more than ten, I'm sure of that."

I am amazed. Helen is telling my mother's story, about how she looked for coins in the ashes after Aunt Kate's burned down. Lydia says her family had very little money, so finding those silver dollars must have been important to them. I can imagine Helen, the baby of the family like my mother, her nose filled with the acrid stench of burned creosote, her little fingers sifting through the ashes for precious coins.

I ask Helen to tell me what happened after the fire.

"We lost everything. The fire basically destroyed us, because we had nothing. Me and my sister and my brother had to go live with my aunt and uncle. That's my Uncle James and my Aunt Estella. My other sister stayed with my Aunt Thelma.

"My mother and father, to be honest, I don't know where they were. I'm sure they were working and trying to rebuild and help us and everything. So we saw them on the weekends, and then we had family dinners together and the whole family would come together at my uncle and aunt's house."

I remember how my Aunt Ruth went to live with relatives in the Bronx after the fire at Aunt Kate's and how difficult that was for her and my mother. The parallel experience Helen is describing haunts me.

"Then a few years down the road," Helen continues, "my father built a new house for us. We didn't have running water in the old house or in the new house. We had the outhouse, as a lot of people in that era did."

"How many people lived in the Lane when you were growing up?"

"I'd say, at most, there were forty-five black people living in Shady Lane in Petersville. It was a dirt road and the farther back you went little houses were popping up and some people lived in trailers. A lot of people didn't have cars. We didn't have a car when I was growing up. We basically used a taxicab. I remember my mom and dad using taxicabs to go and do the grocery shopping, because grocery shopping was a big thing for us. We'd go in the store and get our little groceries and come back home. But everybody was there with everybody; everybody knew everybody. It was like a family neighborhood. If one child got in trouble at somebody's house, you can best believe that the parent of that house was gonna smack you and then you got to come home and deal with your own parents. So everybody was raising everybody's kids, and we learned how to have respect for everybody. Didn't matter who. It was 'Yes, ma'am' and 'No, sir' and 'Thank you.' There was no disrespect.

"And people had gardens. I remember we had chickens. My aunt and uncle used to take us to the orchard and we'd get fresh peaches. My mother would get lots of corn and she'd do a lot of canning and things like that but as far as a garden, I don't remember us ever having a garden. I remember my mother wanting to have a chicken at evening and going out in the yard and grabbing a chicken and wringing its neck and chopping its head off. Then the whole body would be running around like crazy."

Helen tells me that three or four months after the fire destroyed their house, they moved into the parsonage of the A.M.E. Church.

"It was a really, really big house, and we lived there because we had no place to go. But we still owned the land in Shady Lane, and after a while we built a new house on that land."

I ask where their house was located in the Lane and whether they could see the cemeteries.

"We were between the two cemeteries and, yes, we could see them. I remember when they would have Memorial Day and would honor the men in the military. I remember the twenty-one gun salute, all of it."

I mention Lydia's speculation that the graveyards were somehow responsible for people in the Lane getting sick, and how it might have been the water.

"There were a lot of people that died, a lot died from cancer. Just about everyone that lived up there died from cancer. Before my parents built their new house and we built a well by our house, we used to go to my cousins' house down the road and draw water from the well. Everybody drew water from that well. I don't know if you've ever done that but you have a long rope and you just let it go down there and you bring your water up and you fill your bucket up and you tote it home. That's the way we lived, very simplistic."

"Do you think you could ever live like that again?"

"You know, I think if times got hard like that again, I could survive. I'm a survivor, me and my family, my brothers and sisters, we could survive like that. And the people that lived in that neighborhood, they could survive like that. I don't think the average person could do that. I really don't. That was hard living. For the longest time we didn't have lights in our house and my parents had to do with kerosene lanterns. We had a wood cook stove, and, as far as food was concerned, my mother worked for the wealthy people, and when they had their butchering she would bring home meat and things like that. My uncle did butchering too. He'd kill a hog and sometimes during hunting season we ate squirrel. I remember eating squirrels and we had rabbit and they'd go hunting for groundhog. I remember that so vividly. It's the best kind of food you ever want to eat. Ever."

We talk about her great-grandfather and his Native American roots.

"He was Cherokee. That's what my mother used to tell us all the time. I remember my grandmother [Helen] being a tall woman with this white hair and these long braids that she used to twist up in a ring. My mother was fair-skinned, but my grandmother was a red woman. I remember that vividly. And she wore glasses. A red woman. My mother looked exactly like her. She had the high cheekbones. We all have. I have the real high cheekbones and I'm sure we don't have a lot but I think she was part Native American. I'd like to know how much she was, though."

Helen proceeds to tell me that she is named after her grandmother.

"I do remember Mother telling me that when I was born, my grandmother came from wherever she was, and that's why they named me after her. I'm her namesake."

"So you don't have many memories of your grandmother?"

"I have an image of her. I remember her being a tall woman with white hair and the only other memory I have about her is when she died and me and my other sister couldn't go to the funeral. I remember sitting at our kitchen table and looking out of the picture window, because they had her funeral at the Catholic Church. I remember that so vividly, but we couldn't go, maybe because we were too young. But I just remember seeing my grandmother one time and I remember that she died."

"Lydia told me about some of her experiences with racism and prejudice when she was in school," I mention. "What was school like for you?"

"My parents were very strict. We had to go to school and get a high school diploma. That was one thing they were really strict about. Go to school and get your high school diploma, because you're gonna need it. As far as my life, I sing too. I love to sing. It's just been one of my passions and I used to sing when I was in church a lot. My voice is not *great* great, but I can carry a tune very well. I think I get that from my grandmother. I really do. And I also think I get the cooking thing from my grandmother and my mother, because I like to cook. Like I've said, they took care of someone. My mother took care of families and now I'm taking care of someone. So it's like a third generation thing going on here."

"Have you always taken care of people?"

"I used to baby-sit, but I never ever took care of children. Only when I was married and I had stepchildren, then I took care of them. But that was about it. I used to work at National Geographic and I worked for Frederick County. So it's not like I didn't experience things, because I did. I knew when I was growing up that I was not going to stay in Petersville. I knew I had to get out of there because there was nothing to do and I wanted to see the world. And so far, so good. I'm still learning the world and seeing things and exploring. So life hasn't been bad. I just know that I grew up and I was loved and I was fed and we had plenty of clothes and I always remember my mother and father. It was always a family unit sitting down to the table having dinner together. Always. Not like people go through with broken homes now and everything. I never experienced that. I couldn't even imagine that."

"Were you close to your mother?"

"I don't remember my mother that well. As I got older, probably seven or eight, I remember my mother, but before that I don't remember her at all. Lydia told me my mother used to drink but she just stopped when I was born. Then she started up again when I was like twenty-five. It was something I'd never seen, and, when that happened, it just blew my world, because I never seen my mother drink before. So I ended up taking care of my father. We found out he had cancer, so I moved back home to Petersville and was helping to take care of my father and helping my mother because she was drunk all the time. They were my parents, you know, and I knew she was sick. It angered me, but I was supposed to be there. I was supposed to go through that and I've learned a lot, I really have. You have to be compassionate with people. You never know what someone is going through. That's why I always try to speak to people and smile, because everybody needs a friendly word. Everybody. I don't care who it is.

"As for my dad, I remember holding his hand. I would just follow him everywhere; he couldn't get out of my sight. I had to be near my dad."

"Were there any other family members who were important to you when you were young?"

"I had my Aunt Estella and I also had my godmother, who was Lee Fletcher. She was a schoolteacher in Baltimore and she mentored me. She would take me in the summertime. She lived in Baltimore, but she had a home in Petersville, a big house in Petersville, and, in the summertime, I would pack up my clothes and go stay with my godmother at her house. I could run home any time I wanted to, but she exposed me to the arts and music. She played the piano in the church so she knew all the neighborhood kids and was godmother to quite a few kids. And I used to go spend the weekend with her and her husband in Baltimore. I don't know, she just took a shine to me for some reason. And I remember my uncles when I was a little girl—this just popped in my head—they used to iron my dresses for me when I was a little girl and make me look really pretty. I do remember that. You have to remember I was the baby of the family, so I got a lot of little perks. That's probably why I turned out spoiled sometimes." Helen laughs.

As I talk to Helen I wonder what her grandmother, my Helen, would think of her doing similar work and loving music, and her views on life.

I ask if her parents were religious and she tells me that they made sure their children went to church, to the A.M.E. Church, but they weren't really religious. Estella struck me as someone with deep religious faith and I have the same impression about Helen Spriggs, who stayed loyal to the Catholic Church despite the racism of her priest.

Often when I record people for my radio series, I hear stories about a deceased mother or grandparent looking out for someone in the family. When I was eighteen, something happened that put my life in jeopardy, and I believe my father's spirit came and protected me. So when Helen Jackson tells me a story that happened to her, I wonder if her grandmother might have played a part in saving her life.

"I had a really bad experience. It was really horrible. I was at my girlfriend's house and she was going through changes with her ex-boyfriend and her new boyfriend and I just happened to be at her house. Well, the night of December 11, 2002, her ex-boyfriend, who lived next door snuck into her house, broke into her house, whatever you want to call it, and he shot her boyfriend twice, shot her three times. Then he came after me and shot me. But before all of this happened, there was something telling me, I know this may sound strange, most people wouldn't believe it, but something—I know it was God—kept telling me 'Don't go to sleep yet. Don't go to bed yet; keep your clothes on. Don't go to sleep.'

"So I didn't go to sleep and I kept my clothes on. By the time that man came into the bedroom, we were struggling with the gun and everything, then we went into another room and I got a chance to run away, but he still shot me, and that experience changed my life in a way that you'd never believe. I don't think I've ever been the same since. It has changed my life to the point where I know I need to be safe at all times, but by the same token I didn't get angry at this man for what he did. I mean, I lost my best friend of twenty some years, she died immediately from the shots and his intent was to kill everyone in the house. That was his intent, and then he blew his brains out. He went outside and blew his brains out after all this. But I learned from that, and the thing is, I'm not angry at him for what he did, because I know there was something wrong with him. He just knew he was dying because he drank a lot and he had cirrhosis of the liver. I guess his thing was, 'If I can't have her, I'm gonna take everybody and kill up everybody.' But it didn't work out like that. My life has changed to the point where it grew me closer to God, so much closer to Him because I believe in Him for everything. I don't have any fears. I know He's with me at all times, because, trust me, that night He was there with me. It was divine intervention because it wasn't my time to go."

"What happened after the man shot you?"

"Well, he was like really close to me, less than a foot away. He actually shot me in my stomach, in near my belly button. Right in the middle of my stomach. This was so weird too. He shot me, and the bullet actually popped out of my hip and it was in my pantyhose. Isn't that weird? And I was expecting to pass out or just die or whatever and I was like, Lord, I'm still here. I'm breathing. I think my adrenaline kept me from passing out. When I arrived at the hospital, the nurse told me, 'You know what? You are a very lucky young lady because we have the best trauma surgeon here at this hospital tonight to work on you.' So that was divine intervention, too. I know God was with me. I know He was."

"Have you had any long-term effects from being shot?"

"Well, I couldn't move my right leg for a long time and every now and then it'll lock on me. But other than that, I'm okay. I mean, I do suffer from nightmares. I really have some bad nightmares about that night and sometimes I can't sleep. That'll never go away, but I just thank God every day for saving my life because it didn't have to be that way. It could have went totally different. But I had my clothes on. Everybody was going to bed, so I went to bed and God said, 'Don't take your clothes off. Don't go to sleep yet.'

"Now when I think about it, had I been in the bed asleep that man would have come in and probably blew my brains out."

After we hang up, I consider the living conditions in Shady Lane when Lydia and Helen were children: the lack of electricity and how they used outhouses and hauled their own water. I too learned to survive without electricity when I lived on my farm in West Virginia. It wasn't an experiment in early rural folkways, not an intentional experiment at any rate. You could say I lost my electricity because of my Irish temperament.

It was 1971 and I had recently purchased the farm. I was also buying the shoe repair business in the nearby town of Glenville. One day the power company sent a truck out to the farm and turned off the electricity, because I had failed to mail in a twenty-five dollar deposit. I was naive about a lot of things back then, but

I knew they were jerking me around because I was an outsider and a hippie, even though I had cut my hair. So with my blood up, I hung the Be Back in Five Minutes sign on the shop door and hoofed it over to the office, where I confronted the lady behind the counter. She was the twin sister of Ernestine, the telephone operator character created by Lily Tomlin, and her snippy officious manner really got under my skin. Then she made the fatal comment, "Well, Mr. McHugh, if you want to use *our* power, then you have to abide by *our* rules."

"Your power?" I shot back, my voice rising. "You strip these mountains to get your coal and then have the gall to call it your power? Well then, you can just keep your power, for all I care!"

As I stormed toward the door, a dozen ratepayers who were waiting in line behind me, each of them seventy years of age or older, broke out in spontaneous applause. This, of course, was gratifying but then I got halfway down the block and realized what I had done. No electricity meant no lights—or running water, because the well was fitted with an electric pump. Thankfully, the house was supplied with natural gas, that part of West Virginia being rich in natural gas, so I had my heating and cooking covered.

I was also able to swap my electric refrigerator for one that ran on natural gas, a marvel of counterintuitive engineering if ever there was one—you light a small flame with a match in the bottom of the refrigerator and the darn thing gets cold.

For lighting, I relied on oil lamps and hauled water by hand from an older dug well in the backyard. When it was time to take a bath, I did a lot of hauling and heating of water on the gas stove. For laundry, there was a deafening gasoline-powered ringer washer machine, and, yes, there was an outhouse. All of this because I would *not* returnh to the power company office and eat humble pie.

As an aside: even to this day I miss the time of day called dusk. Kerosene lamps work best when there is contrast, the more contrast the better. That is why at twilight it is hard to see using an oil lamp. So I would often sit on the porch and wait until it got dark enough so I could go inside and light the lamps and begin cooking my supper or go back to my leather work. And during that fifteen or so minutes when I was on the porch, the whippoorwill across the creek would begin her singing, and I experienced the day giving way to night. Few people, including myself, experience that transition today.

As I reflect on Lydia's description of life in Shady Lane, I think about Helen and why she came back to Pittsburgh after her grandson died in 1952. I am sure money played an important part in her decision, and there was the promise she made to my mother after my father died. But Estella also said Helen *liked* living with us.

Helen was born sometime between 1894 and 1896, which means she was in her late fifties when she first came to work for us. As part of her employment, she was given her own room in an up-to-date house with central heating and a modern kitchen with all the conveniences. She only had one day off a week, but she could enjoy that day in the city: visit the shops, get her hair done, maybe go out dancing—Estella said she loved to dance. Pittsburgh had a vibrant black community in the early 1950s. The city also had an extensive trolley car system, one of the best in the country, so Helen could get around easily without owning a car. Comparing this to the life she had in rural Jim Crow Maryland, and I see there is something to what Estella said.

On the other side of the ledger, however, her workload was substantial: cooking, mopping floors, doing laundry, and looking after two small children. And as a live-in domestic servant, she was at work *all* the time, 24/7 as we like to say today. Then she agreed to move with us from Pittsburgh to Andover. Not only did she find herself stuck out in the country again, but there were few, if any, black people living nearby. She also had more kids to look after because Aunt Ruth and Uncle George regularly left their

children, Mike and Janna, at our house, often for several days. I
am not sure how this worked exactly, but Aunt Kate's was doing
a land-office business back in the 1950s, and I know my mother,
Ruth and George helped out by waiting tables and tending bar.

When I interviewed Mike and Janna, they both remembered
Helen as the only adult in charge. Janna recalled us carrying
fishing poles across the road to where there was a pond and we
would catch perch that Helen fried up for us. We also had a small
orchard of peach trees, and one of Helen's fresh-baked pies gave
Janna a rash.

Mike, for his part, still nurses a grudge about this familial
arrangement, because Helen often asked him to discipline the rest
of us. When it was time for dinner, for instance, Helen expected
Mike, who was about ten years old, to herd the rest of us to the
table.

Probably the most exciting thing that happened when we lived
in Andover—besides the evening Uncle George showed up with
the athlete's foot medicine—was the day Mike accidentally started
a fire. I have a vivid memory of the event.

Several days earlier, Mike had watched Poppy burn some tent
caterpillars out of a tree and he decided to give it a try himself.
There was a huge tree in the middle of a field next to our house
infested with tent caterpillars, and I remember Mike dragging a
ladder out to the tree so he could climb it. I was playing by myself
in the yard with a toy golf set. It was a hot summer day and between
golf shots I would look up to see Mike crawling along a branch
with a torch of some sort setting fire to the tents. Unfortunately,
some of the embers fell onto the dry grass, and before Mike
realized what was happening a raging fire was heading straight
for our house. Hoses were frantically run out and turned on, and
then Helen, Michael, and seven-year-olds Janna and Ted scurried
back and forth hauling sloshing buckets of water. I remember
everyone, including Helen, being extremely excited. There was a
great deal of yelling and the kitchen screen door slamming as the

wind whipped the flames ever closer to the house. With my five-year-old hand on my putter, I remember feeling blissfully serene and thoroughly delighted; it was a first-rate hullabaloo.

Perhaps there is significance in the memories we carry forward into adulthood, a kind of foreshadowing of what we will become later in life. Storytellers and writers are people who often stand to the side and merely observe and record what is going on. That was my role on the day of the fire. Absolved from responsibility because of my age, I could observe how an adult, Helen, and the older kids, dealt with a serious emergency. I didn't feel any fear because I trusted Helen to take care of us.

Thankfully, a fire truck with sirens wailing and lights flashing pulled up in the nick of time and men piled out wearing big boots and odd-looking hats. Some of the firemen unspooled heavy canvas hoses and others grabbed shovels to dig a firebreak. It is here that God hits the power switch and the memory filament inside my brain dims. I remember Mike and Ted's faces, black with soot, and my mother, Aunt Ruth, and Uncle George barreling up the driveway in our baby blue Buick Special. What happened next is gone. I probably went back to playing golf.

# CHAPTER 14

*DISCOVERY*

Summer comes and goes and I decide to journey again to the East Coast. This time, Paula will join me. Our plan includes visiting friends in Charlottesville, Virginia, giving a lecture on the art of traditional Appalachian storytelling at the University of Maryland, and continuing my research on Helen's family. We arrive at the Baltimore airport in the early evening, pick up a rental car, and drive west fifty miles to the town of Frederick. I was told we wouldn't need a hotel reservation for a Tuesday night, as there should be plenty of rooms available. We discover, however, much to our dismay, that "plenty" is a gross exaggeration. At one motel after another we are informed that there are no vacancies. At last we pull in under the portico of the Frederick Hampton Inn. I go inside and speak to the young woman behind the counter only to receive the same sad story. She has, however, an empathetic nature and offers to call some of the other motels for me. And then: a miracle! She finds us a room at the Best Western across town; perhaps the only available room in Frederick. I assure her that we will take it.

Meanwhile, a middle-aged black security guard drifts over to the counter to observe our little Joseph and Mary in Bethlehem play. He proceeds to follow us out to the car and offers to direct us to the Best Western. Frederick is not the easiest city to navigate, because it serves as a hub for numerous highways fanning out east, west, and south. Also, the city's planning department is not stingy when it comes to one-way streets. So I am thankful for the guidance, and as the guard explains which streets to take to get to the motel, "Turn left onto Patrick Street but then you have to turn right real quick again because Patrick becomes one-way…" an idea begins to percolate inside my brain now that it is no longer awash in anxiety.

"Are you from Frederick?" I ask.

"I grew up here," he replies.

I don't know the size of Frederick's black population, but maybe there is a chance he knows Gail Lee, the daughter of John Harold Thomas, or knows someone who does. I have tried six ways from Sunday using the Internet to locate her without success. Estella couldn't tell me where she lives, nor could Helen's granddaughters: Lydia and Helen. Gail Lee and I were both a year old when we lost our fathers, and I am keen to know what has happened in her life for the past fifty-seven years, since that dreadful night when Helen's house caught fire.

"I'm looking for an African-American woman named Gail Lee Thomas," I tell the security guard. "I believe she has a brother named Bubby. She used to live in Frederick with her mother, Dorothy, but she might be living in Hagerstown now."

"Those names sound familiar," the guard says, rubbing his chin, looking uncertain.

As I open the car door, he says, "My wife knows everybody. I'll give her a call and see if she can find out anything. Do you have a cell phone?"

I give him the number and Paula and I begin our trek across town, following the promise of a soft bed and much-needed sleep. Just before we reach the Best Western, my cell phone rings. It is the guard from the Hampton Inn.

"I talked to my wife, and she thinks Gail Lee lives here in Frederick. She'll talk to some people and try to get word to Gail Lee that you're looking for her."

The next morning we begin driving south toward Charlottesville, but just before reaching the state line we come to the exit for

Route 180 that goes through Petersville and Brunswick. I decide, on the spur of the moment, to take a detour so Paula can see Shady Lane for herself.

A mile and a half down Route 180 we turn onto Shady Lane and drive slowly up the street. It is a stunningly beautiful autumn day, with the leaves in their first full flush of color. We park the car at the end of the street, between the cemeteries, and walk over to the spot in St. Mary cemetery where Estella told me Helen is buried.

"Can you take some pictures of Shady Lane?" I ask Paula, and she returns to the car and gets her camera. As she begins shooting, I notice an elderly black man raking leaves in front of one of the houses. I try to imagine what we must look like to him, a couple of white people in a shiny red car taking photographs of the houses in Shady Lane, including his. Maybe he thinks we are real estate developers. I walk over and introduce myself and tell him about my quest to find Helen's family.

"Yes, I knew Miss Helen," he says with a warm smile. "I was the first black child to grow up in Shady Lane. But then I went into the Army and spent most of my military career in Europe. I was overseas when Miss Helen died."

His name is George Scott, and he lives alone in a house that a local volunteer group built for him several years ago. I have my trusty recorder strapped to my belt, and I ask if I can interview him about his memories of life in the Lane. He agrees, and when I mention what Lydia said, that perhaps the drinking water was responsible for making people sick, George—who insists that I don't need to call him Mr. Scott—tells me that until the 1960s, there was no well for water in that part of Shady Lane.

"We just waited for rain and had fifty-five gallon drums. We put a spout over the roof of the house and let the water run down into the drums. Then they dug the well. I was in the service when they did that, but that was the first time we had a well, ever."

"Was there any other source of drinking water before the well was dug on Shady Lane?"

"Somebody drove a pickup truck into Brunswick every couple of days with empty milk cans in the back to get drinking water."

"Did they ever drink the water out of the drums?" I ask.

"They used that water for washing and stuff like that. But you know how it is. I'm sure they drank that water sometimes, especially the kids."

George's face brightens. "Would you like to see some photographs from when the well was dug?" he asks. "I'm not sure if there are any pictures of Miss Helen—she might have died by then—but there are pictures of her children and grandchildren living here."

He invites Paula and me into his home. The living room is small but comfortable, and he offers us the couch and then goes to retrieve the photographs from a bedroom. I expect him to return with a photo album, like the one Estella showed me, or perhaps an old cookie tin with photographs inside. Instead, he reappears carrying four bound albums, each with beige faux-leather covers.

Paula and I look at each other wondering who should go first; the day is certainly not turning out the way we expected. At last I reach out and lift the cover of the first album to behold a pair of 5x7 black-and-white photographs. One shows a group of smiling black women and children standing under the street sign for Shady Lane. I flip more pages and discover a veritable treasure trove of 5" x 7" black and white photographs: a very old man with a cane walking down the Lane, a boy and a pony both wearing football helmets, a group of women cooking together in a large kitchen, a pickup truck with milk cans in the back, a crowd of youngsters on top of a large well-drilling machine, a young mother holding her baby. A number of the photographs are individual portraits and quite a few are exceptional, true works of art.

"There used to be a Jewish man," George tells us. "His name was Meir Kaplon and he owned the department store in Brunswick. He was the best friend the black people ever had hereabouts. He was always doing things for us, like the water well. He paid for that. He also liked to take pictures. He took these pictures, and because my mother sewed for him he gave me the albums."

Paula is as enchanted by the photographs as I am and we ask if we can take a photograph of the image of everyone standing under the street sign. We realize, as does George, that something special has happened. It is one of those moments when people can't stop smiling. What are the chances, after all, that someone with the soul and eye of an artist would document the life of a small community of black people, spend hours in a dark room painstakingly printing each photograph, and then give the photographs to a man who would, forty-plus years later, decide to rake leaves outside his house when a couple from three thousand miles away show up with a burning curiosity about the history of Shady Lane? I wonder what thoughts passed through the mind of Meir Kaplon as he snapped the shutter of his camera. He must have thought he was documenting something important.

This ripple effect of causality, circumstance, and interconnectedness is part of the allure of family stories. You never know what seeds you plant in life, and maybe that is a good thing, because the marvel of discovery, like the bloom of a flower, is all the more delightful when it happens.

We part company with George and continue our journey to Charlottesville. Just south of Culpeper, my cell phone rings. It is Gail Lee.

"I understand that you are the daughter of John Harold Thomas," I say after introducing myself, "and that he was the grandson of a woman who used to take care of me when I was a child. Her name was Helen Spriggs."

"Yes, John Harold was my father and Miss Helen was my great-grandmother."

"I spoke with Estella Belt and she said you had a brother," I continue.

"I do."

My mother wrote in her letter that John Harold died in a fire and that he had a child who was one year old. There was no mention of other children. So was Gail Lee the one-year-old or was it her brother?

"Is your brother older or younger than you?"

"He's younger. My mother was pregnant with Bubby when my father died in the fire."

Another coincidence: my mother was pregnant with my brother Patrick when my father died, and Gail Lee's mother was pregnant with her brother when her father died.

"I'll be back in Maryland at the end of the week and I was hoping we could meet," I say.

"That would be fine." She gives me her address and we settle on a day and time.

At dusk, Paula and I pull into a bed and breakfast nestled in an apple orchard just outside the village of Crozet, fifteen miles west of Charlottesville. The owners are David and Ginny Wayland. David is a retired Episcopalian priest and Ginny is a retired public librarian. They are also Southerners who love stories. So I tell them about my quest to find Helen's family.

The night before we are set to leave, I wake up at two o'clock in the morning in a state of emotional upheaval bordering on panic. Perhaps the anxiety was triggered by a dream, I can't tell. My mind swirls with a kaleidoscope of Meir Kaplon's photographs of Shady Lane. I am also thinking about George Scott, who seems remarkably fit for his age, but he is getting on in years. Had I set out on my quest eight months earlier, I could have met and talked with James, the last of Helen's children. But James was gone by the time I found his wife Estella. It was that way with my mother. If I had heard about sad brain syndrome on the radio before she died, I could have asked her for Helen's last name and where Helen went after she left us. The discovery of the Kaplon's photos of Shady Lane is providential as far as I am concerned. But what will happen to the photo albums should George suddenly die? He has no children and there is a chance the albums could get tossed in the trash. As the quiet seconds of the Virginia night tick by, I scheme how I might scan the photographs before we head back to Olympia. Time will be tight given the lecture and my meeting with Gail Lee, but I should be able to carve out a window of time, provided we leave Crozet early in the morning. I will buy a scanner somewhere along the way and scan all sixty-five photographs, if George will let me. With this resolve calming my nerves, I am able to fall back asleep.

In the morning while saying our goodbyes, I ask the Waylands where we might purchase a scanner on our way out of town, and David offers to lend us his scanner if I agree to ship it back to him before we get to the airport. This tells me that David and Ginny are as excited about Helen and Shady Lane as we are.

Later during the drive north, Paula calls George Scott and asks if we can stop by and copy the photographs. He says he would be happy to help.

We arrive at his house in Shady Lane in the early afternoon. I have made arrangements to meet Gail Lee at seven that evening. I expect to spend about an hour at George's house, but I have badly miscalculated how long it will take to scan sixty-five photographs at three-hundred-dots-per-inch resolution using David's dated scanner and my even older Mac Powerbook. Two hours pass and we are still at it, and I am guessing we will have to cut our dinner short if we hope to get to Gail Lee's on time. As I have often discovered in life, however, what at first appears as a misfortune is really a blessing, because the extra time allows us to become better acquainted with George. We even play a fiddle and banjo duet for him, and this gets us talking about Helen and old-time music.

"Miss Helen, she loved music. She sure did. And so did my dad. He was half Indian and half Negro and he played the guitar. My dad, I don't know, I never growed up like him, but he was dangerous. He had that Indian blood and stuff in him. But he could play the guitar. He played a lot of music. That's why I'm into so much music now. I've got a basement load of music, old records and stuff that goes way back. I just hold on to them because of my dad. He learned to play the guitar, but he was just so overwhelmed, I think, and angry. He never really did anything. He never went into the service because he was angry. And he took his anger out on my mother and me. He hit me in that old house one time and knocked me down thirteen steps. I was only twelve years old. He hit me up the top of the stairs and knocked me down to the bottom, and I didn't land until I hit the bottom step."

"Did you ever think of running away?" Paula asks.

"Well, that's why as soon as I graduated out of high school, I went into the service. You see, I put myself through high school. He didn't even help me with high school. The high school was all black, so I was a year behind when I went into the service because they give us the books from the white school over at Frederick High, from the seniors from the year before. So when I went into the service, that throwed me a year behind the other boys my age. So for me to get promoted, I had to take my tests over to come up to the equivalence of the boys my age."

"Did your father play his music out in the community?" I ask.

"In them days, we had one old fellow, he would play the mouth harp, and my dad and him would get together and go to nowhere but the black places because we didn't have that many places to go. Sometimes, my dad would go to Virginia, over into Lovettsville, and him and a couple other black fellows over there, they'd get together at the house; play music all night long." George laughs. "That fellow who played the mouth harp could make it howl. I swear but they was *ready*."

"Did anyone play the fiddle or the banjo in the Lane when you were growing up?" I am thinking about the Saturday evening "sit-out" parties that Estella described.

"There was an old man called Francis J. Allen who used to

live here in this Lane. He was the one that built these houses around here, and he was a fiddler. We used to call him F.J., and he was over six feet tall. He was older than my dad, and he never married, but he lived in a house by hisself down here. He tried to learn me the organ. He had an old organ, the one with the pedals you have to pump, and he was teaching me when I was only a kid. I guess I was six or seven years old, and he was giving me free music lessons. But I was so short, and he'd set me up on this stool. But my feet wouldn't quite reach the pedals. And I got tired of pedaling and he told me, 'You learn this because one of these days that organ is going to be the weapon of choice." Again George laughs. "Yes siree, that's what he said, and sure enough this guy Jimmy Smith came out with the organ, and it could make all the different sounds like horns and stuff. So I wish I'd listened to F.J. He was one of the best fiddlers around here."

With the scanner *zzzurrr zzzuurrr zzzurrring* along in the background, I ask George to talk about Brunswick and what race relations were like when he was young.

He begins by telling me that when he was young he worked as a dishwasher at a restaurant that had segregated dining rooms. The boss, a Mr. Coats, told George to keep the dishes separated, one pile of dirty dishes from the white dining room and another pile for the dishes that were used by the black diners. Many restaurants, he tells me, wouldn't serve black people at all. Then after laws were passed requiring restaurants to serve whites and blacks together, some of the restaurant owners would take the dishes black people used out into the alley and smashed them to pieces. They did this so the customers leaving the restaurant would see them and know that it wasn't right to serve food to decent white folk on dishes that black people had used.

"Brunswick had a policeman named Merriman," George tells me. "The black people called him "Babo." They used to have an old wooden bridge coming from Virginia to Maryland. And these white guys from Virginia, they come over to these beer clubs here in Maryland, and they killed a black guy on that bridge. The old bridge was a wooden bridge, and at night you'd hear all these boards clapping as the cars crossed over. One guy, he was like a mechanic. Lincoln Gray, that was his name. He lived in Virginia, but he used to come to Maryland. But me being so young, I don't know what transpired, but they caught him on that bridge over there, and they killed him. Now, this man hadn't did anything or nothing. It was just because he was a black man. There was a couple from Virginia and a couple from Maryland who did that."

"Was this Babo part of that?" I ask.

"Well, he was supposed to be the investigating officer, but he didn't do nothing. The black people started, but they were too scared to say something because of Babo. So you were living under fear. And all this did was bring more bad feelings, bad blood between the races. So then we'd find a white boy around there we didn't like, and we'd whip him. Me and some other boys got in trouble a couple of times.

"But I had a good white friend here in Petersville. His name was Ned Ambrose, and his parents, they was different. I could go right in the house and sit down and eat and his mother would say, 'Come on in, Junior.' They didn't give us class rings at the black high school in Frederick, and so Ned give me *his* class ring. We were good friends, but he died early in life.

"But people in Brunswick, they was different. Brunswick was a nasty little town, to tell you the truth. Now, I have a picture in that book of a white lady." He picks up one of the albums and turns to a page with a photograph of a woman police officer. "She got into the Brunswick police, and she was the first white policewoman in Brunswick. Well, she was my mother's friend and she'd do anything for us. She was just a nice person. She didn't have this feeling that she was superior to you, and that was so nice to know. We never had to ask her for assistance or anything, but the way that she carried herself and the way she reacted with us when we'd have a talk or something. She talked like a human being, like you was a human being to her."

"When did she join the police force?" Paula asks.

"I'd say back in around the fifties. But she was the only policewoman they had in Brunswick, so they made history there. There was a time I didn't trust a white man in Brunswick. No sir. We see how they treated us. So my daddy then—here he was helping to put more wood on the fire—he was telling me, 'Don't you come in this house crying about how some white boy done beat you. If you do, you're going to get another ass whipping.' Good God Almighty, that was enough to scare me right there."

George joined the Army when he was seventeen to get away from his father and the prejudice in that part of Maryland. Because he was underage, his parents had to sign to get him into the service, and the Army sent him to the Far East. The Korean War started not long after that, and he was a member of one the first units to go into combat. After the war, the Army posted him to Germany. He said even though he found prejudice in Germany, it was mostly older folks who mistreated him, not the younger Germans, who had seen what racial and cultural hatred had done to their country. For several years he dated a young German woman. Her father was a soldier and member of the Nazi Party before he died in the war.

"He would have stopped us dating if he hadn't been killed. He didn't like black people. Her mother was much more accepting."

It is plain to see that George loved her. He tells us about buying her a brand new Volkswagen sedan before returning to the States.

"Did you consider bringing her back with you?"

"She wanted to come, begged to come, but I wouldn't put her through the prejudice that was here. You see, I knew what it was like but she didn't. It wouldn't have been any kind of life for her. So we said goodbye."

He asks if we want to see a picture of his German sweetheart.

He goes in the bedroom and comes back with two pieces of a photograph that has been torn in half. One piece shows a much younger George in his Army uniform, and the other a pretty young white woman with a radiant smile.

"I got involved with a gal after I got back to the States and one day she found this picture and tore it in half because she was jealous."

The note of sorrow in George's voice is unmistakable.

Zzzurrr, zzzurrr, zzzurrr goes the scanner, and then it falls silent, its task at last complete. Even though George isn't related to Helen, I have come to regard him as part of the story. Not just because of Meir Kaplon's photographs, but because George has been so open with us, telling us what life was really like for his people back when Helen was a middle-aged woman, working and raising her own children. Paula and I also think that George is remarkable because he isn't bitter, despite the unfair conditions he had to deal with growing up. He saw first-hand what frustration and bitterness did to his father and made up his mind that those emotions would not poison his own soul.

After a lifetime in the military, George lives alone in a house that was built by volunteers. He has his treasured collection of old records, an assortment of ivory figurines he purchased in Japan, and those cherished photo albums of life on Shady Lane.

# CHAPTER 15

## GAIL LEE

Gail Lee's apartment is located in the historic part of Frederick, not far from downtown. Former 19th century row houses, many still showing their original red brick facades, have been divided into multiple living quarters. Gail Lee's ground floor one-bedroom apartment opens onto a narrow alley on the side of the building.

Gail Lee meets us outside riding a motorized wheel chair. A large woman, she is plagued by numerous health problems that make walking difficult. In a moment, two children, a girl and a boy who I judge to be between five and seven years of age, run out of the apartment and circle us, asking us a flurry of questions.

"Who are you? Where are you from? Is that your red car?"

Gail Lee tells us that they are her grandchildren, and I see that they are delighted by our visit. The little boy beams as he shows me his football. He kicks it down the alley, and then gallops after it, so I too can kick it. The girl, in the meantime, is asking Paula what she does for a living, and Paula tells her that she is an artist. This makes an impression on the little girl.

"What kind of pictures do you make?"

Paula has a tote bag with a copy of our illustrated children's book *The Flying Santa*. She takes out the book and hands it to the little girl.

"This is a gift for you and your brother," Paula tells her.

The boy is too busy with the football to notice the book at first.

Gail Lee invites us into her home. The film *Men in Black* is showing on the television in the living room, and the children follow us into the apartment and plop down on the couch to watch the movie. In less than a minute, however, they are off the couch and excitedly asking us questions again. Paula offers to sit with them and read their new book to them so Gail Lee and I can go into the kitchen and talk.

I ask Gail Lee if I can use my recorder, and I set it on the kitchen table between us.

Gail Lee has an open, kindly face that is tinged with sorrow. I suspect she has to struggle for money and has few options in life.

The day I met Estella, she anticipated losing her home. The living room was filled with packed boxes, a landscape of change and uncertainty. And yet even with that loss looming over her, Estella projected an aura of calm assurance, a certainty that everything would be all right. The feeling in Gail Lee's apartment is quite different. Her life is a day-to-day existence, a stream of urgent, immediate problems: paying the rent and utility bills, dealing with health issues, and helping keep her grandkids on the straight and narrow.

Gail Lee has gathered together a short stack of official papers, including her parents' marriage certificate. She spreads these out on the kitchen table and begins a recitation of names, dates, and places in a tone that is surprisingly formal.

"My name is Gail Lee Thomas. My date of birth is July 7, 1951. Born in Frederick. My mother's name is Dorothy Virginia Thomas. She was married at the age of eighteen in Frederick, Maryland. My dad's name is John Harold Thomas, and he was twenty-one when he was married to my mother in Frederick. They were married on July 12, 1951. He worked for the B & O railroad in Brunswick."

"Do you know what kind of work your father did for the railroad?" I ask.

"I never heard what my dad did at the railroad," she replies and then returns to her narrative. "I have a brother. His name is

Eugene Earl Thomas. He's married and his wife's name is Patricia. I'm older than he is. I'm fifty-eight and he's fifty-seven."

"My mother wrote a letter about the fire that killed your father," I tell her, "but she only mentioned one child who, at the time of the fire, was one year old. Was that you?"

"Yes. I was one when my dad died. My mother was carrying my brother."

"My mother was pregnant with my brother Patrick when my father died," I tell her. "But Patrick lived only two days after he was born. What can you tell me about your mother?"

"She was a wonderful mother. She raised us. She was our mother and our father. Where she went, we went. She made sure we had food in our mouth and clothes on our back. She put us through school. She struggled. We never went without nothing. At all. She struggled. Very hard. But she took very good care of us." Gail Lee is having trouble controlling her voice as sobs well up from within. "She missed her husband. It was so hard growing up without a dad. Very hard. A dad to ask, 'What did you do today? What are you going to play?' I often wonder how it would be if he was here. I miss him so much."

We wait for her emotions to settle. "Have you ever seen a photograph of your father?" I ask.

"No. I've never seen my father. I've been asking everybody to give me a picture of him. I'd just love to see him one time. I don't even know where he's buried. I don't even know."

"Did your mom ever remarry?"

"She said, 'I have one husband and that's the only husband I ever had.' She never remarried."

"What did your mother do to make money?"

"She did domestic work. She worked in a canning factory to take care of us. Green beans and corn. She worked, and then when I got old enough, I worked at Blueberry's Restaurant. I then started working cleaning houses down the road. I went to school, though. I finished eleventh grade. I wish I'd finished twelfth grade, but then I had my daughter and I had to take care of my daughter. Her name is Sherry. I have four boys and one girl, but I lost one of my sons. He drowned. The others are all grown now."

I ask her to tell me about her son who died.

"He was twenty-one when he died. It was the Fourth of July. He drowned saving his friend's life. This happened at the Linganore Reservoir off Route 144. It was a whirl, and he got stuck on the whirly; it goes around like this." She shows me with her hand. "It kept pulling him down. The current was so strong he tried to get up for the third time and he couldn't get up. He jumped in from a tree limb to get his friend out. Yep. And then my mom, she just died two years ago. She had congestive heart failure. So do I. Everything my mom got, I inherited everything."

I never dream about my father and I am curious if Gail Lee ever dreams about her father.

"I've never had a dream about my father, but I always dream about my mother. She was my friend. We were the best of friends."

"Was she bitter because of what happened?" I ask.

"I think she was. She really missed her husband."

"Was she religious?"

"She was a Methodist. Me and her went to church together. We sat in the same seat every week because they know it was our seat."

I ask Gail Lee if she remembers ever meeting Helen.

"No, I never met Helen. There's a lot of the family that I don't know."

She pauses.

"I don't have a bad life; it's just my health. I mean, I don't have a good life, but I have a life, because I'm blessed that I wake up every morning, and God gives me the strength to get up and do what I have to do. I can only do so much because I have a bad heart. I have bad diabetes and high blood pressure. I have rheumatoid arthritis and a ruptured disk in my back, in my spine. And every once in a while it twists. But I don't have a bad life. I don't. I just miss my mom." She again begins to sob.

"Do you think she's around somehow?" I ask. "Her spirit, I mean?"

"I think she's always here with me. She died two years ago today, and I really miss my mom today."

"What do you know about the fire in Brunswick in 1952? Was your mother there also, or just your dad?"

"She had just left to go home to her mother's house. I do know that much. I think that Dad lived there in Brunswick and Mom lived with her mother. I think it was because Dad lived there through the week, working for the railroad, and then Mom would go and spend the weekends with Dad. I think that's how it was. I don't think they fell out or nothing like that."

"Have you ever talked to Timmy Jackson about what happened? He was your dad's cousin and he escaped the fire, although he was badly burned."

"I never talked to him but somebody always told me if I wanted to know, ask Timmy because he could tell me things about my father. But I never talked to him. I got one story that when they went back in the house that somebody had tied my dad to the bed. That's what I heard. That somebody had tied him to the bed, and he tried to get loose from the bed, but he couldn't. Then I heard another story that he had tried to jump out the window, but the fire, the blaze, was so bad that he couldn't jump, so he couldn't get out. So I don't know what to believe."

"What did your Mom think happened?"

"Mom never told me," Gail Lee says and then pauses a moment before speaking. "No, I'm lying to you. Mom said somebody had tied him to the bed. She said they were drinking that night, that's what Momma told me. Momma said when they went back to the house, he was nothing but flesh. Momma said she know where he's buried at, but then I asked his family to take me there, and it's always an excuse.

"I just want to go where my father's at, to put a tombstone on my father's grave. That's all I want to do. So I ask them to show me where it is, and Uncle James [Helen's son and Estella's husband] was going to do it before he passed away. My Uncle James, he always do things for me, you know. He was the one who said I had an uncle in Pennsylvania that had a picture of my dad. Before he passed away, he [Uncle James] said, 'I'm going to make sure that you get that picture of your dad so you can see what your father looked like.'"

We talk awhile longer but it is difficult for Gail Lee. As we get ready to leave, Gail Lee lets Paula take a photograph of the two of us.

"You're my brother," she tells me as we pose together in the kitchen. "You're my long lost brother." I am both honored and troubled by the comment.

As Paula and I return to the car, the word "brother" still echoing in my mind, I suddenly make a connection. Gail Lee says she was born on July 7th. That is the birthdate of my oldest daughter Anna.

# CHAPTER 16

## THE YOUNG MIND

I was inspired to look for Helen's family after listening to a radio interview about brain development in young children. The program's guest talked about "sad brain syndrome," and this made me speculate on the role Helen played in my own development. I am fascinated by cognitive and developmental science, and now that I have found members of Helen's family and listened to some of their stories, I want to interview experts on brain development and see what they can tell me.

I begin by contacting the Society for Neuroscience in Washington, D.C., and through a series of referrals I am put in touch with Dr. Daniel Siegel, a clinical professor of psychiatry at the UCLA School of Medicine. Dr. Siegel received his medical degree from Harvard and currently serves as the director of the Mindsight Institute. He is also on the faculty of the Center for Culture, Brain, and Development at UCLA and has authored numerous books that explore how relationships, particularly those during early childhood, help shape the mind and the brain. These works include: *The Developing Mind*, *Parenting from the Inside Out*, and *The Mindful Brain*.

Before reading Dr. Siegel, I used the words "mind" and "brain" interchangeably, but he sees them as distinct from each other. The brain, he explains, is the mass of gray cells inside our skulls along with a network of processing centers located near important organs in the body, such as the heart, liver, and stomach. By comparison, he regards the word "mind" as a verb rather than a noun; a *process* for regulating information and energy flows. The brain creates the mind, but the mind, for its part, has the capacity to shape the physical structure of the brain. There is a third critical component in this dynamic interplay between brain and mind, and that is the sum of our personal relationships. According to Dr. Siegel, our relationships determine how our brain and mind function, for either good or ill. I find it helpful to visualize a triangle with arrows of influence radiating out from each corner in both directions: relationships, brain, and mind. And the relationships that have the greatest impact upon both the architecture of the brain and the quality and functioning of the mind are those that occur between a young child and his/her primary caregivers.

I am fortunate to discover that Dr. Siegel will be visiting Seattle to give a talk for an audience of educators. I call his office and ask if I might interview him while he is in town, and he agrees. The only time in his busy schedule for this to happen, however, is the evening he arrives, so I drive up to Seattle and we meet at his hotel. I can tell he is fatigued from his journey but he graciously allows me to set up my recording gear in his hotel room as he reads the draft prologue of my book so that he will have a better understanding of what I am trying to find out. When all is set, the conversation begins.

"I've never heard of the term 'sad brain syndrome,' so it's probably just somebody making it up," Dr. Siegel says. "But there are studies, actually out of the University of Washington here in Seattle, by Geraldine Dawson, that look at the impact a depressed mother has on the brain functioning of her infant. My understanding is that when the mother is depressed in the first six months of life, and if the depression persists past those first six months, then there can be long lasting negative impacts on how a child's brain functions.

"Your experience was that your father unfortunately died of polio when you were a year and a half old. So I imagine you had a close relationship with your mom for the first year and a half of life, and that would give you a resourcefulness that wouldn't make you prone to what Geraldine Dawson found in infants whose mothers were seriously depressed in the first year of life.

"So that's good news for you. And of course, Helen was present during that time, too. She probably was feeding you and all sorts of things. So I imagine you developed an attachment to Helen, and that attachment served you well when your mother did become depressed with those terrible tragedies of losing your father and losing your brother, all in such a close period of time. And Helen was a continuous attachment figure for you.

"So the fact that Helen was present from the time you were born until you were in first grade was an excellent source of security for you. That's probably an amazing source of resilience in your own neural architecture that you had a continuous caring available person and that is imbedded in your implicit memory.

"Implicit memory is the kind of memory we can't often weave into an explicit narrative of our lives, but we can *feel* it. Like you say in your prologue, you could feel Helen's presence in your life; a loving, open, accepting presence, and that's a great articulation of implicit memory at work.

"You probably also have perceptual memories of Helen, just an image of her that would be hard to exactly grab. What happens by first grade, when you're six years of age, is that the brain is changing a lot. Some kids don't remember what happens before the first six years of life, although during those years they do remember. It's kind of a funny thing. It's called "second phase childhood amnesia."

"Independent of traumatic experiences, you would likely have a barrier to explicitly recalling those earliest years, but you'd have implicit sensations of Helen. So it's interesting that the journey you've been on is a kind of attempt to make the implicit explicit, to really take these inner pre-worded sensations and find a language-based narrative to make sense of your life."

I ask, "Do you think I would have been a different kind of person if Helen hadn't been there, in terms of my brain architecture?"

"Oh yes, but first of all, do we know what your relationship with your mother was in your first year and half of life?"

"I think it was close," I reply, but realize as I say the words that I don't really know—I remember us being very close when I was growing up in Paterson.

"I know she was doing a lot of social things," I add, "I have a photograph of her with my father on a fishing trip in Canada but how much she was traveling, I don't know."

"Assuming you were close to your mother and close to Helen," Dr. Siegel says, "then what we're saying is that you had a loss of your father and your mother at a year and a half, because your father passed away and your mother became depressed. Those would be huge losses for you, and Helen would have been an anchor that would have given you some resilience in the face of those really huge losses. Your mother then came back, emotionally, around when you were how old?"

"From what my brother and cousins tell me, I would have been about five years old before my mother was fully back to being herself. She went to Europe in the summer of 1955, and I think it was after that trip that she was ready to get on with life again."

"Okay, from one and a half to five, that's a long period of time, and if Helen wasn't there, you'd be a different person because you would have lost—assuming you didn't get another attachment figure like Helen—you would have lost an attachment figure.

"You would have been a boat lost at sea without a rudder. Our caregivers give us a sense of being able to calm ourselves and regulate ourselves. They give us a sense of connection, of meaning and purpose, of being seen and feeling safe, really feeling secure. You wouldn't have had any of those, and so you would have had to find some way to survive such a horrible loss, and probably would have become very disconnected from other people, disconnected from yourself perhaps. If loss is unresolved, it can make a person feel very fragmented. So all those things may have been there to some degree, even with Helen present, because you did lose your father. You did lose your mother. Those are serious losses. Your mother came back when you were five, so that's a good repair. But Helen's presence was probably crucial."

I mention to Dr. Siegel that I have no memory of anyone trying to explain to me Helen's departure. I was five years old, and, knowing my family and the times, I doubt much was said about it.

"I often feel insecure," I tell him, "like I don't belong. Maybe everybody feels like that to some extent, but I've lived a life that has been largely outside of mainstream society. I was kicked out of high school, and I left college after only one semester because I couldn't get along with the priests who ran the school. I took drugs, marijuana and LSD, and I traveled around the country before settling in West Virginia. Do you think Helen's leaving, along with everything else that happened when I was young, affected me in some deep way?"

"Helen's leaving was definitely a loss. You get your mother back, but you lose Helen. So loss would be a big deal in terms of what your brain was trying to adjust to. We weave these attachment figures into the neural architecture to create a sense of wholeness. In the psychological literature, it's called a "self-object," meaning a person who helps you define yourself. In the brain's terms, we literally weave the interactions we have with caregivers into the fabric of who we are, and you had those fabrics ripped apart at different times, three different times. Your father, your mother, and then Helen. At some point a person just tries to pull inward, maybe not depend on other people or feel like things are reliable. You have a sense that things could be ripped apart at any time. Those would be kind of implicit sensations of fear of abandonment and, really, of terror—of things falling apart. So given the stress of facing high school, for instance, or college, if that felt too stressful, then you'd take off. And certainly turning to drugs, those could be used for self-medication, to help regulate your state. I don't know if those were your experiences, but they certainly would be predictable by what happened to you."

I feel as if Dr. Siegel has shot an arrow into my soul, allowing the grief to flow out like warm blood, but I do not feel sorry for myself. Instead, I feel sorry for this little kid. I can see him in my mind's eye. He is five years old, and he wants nothing more than love, cookies, and a chance to go outside and play. But people keep coming and going until he can't make sense of it all. He aches for his brother's attention and friendship, but Teddy has his own issues to deal with and the last thing he wants is a needy younger brother.

I tell Dr. Siegel about my attraction to Appalachian music. I explain how the music is a mix of Celtic and African-American traditions, and I ask him whether Helen's influence might have played a part in my decision to pursue this relatively obscure, but evocative, style of music.

"Wow, that's cool," he says. "That would be a great example of implicit memory, and your affinity could easily be a resonance that was deep in your implicit memory. Along comes this Appalachian music from your place in West Virginia, and yeah, you'd really resonate with that. Absolutely. It would feel like a memory trigger that was giving you a sense of familiarity, and that's exactly what implicit memory brings up."

It is getting late and I know Dr. Siegel has a long day ahead of him. But one question nags at me. There have been so many remarkable coincidences, moments of serendipity, attending my quest to find Helen.

"Your work explores how relationships shape both our brains and our minds," I begin. "Do you think there might be other dimensions to our relationships? What I mean is, do we at times interact with unseen entities, be they ancestors, angels, or demons, and do these relationships also play a role in shaping our brains and minds? Science dismisses these kinds of influences, but that's not what I've been experiencing. I sometimes feel that my mother and Helen are walking beside me, guiding me. Do we limit the field of our understanding because we won't, or can't, accept and discuss these other realities?"

"That's a great question," Dr. Siegel responds. "I don't have any answers for it, but there is a book you might want to read. It is called *Extraordinary Knowing* and was written by Elizabeth Mayer, who was a clinical psychologist at U.C. Berkeley for many years. It's about all that kind of thing. There's got to be huge amounts of interconnected fields, of processes we can't see but that are absolutely real. So I'd read that book. It's a great book."

I decide to contact another expert in the field of early childhood development that I met at a juvenile justice conference in 1999. His name is Dr. Bruce Perry and he currently heads the Child Trauma Academy in Houston, Texas. He attended Stanford and Amherst College for his undergraduate degree and afterward earned both M.D. and Ph.D. degrees at Northwestern University. He completed a residency in general psychiatry at Yale University School of Medicine and a fellowship in Child and Adolescent Psychiatry at the University of Chicago. His research has been instrumental in understanding how childhood experiences, including neglect and traumatic stress, change the biology of the brain and impact a child's health. He is the author of numerous articles and books, including *The Boy Who Was Raised As a Dog* and *Born For Love: Why Empathy is Essential and Endangered.* Given the distance that separates us, I set up a time to interview him by telephone.

"I think the thing that strikes me the most," he says as we begin the interview, "is just how open young children are to positive experiences, and their ability to absorb positive regard from whoever presents it—just their malleability, the ability of an individual to essentially soak up the good things that are being offered. I thought about it a lot in context of all these kids you worked with in the juvenile justice system who don't have that opportunity. They don't have the ability to make a consistent, relationally enduring connection with somebody. They may be taken out of a really bad environment, or they lose a parent or something like that, and then there will be a set of replacements, all of whom have good qualities, or at least adequate qualities. But what we tend to do in our culture is shift these people. We move them from a bad environment to a better environment, almost as if the important part is not them, but rather where we put them.

"In our work, one of the things we're looking at really carefully is the quality of the original relational interaction and the consistency of the interactions. As a newborn, your brain really has not made the connections between people and any attributes. You don't know what people are. Over time, if you have an attentive, attuned, loving caregiver, your brain begins to make these associations that people are good. When this person goes away, they come back; when I cry because I'm hungry, she shows up; she not only shows up, but I get all these wonderful physical feelings: I get full, I get embraced, I get rocked. And your brain starts to make associations between people and pleasure and people and safety.

"But if you have a caregiver who comes and provides really good stuff for you and then they don't come back, and, all of a sudden, somebody different comes, your brain starts to make associations between people who meet your fundamental needs but who are fleeting; they're always going to go. This is a prominent part of what contributes to that flat affect you experienced in the young people you worked with. When these kids engage you, behind their eyes their brain is saying, 'Well, this might be good, but it's fleeting, it's gone.' It's a melancholy, bittersweet engagement, and you feel it with these kids that have a flat affect. They're almost afraid to be joyful about something, because why celebrate when this person is going to leave my life anyway? But when you have a solid set of associations when you're little, and then later when people come in and out of your life, you're able to use a higher part of your brain to make sense out of the fact that they went away—they didn't go away just because they didn't like me. They went away because that's their job, but they're not gone. I just have a different relationship with them now.

"So as the cortex of your brain begins to develop, you can make more mature associations. You're able to adequately handle absences and sort of make sense out of them. But when you're little and you organize yourself around loss and the fleeting nature of human relations, it's kind of like you grow up with an existential brain. Why and how should I engage when all life is fleeting? You grow up with a gloomy perspective on life."

"If the mother is depressed," I ask, "does the child's brain mirror that emotional state in the way it grows and organizes its neural pathways?"

"Particularly for young children, the emotional climate, the relational milieu, is something that is essentially like contagion. So if the predominant person in your life is depressed, that's essentially going to have an impact on you. If they're sad, if they're angry, whatever their affect is, the brain will begin to reflect that. It's one of the things we see all the time, vicarious depression, vicarious trauma. A lot of kids are never maltreated, but if their mother is in a domestically violent relationship, if she's all over the place, then the child's own affect regulation becomes abnormal. Some of the earlier studies that were done on the children of Vietnam vets, these kids develop essentially what you call Post Traumatic Stress Disorder with combat-specific cues. Obviously, they weren't in combat, but they were vicariously absorbing what their parent was experiencing.

"The word I would use is 'dosing.' I think there are moments when the emotion of one person doses another. It's these little bursts of experience when you engage—you feel their pain—and then your brain protects itself and you disengage. You'll go play and then you'll go back and try to engage again, and, if they're depressed, then you have another little burst of that affect. Your brain tries to modulate the negative input."

"So you're saying Helen was essential to my well being, both then and now."

"Well, I think you're right in that the presence of that woman in your life made a significant difference in the way you grew up. Now the question that is always hard to answer is, could there have been a substitute? Could there have been another person who would have stepped in and been able to provide comparable structure, nurturing, positive stuff? And you don't know for sure. What happened between you two was related to what you brought into the interaction and what she brought. It created the special stuff that made you who you are. And there were multiple trajectories out of that, and she played a major role in the trajectory that you took. But it's always interactive. You elicited things from her and she elicited things from you, and that's the magical thing about relational interactions. When there's a good fit, it can be tremendously positive.

"Sometimes you can have a truly decent caregiver and a child who has lots of potential, but, for whatever reason, the kid pushes that caregiver's buttons, and then it's a bad fit and so the same magic doesn't happen."

"Why do you think we see so much mental illness in children today?"

"Our culture has shifted. Relational permanence is much less common than it used to be. I don't want to sound like a moralist, but when you look at human life, at the death rate, the loss rate of any living group all the way through most of the history of humankind, it has been quite high. So it's not necessarily about death and loss. But almost no culture up until the modern time was as relationally fragmented as ours. Even though all kinds of bad stuff happened, you still stayed essentially with the same group, the same community, and the same neighborhood. Very few people left their group and went off and explored the world.

There were some merchants, some explorers, but that was a really rare phenomenon. And so in the United States and in the West, we've become increasingly mobile, increasingly have divorces, increasingly move away from extended family, because that relational permanence is almost gone.

"Then you fold in the relational fragmentation that goes with the normal child-rearing practices. That relational permanence, even if there's not fragmentation in your own family, is really quite rare. You spend the first eight weeks maybe with your mom, and then your mom and primary caregivers become, basically, a bunch of transient folk who are in and out of your life. Sometimes you might have kinship care, or you might have the same babysitter for eight years or so, and that's actually really powerful, even if that babysitter is neutral. Neutral permanence is better than positive impermanence for the development of some of these important relational associations.

"The way we're raising our children and the way we're organizing our culture makes it very difficult to maintain meaningful relationships. Then you add in the incredible, almost explosive, increase of screen-time, and that cuts away from these traditional modes of communication like storytelling and verbal communication and non-structured play. All of these things organize the brain.

"Humans are neuro-biologically biased to communicate. We don't do that anymore. We have a very passive style of absorbing somebody else's story, and it's not good for us. At the heart of what you do, you probably see this all the time. You ask kids to try to tell their story and they're almost inarticulate. They don't know what you're talking about."

Since setting out on my quest, I have been trying to understand the mechanics of brain development in young children, how tendrils of neurons grow into neural pathways. These pathways are the superhighways, service roads, avenues, streets, and alleyways down which electrical pulses carry vital information from one part of the brain to another. The more neural pathways there are, the greater the brain's capacity for making sense of the world and coming up with the creative responses necessary to deal with life's whirlwind of challenges. The word "infrastructure" is as good a word as any for describing these physical structures inside the brain.

Not long ago C-SPAN broadcast a ceremony held inside the United States Capitol. A number of elected officials were present, including the Speaker of the House and the majority and minority leaders of the Senate. Also in attendance were members of the Congressional Black Caucus. The solemn assemblage dedicated a plaque acknowledging the fact that African-American slaves constructed the outer walls of the Capitol. Now, this is only one example of the significant contributions made by African-Americans to the building of our nation.

During centuries of enslavement, and thereafter as poorly-paid laborers or chain gang workers convicted of crimes under the corrupt Jim Crow laws, African-Americans cleared the land, tilled the soil, and harvested the crops. They dredged the harbors, built the plantations, laid the tracks, drained the swamps, and dug the coal. Without the toil, sweat, and ingenuity of countless black people building the basic infrastructure of the country, often without pay or recognition, we would not have achieved the economic and political prominence we enjoy in the world today.

I believe the same recognition is owed the legions of black women who cared for other people's children for generations, the children of elite and middle class families who relied on these women to teach their children how to live in the world. While these parents were occupied commanding armies and making laws, building factories and breaking labor strikes, attending fancy parties and playing golf, black women were in their homes building the vitally important neural infrastructure of the brains of their children.

It is one thing to talk about how Lucille taught Mary how to brush her hair, how Bernice showed William how to catch lightning bugs and put them in a jar, or how Matilda helped Howard tie his shoes and dried his frustrated tears when he couldn't get it right at first. Inside a child's skull, a mass of living tissue crackles and snaps with electrical pulsations bringing forth a cornucopia of thoughts and feelings, as new strands and clusters of neurons grow like ivy, increasing the brain's ability to process experiences. And the catalyst and conductor of this remarkable process is the child's primary caregiver. The black woman who was owned and regarded as property during centuries of slavery and, since emancipation, was given a meager salary and a room with a bed and a chair—paid less than the gardener or the chauffer because of her gender—she was the one entrusted with her employers' most precious and vulnerable treasure: their children.

Consider for a moment the formidable combination of energy, time, health, temperament, household skills, dependability, discretion, nurturing, sobriety, and moral rectitude these women possessed. A person with such qualities is a valuable resource for any community, and yet how often the lion's share of the benefits flowed to one group of people in society, mostly well-to-do white families, at the expense of another group of people, African-American families.

A close friend of mine named Joanna grew up in the 1950s in Glencoe, a wealthy suburb north of Chicago. She vividly remembers winter mornings when she would look from her bedroom window at the train station across the street. There she watched companies of white-skinned men in business suits and thick wool overcoats board trains that would take them into the city while scores of black women stepped off the trains. These women then fanned out and headed to different homes and streets all throughout her neighborhood, their rubber-clad shoes leaving tracks in the snow. The scene was reversed in the evening when white men got off the trains and hurried to waiting cars, gray vapor trails from tail pipes wafting upward in the gathering dark, as the black women congregated on the snowy platform to board the trains heading back into the city. Even though my friend was very young, she remembers a feeling of sadness as she watched the tired black women climb onto the trains and return to whatever world they came from.

When I lived in West Virginia, the sordid business of exploitation was close at hand. West Virginia is a land rich in natural resources—timber, coal, oil, and natural gas—and yet the people of that unfortunate state received scant benefit from all the cutting, mining, and drilling of these natural treasures. Worker wages were seldom enough to lift families out of poverty, and even though the modest taxes collected by the state did build some roads, bridges, and schools, the real wealth went north to Pittsburgh and Cleveland, or east to Philadelphia, Baltimore, and New York. There the living deities of industry enjoyed their days in elegant mansions and grand churches and appreciated their social equity by endowing museums and symphonies.

Meanwhile, West Virginians are left with a scarred landscape, eroded soils, and poisoned waterways. I know this is an old story, nearly as old as humankind itself. Social Darwinism, a philosophy much in vogue when my paternal grandmother was coming of age at the turn of the twentieth century, argues that this is how things should be. Natural selection favors the strong over the weak. But we humans have in us an alternative, internal narrative that urges us in its quiet, gentle voice to be fair and, yes, even kind. The great spiritual teachers call our attention to this inner directive. They tell us to be compassionate, to care for the less fortunate: the widow, the orphan, the prisoner, and the stranger.

My mother carried a burden of regret for many years because she felt she treated Helen and Joe Walls badly. These regrets, I believe, came from her listening to the call of this moral narrative. She liked to say that even though she was a Catholic, it was Charles Dickens who formed her character. In Dicken's classic novel, A *Christmas Carol*, the tormented ghost of Jacob Marley challenges his former business partner to reflect upon what is most essential in life: *"Mankind was my business. The common welfare was my business; charity, mercy, forbearance, and benevolence, were all, my business. The dealings of my trade were but a drop of water in the comprehensive ocean of my business!"*

From Drs. Siegel and Perry I have gained a deeper appreciation for Helen's place in my life. But the larger social issues continue to trouble me, so I pay Dr. Stephen Bezruchka a visit at his home in West Seattle. Dr. Bezruchka is a recognized expert on the impact of socioeconomic determinants of the health of populations. He is a senior lecturer at the University of Washington School of Public Health and a popular TED (Technology, Entertainment, Design) presenter.

I begin the interview by relating details about the deaths of my father and my brother Patrick and the emotional impact these losses had upon my mother.

"When I was two, I had a brother age four, and he died very quickly," Dr. Bezruchka tells me. "One day he got sick, and my mother took him to a doctor. The doctor wrote some prescription, and she went to a drug store and brought the medicine home. She then gave it to him, and two hours later, as she held him in her arms, he said something like, 'I'm dying,' and he died.

"Until I went to school when I was six, I remember only one night when my parents weren't at home; they went out somewhere and somebody else babysat. So I was always with my parents and I was well-nurtured. I also think of myself as being securely attached until age two, and then my brother died, and my parents never stopped grieving, my mother more so than my father. I can't imagine what the house was like at that time. My earliest memories of our family are the weekly trips to the cemetery. That's what we did as a family. I think I'm reasonably well-developed, but I think the kinds of issues I have are related to this experience of everything going along quite well, and then this tragedy occurs at age two that sort of affected my subsequent development."

"So what have you learned about what makes a society healthy in your research and medical practice?" I ask.

"I've learned that the structure of society that promotes caring and sharing is the most important factor that produces good health. Once everybody has enough to eat, clean water, a roof over their head if they need it, once these basic needs are covered, then it's the nature of caring and sharing relationships that produce health in society. And caring and sharing are most important sometime between conception and before you go to school. We have a saying in my field: 'Early life lasts a lifetime,' which means that the conditions of early life are there with you forever.

"Having been a scientist and a clinician—I used to be a mathematician and a physicist—I want to be able to explain what happens scientifically. That's the exciting part, because we are learning more and more about how these early life factors are programmed into human biology and how they're transmitted from one generation to the next. It's a critical thing that happens. Namely, your health depends on the health of your grandparents, and your great grandparents. We can only go back about three or four generations scientifically, but if it goes back three or four, why not ten? You have to take that perspective to understand why African-Americans in the United States don't do well, healthwise. They don't do well even if they do all the right things. That's a really tough thing to appreciate, but that's because if health is transmitted intergenerationally, then we have the legacy of centuries of slavery and mistreatment. So they don't do well.

"We also have studies just emerging in Washington state looking at what are called adverse childhood experiences, ACEs, that show that if you're abused in early life, you're not going to do well either. So the science is coming together in a remarkably coherent, systematic way, but it's almost impossible to engage people to take these ideas seriously."

"So the critical period in all of this is early childhood?" I ask.

"The new acronym for this is DOHAD, Developmental Origins of Health and Disease. People characterize this developmental period as minus nine months to twenty-four months. And what are you going to measure as an indicator of what happened, for example, for the first nine months? Well, one is, did you spend all nine months in utero and what was your birth weight? Obviously, if you had a low birth weight, by low I mean less that 6.6 lbs. (2,500 grams), then there was something going on and you didn't get adequately nourished. I subscribe to the 'room with a view' hypothesis; namely, the fetus senses the world outside—and we know how it does this—and if it's going to be a tough world out there, well then maybe it better pop out early and do the best it can. Nutrients are the traditional way of thinking about it. We sort of felt, for a long time, that no matter what the status of the mother, the fetus will starve the woman to get the nutrients it needs, but it's not quite like that.

"So this gets into medicine, population medicine. What are the medicines that can produce healthy outcomes? Well, they're not pills, and they're not surgical procedures in the sense we consider them. Instead, they are providing the first nine months to be a period without undue stress, with adequate nutrition, and in a caring environment. Caring and sharing.

"There's a whole host of studies linking stress on the mom while she's carrying a fetus to later health outcomes for that son or daughter. For example, the latest studies involved girls in their twenties, with no bad behaviors, and who are not sick in any way. The researchers looked at circumstances their mothers faced when they [the girls] were in the womb, and those whose mothers had stressful experiences between twenty-two and thirty-five weeks of pregnancy. Those mothers who experienced the death of a close family member, eviction from the household, denial of paternity, and a few other major stressors—not just a bad hair day—the daughters now in their twenties already have biomarkers for trending worse health—inflammatory markers. They're going to have changes in their stress response; they're going to have short-term memory loss, be more prone to diabetes, all kinds of problems. There are scores of studies that validate the importance of early life."

Hearing this, I think about my brother Patrick, who died shortly after his birth. He was inside my mother when she lost our father. What long-term health problems might he have suffered had he lived, given the stress my mother endured when he was in the womb?

I ask Dr. Bezruchka, "Can you talk about what happens following the first nine months of life? What role do the mother and other caregivers play in a person's future physical and mental health?"

"Well, that's harder to study conceptually, because it's very hard to have data on large numbers that show what conditions were like that the infant was raised on. Was there adequate nutrition? Was a parent there? Were there environmental influences? Was there abuse?

"So it's not like we have studies where there is somebody in the home to monitor these conditions for these first few years. There are, however, experiments.

"The best experiments are with orphans. You can look at those orphans and study how they were reared, what the conditions were like for those first few years. Now, these experimental opportunities don't come around too often, but after the Second World War there were lots of orphans. So John Bowlby, a British psychiatrist, studied groups of these orphans and found that orphan babies who were in the care of a single caregiver who was there for almost all of the first year later did very well. In the second year he found that you needed not just one person there, you needed another person in their lives. So if they had a single person in the first year and an additional person in the second year, then things were better down the line. John Bowlby coined the term 'secure attachment.' If a baby was securely attached, he posited, there had to be a single caregiver, a single pair of eyes in that first year.

"Now, when I present this to people, I always say, 'Just think about a pair of eyes. Think of the pair of eyes on the cover of National Geographic of that Afghani woman photographed by Steve McCurry in 1984,' and everybody knows those eyes.

"You could also sense what the eyes of your mother looked like, most of us. So we imprint on those eyes. Konrad Lorenz in the early 1900s, he had this experiment. He got some baby ducks and just had his face in front of those baby ducks soon after they were born, and they followed him everywhere. They wouldn't leave him. So this idea of being conditioned to feeling comfortable around a pair of eyes is critical. We're the only primate species with whites in our eyes. So high contrast seems to be very important for human interaction. If you were sitting there with sunglasses on, we wouldn't interact as well. So why is it that we have white sclera? When babies are born, they don't have good vision. The one thing they can see is contrast. They can sense black and white.

Dr. Bezruchka laughs. "I used to think the key black and white they had to sense was the pupil of the eye framed in white. But after I said this at a conference at Hunter's College in New York, a man came up later and said, 'There's another really important contrast that a baby has to see and that's the pigmented areola of the breast.' I hadn't thought of that. The breast nipple does become very dark and that probably helps the baby to identify the breast. The man had just had a baby, and I guess he realized how important this was.

"So the physiological changes we undergo at various stages of our life are there for a purpose. And they are evolutionarily selected. So I think eye contact is very important for human interaction. It's doubly important very early in life. When I'm giving a talk on this subject, young women often say, 'Oh, you're telling me I've got to stay home and mother my baby.' So I ward that off by saying, 'It doesn't matter who the pair of eyes belong to. It could be the nanny. And in the second year, when you need another pair of eyes, it could be her boyfriend. Because I think Bowlby's studies are very clear with orphans: it doesn't have to be the mother. In the second year you need somebody else around. Babies and two-year-olds don't socialize very well—you know, the 'terrible twos.' It's not until they're around three that they socialize, and then you need a bunch of eyes. Interacting. Other kids.

"That then asks the question: what's a society going to do with this knowledge? Well, first of all, you need paid antenatal leave. You need time for the mother not to be wigged out, stressed out with her pregnancy. And you need paid maternity leave. And paid paternity leave. Then you need the social circumstances for the then three-year-old to engage with others.

"So take Sweden, that nation has very good health outcomes. In Sweden, it's mandatory to take a year's paid parental leave—at full pay. It's really hard, I know," Dr. Bezruchka quips, "but most people seem to accept it. And if the mother takes the full twelve months, the father has to take twelve weeks. So they recognize the importance of getting the dad involved. And they're paid. They get their salary from the Swedish government for this."

I am curious. "Does the father take the twelve weeks at the same time his wife is taking her twelve months?"

"The actual twelve months can be split. Mostly it's women that take the time, but Sweden is a very progressive country in terms of gender issues."

"But does the second person take the twelve weeks simultaneously with the person taking the twelve months?"

"Yes, Sweden is very concerned about this. You want to have both parents involved with the newborn. That's really key. And here's something to think about: there are only four countries in the world that don't have a law saying that women are guaranteed some paid leave after the birth of a child—the United States, Swaziland, Liberia, and Papua New Guinea. They are the only four countries in the world without a paid maternity leave policy.

"So in Sweden, the second year is optional at only eighty percent pay, and the third year, if you want to go back to work, you can put your child in a Swedish government-run daycare center that's free. And one requirement to work in a Swedish government-run daycare center is that a person has to have an advanced degree in play, because what is daycare all about? It's socializing the kid. And what are our requirements in the United States? No recent history of sexual abuse of children, I guess."

It is after midnight before I start for home, and all I can think about is how ashamed I am of my country. We are in the same league as Swaziland, Liberia, and Papua New Guinea when it comes to how we care for our children. The politicians are keen to tell us that children are our future, our most valuable resource. But the rhetoric fails to match the reality. We are so focused on short-term profits, pleasures, and poll numbers that we cannot see the big picture, the longer story. Early Life Lasts a Lifetime. That is a good slogan. Maybe we should put it on the dollar bill.

Estella Belt and Joe

Poppy, Helen, Uncle George, Joe, and Michael Carey

James and
Estella Belt

Gail Lee Thomas and Joe

# Photographs Taken by Meir Kaplon of Residents of Shady Lane, MD - 1968

Diane, Margaret, & Karen Lipscomb, Cynthia & Kevin Michael Jackson, Keith Sparrow, Timothy Jackson, Bernie Lipscomb, Deborah, Vivian, & Mary Jackson

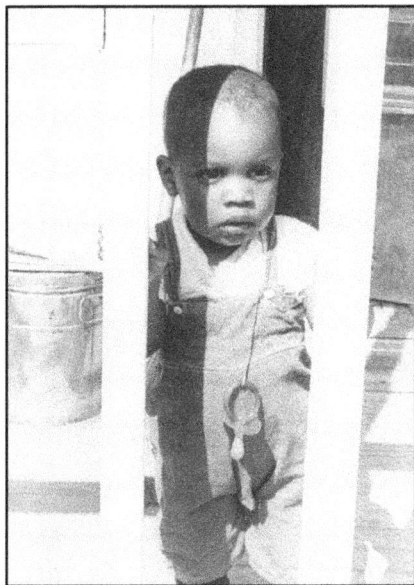

Antonia Jackson-Helen's great-grandson

Keith Sparrow & Bell the horse

Mr. Thom Woods

Melissa Anderson

Sharon Scott, Karen Lipscomb, Cynthia Jackson, Barbara Scott,
Timothy Jackson, and Gary Scott

Velva Cooper

Jeffrey Ramey

Randolph Cooper

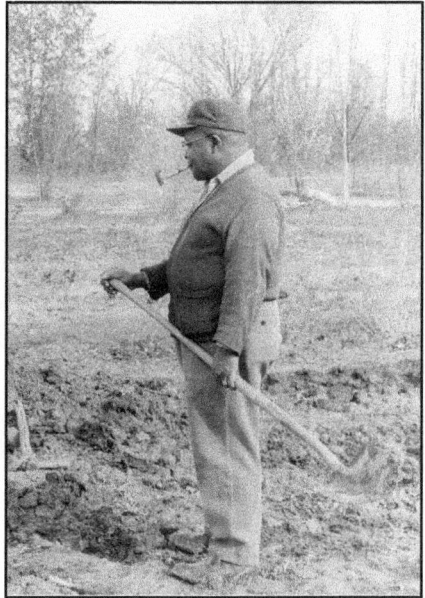
Mr. Scott - George Scott's father

Marie Virginia Spriggs - married to Helen's brother-in-law

Helen Jackson,
Helen's
granddaughter

# CHAPTER 17

## PITTSBURGH

*"Not until the loom is silent, and the shuttle ceases to fly,*
*Will God unroll the canvas, and explain the reason why;*
*The dark threads are as needed, in the Weaver's skilled hands,*
*As the threads of gold and silver, in the pattern He has planned."*

—from the poem *"The Loom of Time"* - author unknown

It is ten o'clock at night as I descend the long grade that leads to the western entrance of the Fort Pitt Tunnel. Like a massive cannon, the tunnel will shoot me out onto the Fort Pitt Bridge, where I will be greeted with a spectacular nighttime vista of downtown Pittsburgh. Few cities sneak up on you like Pittsburgh. Following the highway from the airport to the tunnel entrance, most of what you see are rolling hills dotted with drab, boxy office buildings, staple-shaped shopping malls, and assorted franchise restaurants and hotels—predictably unimpressive buildings for the most part. Then you emerge from the tunnel onto an elevated bridge and smack dab in front of you is the city, a cluster of illuminated skyscrapers that looks like some mythical kingdom squeezed into an arrow point by the convergence of three great rivers: the Monongahela, the Allegheny, and the Ohio. It has been ten years since my last visit to Pittsburgh and I relive the sweet anticipation I experienced as a child whenever we visited Nana and Papa.

Paterson and Pittsburgh were worlds apart when I was young. Nana made sure there were always exciting things to do when we came to her city, such as visiting the Buhl Planetarium, attending Pittsburgh Pirates games at Forbes Field, or spending the day at Kennywood Amusement Park where we ate cotton candy and rode a centrifugal ride called "The Whip."

What is more, my brother, cousins, and I had the entire third floor of Nana's house on Devonshire Street to ourselves. It was outfitted toy cars and trucks and elaborate sets of cowboys and Indians, knights and dragons, British redcoats and American Continentals; many of them delicately painted lead figurines. Nana also owned a pair of dollhouses as tall as I was, each with leaded windows, hand-turned banisters, electric lights, and working dumbwaiters. The interiors of the dollhouses were tricked out with a variety of exquisite miniature objects including tiny hairbrushes and candlesticks.

Our third floor at 700 Devonshire Street was a child's wonderland where we whiled away the hours lost in realms of our own imagining. To this day, I associate the smell of wool with safety and pleasure, because wool was everywhere at my grandparents' house. The blankets, carpets, and upholstery on the sofas and stuffed chairs were all made of wool—even the seats inside Nana's Cadillac were wollen. When I crouched inside closets during games of hide-and-seek, a mixture of wool and mothballs tickled my young nostrils.

The city of Pittsburgh in the 1950s and 60s had its own distinctive smell as well, an acid-sweet aroma that I found appealing because I associated it with so many good things. Now that I am older, I realize the source of the smell was coal smoke belching from the city's many industrial steel mills; Pittsburgh's air during those decades was among of the most poluted in the country.

Traffic is light as I reach the foot of the grade and enter the tunnel. Tomorrow is Mother's Day and the *Pittsburgh Post-Gazette* will publish an article about my quest to find Helen's family.

The reporter, Mary Lynn Pitz, interviewed me several times by telephone, and I emailed her half a dozen photographs, including the one of Estella and me standing outside her house in Petersville and the photo of Helen in her straw hat. The timing of the article couldn't be better. Not only is it Mother's Day, but the following evening, I will give a talk at the Carnegie Library in Homewood, a predominately black neighborhood in Pittsburgh, where I hope to meet people whose mothers and grandmothers worked for well-to-do families in the city.

I exit the tunnel and sweep out onto the Fort Pitt Bridge. For a second or two, all I see before me are the glittering towers of the city. Then the night sky erupts into a riot of crackling colors and concussive explosions, patches of reflected light bouncing around inside the car like a family of sprites on holiday. I am all over with goose bumps. The fireworks seem to be welcoming me home.

Then the rational part of my brain kicks in and tries to figure out what is really going on with the fireworks display. I take the first exit after the bridge into downtown. I am hungry and hunt up a pizza joint, and the owner tells me that Three Rivers Stadium, which is just across the river, sets off fireworks when the baseball games end. Mystery solved, but I can still pretend that the celebratory pyrotechnics were meant for me.

It is Sunday morning and I pull up in front of my grandparents' former home on Devonshire Street. The house is a stately L-shaped Tudor revival of white stucco and brown timbers, with dormers set into a steeply raked slate roof and a pair of red brick chimneys.

I am early and, while I wait for my cousin Ty to arrive, I take photographs of the house and grounds. It is a gorgeous May morning, the grass is thick and green, the trees are pushing out their first leaves, and the sky overhead is washed blue.

700 Devonshire Street holds a unique place in my heart, as I know it does in my brother's. It is not the most impressive house on

the block—next door are the mansions of some of the city's most influential citizens—and yet it exerts a profound influence over all of us. I am sure my grandparents' personalities play a part in this, but there is also something special about the structure itself, a subtle combination of beauty and grace given form through the efforts of a gifted architect and a cadre of skilled artisans. Looking up at the house, I suddenly feel like the exiled prince who has been doomed to wander the world, never at home, never truly at peace.

A jet airliner passes overhead. I rouse myself from this strange and unexpected bout of melancholy with the thought that all the earth is my home and all rivers flow to the sea. I take a few more photographs. I even go up on the porch and ring the doorbell, but the current residents must be away.

Then Ty pulls up in a shiny new Mercedes sports car. We talked several times on the telephone, but have not seen each other for many years.

"Cousin Joey," he says. "How've you been?"

No one but family calls me Joey his greeting snaps me into a different frame of mind. "This is some car," I say.

"It was a birthday present from my kids. Get in, we've got a busy day ahead. I want to show you some of the old haunts."

By haunts, I assume he means places that played a significant part in my family's life in years past.

The car is built so low to the ground that I have to fold myself into the passenger seat, dipping my neck to keep my head from striking the top of the doorframe. We then head over to a section of the city called Oakland.

"I'm glad our schedules worked out," Ty says, "I only got back last night from France."

"What were you doing in France?"

"Every year we take a group of sick children to Lourdes."

Lourdes is where many Catholics believe St. Bernadette beheld a vision of the Virgin Mary. There is a grotto there with baths thought to have miraculous healing powers.

"Who organizes the trip?" I ask.

"The Order of Malta. I'm a member."

He tells me the Order of Malta was founded during the Middle Ages by a troop of Crusaders. On their journey back from Jerusalem, they decided to settle on the Isle of Malta in the Mediterranean.

"The order is dedicated to helping people with medical problems. We raise money for hospitals and other programs and, once a year, we take wounded veterans and children and others with serious illnesses to Lourdes so they can bathe in the water."

My brother and cousins on my mother's side of the family were all raised Catholic. Like me, the nuns at St. Therese's Elementary School drilled them in their catechism and glowed with pride as they marched up the aisle of the church to receive their First Communion dressed all in white, their little hands held in the gesture of prayer against their breasts. Each of them then went on to graduate from a Catholic university. Despite this, however, none of them today are practicing Catholics, let alone a member of an ancient order, like the Knights of Malta.

"How old is the Order of Malta?"

"It was founded in 1066. The men are called knights and the women are called dames. In Europe you have to be descended from aristocracy to be accepted into the order but since we don't have aristocrats in the United States, I was able to become a member."

I translate this to mean, if you are wealthy, they let you in. Europeans honor blood, we honor money.

We pull into the parking lot behind the clubhouse for the Pittsburgh Athletic Association. No ordinary clubhouse, the massive five-story building takes up an entire city block, its architecture inspired by the 16th century Grimani Palace in Venice. On the opposite side of Fifth Avenue stands the University of Pittsburgh's iconic Cathedral of Learning. At 535 feet, it is the tallest educational building in the western hemisphere. Looking southeast, across Bigelow Boulevard, I behold the Soldiers and Sailors National Military Museum and Memorial.

Ty climbs out of the car and gives the car keys to an elderly black attendant. I can see Ty has trouble straightening up. He rubs his lower back as we walk toward the rear entrance to the clubhouse.

"Is your back giving you trouble?" I ask.

"Yeah, it's bothered me for years. I was exercising my fox hunting horse out in Ligoneer, and we went across an old bridge and one of his legs went through a rotted board. He reared up and lost his balance and went over on his side, with me underneath. I banged up my hip pretty good. Do you remember this place?"

We are now inside the PAA and the aroma triggers a stream of youthful memories. Maybe it is the wool carpeting with the hint of chlorine from the indoor pool on the third floor. One of my most vivid recollections is of Christmas at the PAA, when the members brought their children and grandchildren to the clubhouse. A portly, white-bearded Santa in a velvet red suit and black leather boots handed out gaily wrapped presents from a great red sack. There were scores of children, each excited enough to burst, and the presents were of the first order: metal airplanes and trucks for the boys and talking dolls for the girls.

"Your dad took me to dinner here once when I was in town performing at the Carnegie Museum," I tell Ty as we stroll down the hallway past the dining room with its crystal chandeliers.

"Yeah, he loved this place," Ty says.

We wander around the building for several minutes before returning to the car. We pull out onto Fifth Avenue and head back toward Shadyside along Ellsworth Avenue, passing Nana's house before reaching the business district on Walnut Street. Here we grab some coffee and pick up a newspaper.

The *Post-Gazette* article is well-written and accurate. I wonder if Ty is impressed with his long lost cousin. He then goes back into the store and buys twenty dollars' worth of newspapers and hands them to me.

"Give these to your children and your friends," he says after peeling off a copy for himself.

We cross the Allegheny River by driving over the Highland Park Bridge and wind our way through the town of Aspinwall and ascend into a neighborhood of wooded hills and handsome homes called Fox Chapel, named, I have recently learned, not after moneyed people on galloping horses but in honor of an early settler named John Fox.

I have downloaded a map to direct us to my old house on Shady Lane and, after a few wrong turns, we find it. The lane is much as I remember it, a narrow road with a latticework of tree branches reaching out from both sides, the gray asphalt in front of the car dappled with patches of sunlight.

When we moved to New Jersey in 1954, my mother sold our house to my Uncle Mack and Aunt Nancy. They lived in the house for the next five years, and we visited my cousins at our old house whenever we came to Pittsburgh. That is why everything is so familiar. Shady Lane is a short street with only a couple of houses on each side and our house was at the end, perched upon the shoulder of a hill.

When I went to see my brother at the beginning of my journey, he gave me a digital copy of an eight-millimeter home movie from when we were kids, a collection of short scenes shot by my Uncle George over several years. One scene from the summer of 1951 shows my brother, cousins, and me next to a large swimming pool with my father, mother, and Aunt Ruth. The pool is at the Field Club, a country club in Fox Chapel that we used to belong to, and my brother is running in and out of the water with Janna, who keeps trying to kiss him. There are several seconds of my father teaching my cousin Michael how to swim. On the grass next to the pool, I am just learning to walk. I am holding up my arms in an effort to keep my balance and am having a grand time. My mother, sitting on a beach towel, is very pretty in her swimsuit and wavy black hair, and she is smiling the way you do for home movies. Unfortunately, there is no sound; I would give much to hear my father's voice. When I watch the film I cannot get out of my mind the fact that he will be dead within months. Then the film jumps to the driveway in front of our house on Shady Lane. It is late autumn or winter, the trees have dropped their leaves, and my father is gone. It is just my mother, Aunt Ruth, and my grandparents, Nanny and Poppy. There is also a brief shot of Helen standing next to the porch in her white uniform. My brother and I are in the scene as well, and I am pointing and shooting a pair of silver cowboy pistols at the camera.

I cannot adequately describe the look on my mother's face. She is forcing a smile, but she is a walking ghost, her charmed life shattered into a million pieces. Nanny and Poppy are also smiling, bravely and awkwardly. I suspect they are getting ready to drive back to New Jersey. The film has that "let's take a group photograph before we leave" quality to it.

I can only guess at how Nanny and Poppy must have felt leaving their youngest daughter in a house hidden in the woods with two small children and a black maid.

As I mentioned earlier, my cousin Chris, Ruth's youngest child, found a packet of letters among his mother's possessions after she passed away. The letters, three dozen in all, were written by my mother while she was living in Pittsburgh. Half of the letters are addressed to Ruth, and the other half to Nanny. The letters to Ruth provide a more complex glimpse into the ups and downs of married life for my mother, because they include the kinds of concerns and frustrations you don't share with your parents. In some of the letters, my mother complains about my father's lack of interest in the arts, music and literature in particular. She writes about how he won't go with her to hear the Pittsburgh Symphony Orchestra perform; instead he goes bowling with his father. Even getting my father to go to a movie was a chore; he preferred to stay at home and work on his model train setup in the basement.

Some of my mother's letters ache with homesickness, especially the ones written in the months leading up to Christmas. For the first couple of years of their marriage they drove or took the train to New Jersey to be with my mother's family for the holidays. But then my father "put his foot down." Pittsburgh was their home and that was where they would celebrate Christmas in the future. The tone of the letters leading up to those first Christmases in Pittsburgh swing from sorrow to anger and back to sorrow.

But there are happy letters, too. A letter from December 1947, six months after my brother's birth, shows how much she delighted in being a mother.

*"Your nephew is really cute these days, Ruth—and so good! He amazes me at times. He has accomplished the art of blowing his nose—he blows when I hold it, then grins at me in pride. It really is funny—he makes so much noise. He also usually gets my fingers all over with boogies, but wotthehell! He's about 17 lbs. and as solid as a pound of butter fresh from the icebox. He isn't too energetic—he still turns over sheerly by accident and he can't seem to figure out how to creep, but that can wait. I think he's heavy, which holds him up, and I don't dare let him stay on his stomach much because he spits up awfully. Sometimes I think I love him too much—I can't seem to handle him without gritting my teeth. You know that feeling? But he really is cute—sunny and bright and affectionate."*

Another letter written in late 1947 includes a paragraph that shows how uncomfortable my mother was having a maid, given her working-class background growing up around Aunt Kate's. The maid's name was Lillian; Helen replaced Lillian some time later.

*"Ted is doing fine. I took him into the doctor's today for a postoperative check-up—at his age! I took Lillian with me to help me. It's so hard to find a parking place and cart him all over. She had her uniform on and I started to feel silly. I must have looked quite spoiled. Me, Beverly Quinn, who's slung beer and brushed past drunks with the best of 'em. Funny thing life—I'd almost rather be back drawing beers and be near to you all again. Oh me—you never quite get the brass ring, do you?"*

A later letter written in the spring of 1948 mentions Lillian again, but this time my mother is wrestling with a dilemma. The letter starts off with my mother complaining about being cooped up at home when she had hoped Ed would take her out to a movie or concert. She is twenty-three years old, a wife and mother, struggling to make sense of her place in her new world.

*"Ed just got up to make a drink and I found out some news that put the final kibosh on the night. He marked the liquor bottles just to check, and sure enough, there were about two drinks gone. Honestly, it's made me sick. I was so sure we could trust Lillian, but now it appears she's been helping herself right along. Ed says just to lock the liquor up and not say anything, but I'm not so sure. I don't want to lose her, but still, it's made me doubtful about leaving the baby in her sole care anymore. Damn, damn, damn! I'll let you know what I decided to do when I write again."*

Thus the stage was set for Helen's arrival. Somehow the sporting man, Mr. Robinson, got wind that my parents were looking for a new live-in maid, and he convinced Helen Spriggs to leave Brunswick and go with him to Pittsburgh and apply for the job. She did, my parents hired her, Mr. Robinson's eye fell on another and he took a powder, and I was born. Thus fate played its hand in making sure we would survive the hard times ahead.

# CHAPTER 18

## *THE BLACK OPAL*

Ty and I drive through the entrance of the Field Club in the early afternoon, the road a black velvet ribbon meandering its way through manicured golf links. At the top of a hill sits the clubhouse, guarded by a phalanx of white and red oaks under the command of a majestic Dutch elm, one of the few to survive a fungal disease that arrived in North America from Europe in 1928 and gradually killed most of the Dutch elms in the country.

The architecture of the clubhouse is a mixture of Colonial American and Antebellum Plantation with a wide, lazy porch looking out upon the broad fairways and a horizon of wooded hills to the east. We pull up before the portico and a peppy young valet takes Ty's keys and zooms away in the silver Mercedes. We enter the clubhouse and turn down a hallway decorated with photographs of smiling golfers, until we come to the entrance of a wood-paneled dining room. The room is packed with families celebrating Mother's Day, but it lacks the din of a family restaurant. Luckily, I brought along the required sports jacket and tie, but Ty must borrow his from the maitre d'.

Ty smiles and waves to this member and that as we are shown to a table. All the while a flood of childhood memories rush through me, recollections of going out to dinner in finely appointed rooms with my grandparents. Nana and Papa were members of the Field Club, as well as the University Club and the Pittsburgh Athletic Club. By contrast, we never belonged to any club when I was growing up in Paterson. As a family, we were on our own when it came to official clan affiliation except for being Roman Catholics, and I remain largely a non-joiner to this day.

The dining room is familiar and inviting, but it is also a tad suffocating. The suffocating part I remember well. Nana and Papa took us to dinner at these clubs, most often at the Pittsburgh Athletic Club. My mother would dress me in dark wool pants that scratched something awful. The African-American servers moved into and away from the table with an economy of movement that made them nearly invisible, which I suspect was the point. The club silverware was heavy and laid out just so: two forks of different size on the left and a knife, with the club crest engraved in the handle, and a pair of spoons on the right. The tablecloth and napkins were of starched white linen. My brother and I—and the Sexton kids if they were in town—said little during these meals. I am sure the adults laughed and enjoyed themselves, but I don't remember, because all I wanted was to free myself from the requirements of proper table manners, to steal away from the thick carpets and ornate chandeliers, the little balls of butter resting on ice in their silver dish, the sweating water glasses, the tired Brussels sprouts, and the muted conversations of the members who dutifully sawed away at their prime ribs and lamb chops. I guess I was supposed to appreciate the fact that this was elegant living at its finest, the prize for working hard, following the rules, and being lucky.

How different these tedious affairs were from the family meals we enjoyed at Aunt Kate's. There the talk was loud, the interruptions constant, and the consuming of food was interspersed with fits of laughter and the singing of familiar songs. I doubt the country club set would have appreciated Poppy putting cherry tomatoes in his eye sockets while us kids tried to stick spoons to our noses. Then after the meal, my brother, cousins, and I would head to the snack bar for desert, which, at that time of day, was closed to the public. As the owners' grandkids we had the run of the place and I have a mouthful of silver and gold fillings to prove it.

Ty and I join the buffet line and heap our plates with waffles, sausages, fresh strawberries, and slices of cantaloupe. Ty continues to exchange pleasantries with his fellow members, asking a considerate question or bemoaning the condition of the economy. We return to our table and I pull out my recorder and place it between us because Ty is a font of stories about this side of the family.

He begins by telling me how my great uncle John McGraw served as president of the Field Club back in the day and was responsible for building an elevator.

To be honest, I am under impressed by this tidbit of family lore, until I realize he is not talking about an ordinary elevator, but a stand-alone exterior elevator located in the woods next to the eighteenth green.

"It's an uphill hike from the eighteenth hole back to the club house and the old guys kept having heart attacks," Ty tells me. "So grandpa decided they needed an elevator. I think only one other golf club in the country has one."

John McGraw was my grandmother's oldest brother. He and his wife adopted Ty's mother, Susan, when she was a little girl. Tom Freyvogel met Sue McGraw on his way to my father's wedding in New Jersey. Tom was my father's best friend. Ty is their first-born and John McGraw was his grandfather.

"My dad was very close to your dad," Ty tells me. "They were going into business together, did you know that?"

I shake my head. All I know is that Tom Freyvogel—we always addressed him as Uncle Tom—ran a successful funeral home and that his sister married a Hanna whose family runs one of the largest real estate companies in the Pittsburgh area.

"My dad's parents owned a funeral business and it was expected Dad would become a mortician. But he was a born salesman. That's what he loved doing."

This all makes sense. Ty is a gifted salesman in his own right. Over the years, he has started and sold numerous independent businesses and franchises. He also led the effort to create a Center for Entrepreneurship at a private college in Ohio.

"The plan was that your father would take over the wool company, which is what the McGraws wanted, and he'd be the inside man, responsible for all aspects of the manufacturing process, while my father would be the outside man, in charge of sales. They had it all worked out and my dad was already signing up new accounts when your dad died. It was a tremendous shock for my dad. He never really recovered from it."

As Ty leaves the table to refill his plate, I think back to the day I interviewed my mother. We had been talking for almost two hours and I knew she was tired. But I wanted to hear the story of my father's death. I knew the general outline of the story but I wanted the details.

"Can you tell me what happened step by step?" I asked.

She was quiet for some moments and I felt perhaps I had gone too far. Then she began talking about a black opal ring that my father gave her after returning from a trip to Australia. She had never mentioned an opal ring as far as I could remember, and I couldn't see what it had to do with my father's death. But I resisted the urge to interrupt her, and, as the story unfolded, I began to see my mother in an entirely new light. I had always regarded her as the dutiful and clear-eyed child of the Age of Reason who placed her trust in the exercise of free will rather than fate. She never talked about ghosts, premonitions, or miracles, nor did she glance at her horoscope in a newspaper; her sole interest in the entertainment section of the *New York Times* was the crossword puzzle, which she did in ink, even on Sundays.

True, she was a Roman Catholic for most of her life. And she was a Celt, which meant she never gave someone a purse as a gift without first depositing a coin inside so the new owner would always have wealth. Likewise, when someone gave her a sharp object as a gift, a set of bone-handled steak knives or a pair of sewing scissors, she made sure to hand the giver a penny under the pretense of having "purchased" the knives or scissors; that way the friendship would never be cut. She also knocked on wood whenever she made a bold statement about the future, and she threw salt over her right shoulder after accidentally knocking over the shaker. But these were autonomic, culturally ingrained behaviors. They were not, generally speaking, precautions she took seriously.

Ty returns to the table and I decide to tell him the story of the opal ring, because his own father played a part in it. It is also Mother's Day, and, although it is a strange and sad tale, I again sense my mother at my shoulder, hear her voice in my ear.

The story begins in early 1951 when my father traveled to Australia on business. An important part of his job for the McGraw Wool Company after the war was inspecting and purchasing lots of cured sheepskins. He did this by traveling to Scotland, South America, New Zealand, and Australia. On this particular trip to Australia, my father became fascinated with black opals. Someone told him that the only place these mysterious stones were mined was deep in the outback. This gave my father an idea. He would seek out and purchase the most beautiful black opal he could find and give it to my mother. The stone he eventually settled on was large and exceptional. He took it to a jeweler in Sidney who set it in yellow gold with three small diamonds on each side. Later, when he got back to the States, he presented it to my mother.

"You know, Bev," he said, "there's a superstition that black opals are bad luck, but I don't believe in that."

My mother replied, "I agree. It's stunning."

Thrilled as she was with the gift, she discovered that it was too large for her finger, so she took it downtown to a jeweler to have it resized. Meanwhile, my father flew to Boston to inspect a shipment of sheepskins from Scotland.

When he got off the plane after returning from Boston, he felt ill. My mother drove him home, gave him a couple of aspirins, and put him to bed. The next day, Saturday, he went to work but he came home at lunchtime feeling even worse.

"He was running a temperature," my mother said, "and I thought he had the flu. It was the trip to Boston and all that. He just needed a few days in bed. But then he started vomiting, so I called his mother."

My grandmother volunteered as a Pink Lady at Penn Hospital and always encouraged her family members to go to the hospital at the first hint of a problem. My mother said my father and her used to laugh about Nana being so overly cautious, but Nana had her reasons: she lost two daughters to illness—Alice was five when she died, and Patricia was three. Both were victims of spinal meningitis.

"I think you should take Ed to the hospital," Nana told my mother.

"I'll ask Ed what he thinks and let you know," my mother said and hung up.

She told my father what his mother recommended, although she never expected he would take his mother's advice. But he said, "You know, Bev, maybe that's a good idea. If I go to the hospital they can give me something for my stomach and I'll get some sleep."

So my mother drove him into Pittsburgh, where he was admitted to Penn Hospital and given a private room.

"The doctors there examined him, and I presume they gave him shots, and he started to feel a little better. I sat there with him and then I went down and had lunch and came back. I was reading to him to amuse him. This was Saturday at around six or seven o'clock and he said, 'Bev, I really feel lousy. Why don't you go home?'

"And I thought, he just wants to sleep and, you know, hunker down, and he doesn't want any company. So I said, 'Okay, I'll go home and I'll be back tomorrow.'"

As my mother gathered up her purse to leave my father said, "You know, Bev, I'm glad I did the mission at the church."

The comment surprised my mother, because my father seldom talked about his faith. A month earlier, however, he had attended a men's mission at their church, but he said little about it at the time. Now he was bringing it up with an intensity that made an impression on my mother.

"So I said I'd see him in the morning, kissed him goodnight, and left."

My mother went home and watched a funny television show starring Sid Caesar and Imogene Coca before going to bed. The next day was Sunday, and she decided to visit my father in the hospital and then go to Mass afterwards.

Several days earlier she had picked up the opal ring from the jeweler, but she hadn't worn it yet.

"It was sitting on the dresser and I thought, I'll wear it because Ed gave it to me. It'll help cheer him up." So she slipped the ring on her finger.

She expected that my father would be feeling better, and the doctors would send him home. She went to his room but, when she tried to open the door, it was shoved back abruptly in her face.

"There was a whole bunch of people in there. I still didn't get it because I thought maybe they were washing him. There were nurses and doctors and they wouldn't let me in. So I thought, what's going on? And as I turned around I saw his mother coming down the corridor. And I knew right away it was serious trouble. She came up to me and said, 'Bev, it's very bad.'"

That was the moment my mother first thought that my father might die, even though the words—It's only the flu; he's not that sick—repeated themselves over and over inside her head.

The diagnosis, however, told a different story: bulbar polio, the worst strain of that awful disease. Bulbar polio destroys the lining of the nerves and paralyzes the lungs. It is also highly infectious. In fact, had the doctors at Penn Hospital realized that my father had polio, they never would have admitted him. They would have sent him instead to a hospital reserved exclusively for polio patients.

"If you had polio, it was almost like having the plague back then. You were confined to a certain area. But because Ed was already there, and because they needed what they called an 'iron lung' to keep him breathing, they telephoned his mother. She was quite a bigwig in the hospital auxiliary and she got in touch with Tommy Freyvogel, who was Ed's best friend. Tommy's family was in the funeral business and they also ran an ambulance service."

The doctors at the hospital tried to find an iron lung in the city, but none were available. This was at the height of the polio epidemic, and iron lungs were in high demand. After more calling around, they located one in the town of Greensburg, thirty miles southeast of Pittsburgh. So Tommy grabbed a Freyvogel ambulance—he knew the police and they agreed to provide an escort—and in the middle of the night, with lights flashing and sirens wailing, he raced to Greensburg to get the iron lung for my father. The doctors were putting my father into the mechanical lung when my mother arrived at his hospital room. She never heard his voice again.

"The iron lung kept Ed going for a while, but he died around three o'clock that afternoon. At the time, I was pregnant with what would have been my third child, and so, of course, in the awful, awful times that followed, I was trying to take care of myself so the baby would be all right. Because everyone was so afraid of spreading the polio, Ed couldn't be buried from our house on Shady Lane, which was across the river from Pittsburgh in Fox Chapel. Instead, he was buried from his parent's home. He was buried, incidentally, on his thirty-third birthday. Got all through the war, been wounded, done everything you could name. Worst of the fighting. Then he comes home and this happens. Well, anyway, when I got back to the house I looked at the ring and got this feeling like it was bad luck. I put it back in the box and put it in my dresser drawer and then I went on with my life."

Four months passed, and my mother went into labor with her third child a month early. She called Nana, who drove out to Shady Lane to take her to the hospital. As my mother was removing some things from the dresser to take to the hospital, she came across the ring, and the sight of it made her nervous. It also made her angry because she felt nervous.

"'It's superstition,' I told myself. 'It's absolutely crazy that a stone can be bad luck.' So I made a deliberate choice. I took it out of the drawer and put it on so I could break whatever I thought about it, and then I went to the hospital.

"Well, as it turned out the baby was what they called a 'blue baby,' born early, and he only lived for forty-eight hours. I saw him just once and then he died. Unfortunately for me, that ring had become what people said it was. It brought disaster on me. Now I was stuck. I couldn't wear it and I couldn't think of giving it to someone else. I wouldn't sell it because I wouldn't want to sell bad luck to someone else. So it still sits in my jewelry box. I haven't looked at it in a long time. But I will not wear it, I will not give it, and I will not sell it. I don't know what I'll do with it. Maybe I'll have it buried with me and be all done and finished with it."

My mother was quiet for a long moment. "Yep, it's sad. It was bad. I'm not a superstitious person, but that ring … I can't touch it. Fifty years later, I can't even handle it."

Three years after my mother told me this story, Paula and I were staying with her in her apartment in New Jersey. She was close to the end, receiving hospice care, and one evening she asked us to get her jewelry box so she could tell us which pieces went to which daughter-in-law, granddaughter, and niece. That is when I pulled out the ring with the cracked stone that Bob Murphy had given her before the war, the man whose hand in marriage she turned down so she could marry my father. There were other rings, necklaces, bracelets, and pendants. The last ring to come out of the box was the black opal. I had never seen it, nor was I keen to even be in the same room with it.

"Do you still want the ring to be buried with you?" I asked.

My mother was quite definite. "Yes. That's what I want. Maybe that will end the bad luck."

A waitress approaches the table with a pot of coffee and asks if we would like her to refill our cups. We both nod.

"Did you know my dad had a chronic back problem?" Ty says after she leaves.

I shake my head thinking about Ty's own back problem.

"He threw it out lifting the iron lung into the ambulance. That's what happened."

I am stunned. I didn't think Ty knew about his father driving to Greensburg to get the iron lung for my father. That is what got me to tell him the story.

"He ruptured a disc or something and had trouble with his back for the rest of his life. You know, he really loved your dad."

# CHAPTER 19

## *WOOL PULLING*

Monday morning is my last day in Pittsburgh, and I drive across the Allegheny River to the Northside neighborhood. Northside is a level strip of land fronting the river, flanked by steep, high bluffs. My destination is Troy Hill, a working class neighborhood of modest homes snugged together along the street like piano keys, with patches of grass here and there to break the monotony. Troy Hill was once home to the employees of the Patrick McGraw Wool Company and other companies whose factories were located down along the river. I have an appointment to meet with Father James Garvey, pastor of Most Holy Name of Jesus Church. Fr. Garvey is the unofficial historian for the Catholic Church in Pittsburgh. He is often assigned to parishes that are slated to close, and he has taken it upon himself to preserve as much of the history of these parishes as possible.

When I meet up with Fr. Garvey, he hands me a thick packet of documents he collected about the Patrick McGraw Wool Company. Included are articles on the wool industry in Pittsburgh, with frequent references to my family's business. There are also copies of land plats that show where the mills once stood. Fr. Garvey then takes me on a driving tour of Pittsburgh's Northside. In earlier days, the industrial district was home to dozens of slaughterhouses and tanneries. We drive past the original Heinz (of ketchup fame) factory, a sprawling red brick complex sporting a pair of distinctive towers, and pull up in front of a modern warehouse.

"The McGraw Company had two mills," Fr. Garvey explains. "One was here, next to the Heinz plant, and the other was a quarter mile upriver, across from what was once called Pig Island. That's where the livestock was brought in on the trains and held before being butchered."

"Who owns the warehouse?" I ask.

"Heinz. There was a big controversy when Heinz announced that they were going to tear down the mill and build a warehouse. A number of historians wanted the mill preserved, since it was the last remaining wool-pulling plant in the city."

"What's wool-pulling?"

"It was a tannery. The raw sheepskins came in by train, and then the wool was removed and the skins were put into vats to be cured into leather. The wool was then taken to the other mill where it was spun into thread and yarn and woven into cloth."

This is a revelation to me. I always heard that my family produced wool cloth, but no one ever mentioned that we also ran a tannery. For nearly ten years I made my living as a leatherworker. There was a wholesale leather distributor in Charleston, West Virginia, an hour's drive from my farm, where I could have gone to purchase my leather, but instead I preferred to drive almost three hours to a tannery in the eastern part of the state. I enjoyed roaming about inside the large building selecting the best hides from stacks of newly tanned hides, all the while absorbing the sounds and smells of a working tannery. My mother told me that her parents tried their hand at farming when they were young adults, something I did in my early twenties, and now I learn that tanning leather was an integral part of my father's family business. It makes you wonder.

Fr. Garvey is a charming and enthusiastic tour guide, and stories spill out of him like water from a clear spring as we wind our way through the narrow streets where families from Germany, Lithuania, and Croatia first settled after arriving in America.

"I understand the pollution from all the mills was terrible," I say. "It must have been hard on people's lungs."

"Pollution was everywhere. I grew up in McKees Rocks, and St. Francis De Sales Church was our local church. It was built in the late 1800s, I can't remember exactly when, but it was more than a hundred years old by the time they closed it. As far as anyone could remember, the church was made of black stone. Then they had to get the building pointed, so they also got it cleaned. In the process of cleaning it, they discovered that it was constructed of beautiful white stone, but the accumulation of industrial pollutants in the air darkened the building over the years, and nobody could remember when it had been anything but black."

As we head back to Most Holy Name Church, Fr. Garvey tells me that he made an announcement to his congregation that he was looking for anyone who had relatives who once worked for the McGraw Wool Company.

"Two people have gotten in touch with me," he tells me. "I put their names in the packet I gave you. I'm sure they'd be happy to talk to you."

He then tells me about the Printers' Mass.

"Most of the ethnic groups—the Germans, Greeks, and Lithuanians, the Italians, although they came later—they all had nationality newspapers, including the blacks. The Pittsburgh Courier was a wonderful newspaper. It was perhaps the best paper in the nation serving the black community. But at that time in Pittsburgh, there were twelve or fifteen different ethnic publications that came out either weekly or monthly that were written in the language of that particular group. So it might be Greek, Italian, Slovak, or Polish. And most of those publications were located in what's called the Lower Hill district, which is just across the river where the Civic Arena is now, and many of these people were Catholic. So they approached the new pastor at Epiphany Parish—I think Epiphany was opened in 1903—and they said to him, 'Look, we work all day Saturday to get the paper out and we have to work into the night. We don't finish until maybe twelve-thirty or one o'clock in the morning and then we go home and can't get up to go to Mass at six-thirty in the morning. Can't we have a Mass when we get off the job at about one-thirty or two o'clock in the morning?'

"And the priest said, 'No, you can't, because the only allowance for Mass other than between dawn and noon is Midnight Mass on Christmas Day.'

"And they said to him, 'But we still want it. What can you do?'

"He said, 'I'll have to write to Rome.'

"And they said, 'Then write to Rome.'

"So the pastor—his name was Father Larry O'Connell—writes to Rome and explains the situation, but he doesn't hold out much hope for these people. Then, lo and behold, Rome says, 'Well, that's a pastoral need; you can have Mass at two o'clock in the morning.'

"So it was called the Printers' Mass and they came from the printing shops all around the Lower Hill. These were people who did old-time linotype printing, and they had to set that stuff upside down and backwards and leave spaces and put in the punctuation. It took a lot of skill to set type.

"Well, it doesn't take long to walk from Duquesne University, which is up on the top of the hill there, to Epiphany Parish. It's a five or ten minute walk. Soon the students at Duquesne found out that there was a Mass they could go to at two o'clock in the morning. If they were out partying, they said, 'Let's go to Mass tonight and then we'll be able to sleep in tomorrow.' Well, it didn't take long for the word to get around, and, if people were partying at the hotels downtown or the nightclubs, then they appeared at two o'clock in tuxedos and the ladies were all decked out in their finery to attend Mass.

"There was a policeman who always attended that Mass, and some of the people that came in were so well-advanced along the route of alcohol that if you struck a match near them they would catch on fire. So he always kept order, and they never had any trouble."

"Do they still say the Printers' Mass?" I ask.

"No, after the Vatican Council you could have Mass on Saturday evening and Sunday evening. I was the pastor at Epiphany Church when the church celebrated its one hundredth anniversary and I brought the Printers' Mass back for one night only. And you'd be surprised at the number of people who showed up and said, 'Father, when we were dating, we used to come here for the two o'clock Mass.' And they brought their grandchildren and, of course, the grandchildren fell asleep in the pews, they weren't accustomed to being up at two o'clock in the morning."

As I get into my car, I wonder if my grandparents or parents ever attended the Printers' Mass after a night on the town. I see it with my mind's eye like a scene from a Fred Astair film: the men in evening dress with top hats and the women in chiffon gowns and high heels climbing (or perhaps weaving) their way up the steps of the church to crowd into the pews, the aroma of Chanel No. 5 and Old Spice intermingling with the scent of incense and burning candles, and the sobering shift from jokes and gossip to liturgical responses in the ancient Latin tongue.

My next stop is the city's historical museum, which was named for the Heinz family, who helped fund its construction. I am here to meet with David Grinnell, the museum's head archivist. We meet for lunch and David talks about how Pittsburgh became an industrial powerhouse.

"One reason was its proximity to natural resources: timber, coal, natural gas, and abundant water. Also, because of the rivers, and later the highway systems, it was easy to transport goods in and out of the city. Before the Civil War, packet boats regularly brought raw cotton up from the South, so it could be woven into yarn and sheeting in the textile mills that lined the north shore of the Allegheny River. And the same factor that made it easy to ship goods in and out also made Pittsburgh a place to transport people in and out. We like to call Pittsburgh America's first gateway to the West. Long before St. Louis, Pittsburgh is where you came to go West. Another factor not to be overlooked was the ability to get capital. Because Pittsburgh had an entrepreneurial bent to it, many of the people who made money were willing to invest in new ideas. You particularly see that with the formation of the Mellon Bank by the Mellon family. They were very much on the front edge of providing capital for these new ideas and new inventions. Lastly, Pittsburghers worked hard, especially in the earlier years. They were always trying to make life better. Much of this I think had to do with the Scotch-Irish work ethic that came with the early Presbyterians who ran things in the city, like the McKees and Grogans."

David then talks about how the Civil War changed Pittsburgh.

"The Civil War created immense wealth in Pittsburgh. Right across the street from the history center is where the Fort Pitt foundry was. They produced fifteen to twenty different types of cannon there, including the Rodman Gun, the largest artillery cannon produced during the war. The foundry was an immense operation. Uniforms were also produced here in Pittsburgh, and I believe, although I'm not a hundred percent on this, a lot of the carriages and the caissons and stuff like that."

"So war was a good thing for Pittsburgh?" I ask.

"It certainly was. During WWII, the Heinz Company converted part of their plant so they could make gliders for the Army. Pittsburgh really does change on a dime for war production. They've done it for every one of the big wars."

This portrait of Pittsburgh as war profiteer intrigues me, given my own family's history. I always heard that the McGraw Wool Company thrived during the Second World War, manufacturing wool cloth for blankets and uniforms. The good times, however, came to a crashing halt with the end of the war. Anticipating the invasion of Japan in 1945, the company seriously extended itself purchasing raw sheepskins. Then the United States dropped atomic bombs on Hiroshima and Nagasaki, and the war abruptly ended. Standing orders from the Army and Navy were cancelled without warning. The company was essentially bankrupt, stuck with warehouses full of cured sheepskins.

That was the situation my father faced when he returned from Europe onboard the Queen Mary: globs of red ink and everyone looking to him to figure out a way to save the company. He talked old customers into buying more wool than they needed. He borrowed from Peter to pay Paul. He enrolled in textile school and fretted over schemes to retool the upper mill so it could manufacture new synthetic fabrics. It must have been a trying, even humiliating, time for him, but somehow he helped the company regain its financial footing. In one of the letters my mother wrote to Nanny in 1948 I found this passage, which gave me a sense of the kind of pressure he was under.

> *"Today Ed had to get up real early and dash down to the mill. The river is rising—it's on the street already—and they're afraid it'll hit the mill. Not badly but enough to damage about $100,000 worth of wool. He said he'd call and tell me what the case is, but I haven't heard yet and I don't want to call for fear he'll be too busy to talk."*

My mother said my father often talked about moving the company from Pittsburgh to a small town. He said he wanted to be a big fish in a small pond. But perhaps the real reason was that he feared the company couldn't continue to handle its labor costs. If he moved to a right-to-work state, then at least he could stop worrying about the unions. That was the idea but then polio ended his life and he never got the chance. Not long afterward, the mills were sold and the Patrick McGraw Wool Company ceased to exist.

David takes me to a room where we flip through old plat books until we find where the McGraw mills once stood. He then takes me up to the fourth floor to see an exhibit on the wool-pulling industry in Pittsburgh. There is a canvas wool bin and a chalkboard for rating the quality of the sheepskins. David tells me these items are from the former McGraw tannery, which was bought by the Pittsburgh Wool Company when the family sold the business. There is also a video filmed inside the mill that shows the wool-pulling and tanning process. This is where my family made their living, here in the tannery and up the road at the spinning and weaving mill. It is one thing to have someone explain it to you and another to see the work being done. All that is missing is the stench of damp wool, raw animal hides, and tanning chemicals. It must have been overwhelming, especially during the hot, humid months of summer. No one in my family ever talked about money. It was just there; Nana and Papa must have had piles of it. It helped pay for all those elegant suppers at the University Club and the Pittsburgh Athletic Association Club—as well as all those wonderful presents Santa pulled out of his magic sack—and the box seats behind home plate at Forbes Field. There was money for my brother and me to go to the same summer camp on the shores of Lake Chautauqua where my father and his sisters were once campers themselves. And all those great toys on the third floor, the painted lead soldiers and wooden train sets, the Irish crystal and fine china, delicate silk window curtains and yard upon yard of wool carpeting. These treasures, and many more, not to mention the sweat of servants to maintain them, were all paid for with money earned inside the dirty, hot, and noisy tannery and spinning mill.

Later that afternoon, I call the people Fr. Garvey found whose relatives once worked for McGraw Wool Company. The first is David Bukovan.

"Yeah, my dad worked for Paddy McGraw," he says with a

laugh. "I used to take him his lunch there at the mill. I was just a kid."

"What was it like, the mill?"

"There was so much wool lint flying around in the air that it would get stuck in my teeth as I ate my sandwich and I had to pick it out. The air was white with the stuff."

"How long did your dad work for the McGraws?"

"A good while, but then he began to lose weight. He got really skinny and he went to the doctor's and the doctor told him it was from breathing all that lint. He told the McGraws that he had to quit working there and find another job, and that's what he did."

Next I call Roseann Berube, who tells me that her grandmother used to work for the McGraws and was once thrown into a paddy wagon and hauled off to jail for participating in a labor strike at the mill. I press her for more details about the strike, but that is all Roseann knows.

"My grandmother also worked for the Heinz Company," Roseann tells me as an afterthought. "Her job was to wring the necks of the chickens that went into the chicken noodle soup. She did that all day long, one chicken after another. She told me that she didn't let her young children sleep in the bed with her because she was afraid she might wring their necks one night in her sleep."

It is time to head over to the library in Homewood for my evening program. As I drive along the banks of the Allegheny River under the shadow of Troy Hill, I think about all the hardworking individuals who helped make the lives of those of my family easier. Whether the geographical separation is only a neighborhood or two, the distance, for instance, between Shadyside and Troy Hill, or between Olympia, Washington, where I now live, and a city in Malaysia or China where my shoes and underwear are made, the worlds of the privileged and the working class are bridged but

# CHAPTER 20

## HOMEWOOD

My presentation at the Homewood Library is well-attended, thanks in large part to the article in the *Post-Gazette*. I use a projector to share some of my own family's photographs along with those Meir Kaplon took of the families who lived in Shady Lane in Maryland. I conclude by talking about the influence of Irish and African-American culture on Appalachian music and demonstrate this by playing a medley of old-time mountain fiddle tunes.

Afterward, a number of people come up to talk to me about their parents and grandparents who worked for white families. An elderly black man tells me about his father who was a chauffeur for a wealthy family.

"They didn't like to drive their own car. They liked owning a big car but they got my father to drive it. And he had to wash it, too, and polish the chrome." The man smiles. "My dad was proud of the way he kept that car. There wasn't a scratch on it."

There are more stories; everyone seems to welcome the opportunity to reminisce. There is one black woman, however, who becomes sorrowful as she tells me her story. For many years, she worked for a white family in Squirrel Hill, a Pittsburgh neighborhood next to Shadyside.

"I raised their children—two girls—from the time they were born until they went off to college," she tells me, her voice quavering with emotion. "But I've never heard from them or their family since. I don't know what happened to them. I would like to know. I think of them as my children."

An elderly white couple waits to speak to me, the man carrying a large canvas bag. When at last they step forward, they introduce themselves as Donald and Gay Reigel. Donald tells me he is a retired pediatric neurosurgeon.

"We read your story in the newspaper and wanted to meet you," he says. "You see, we bought your grandparents' house on Devonshire Street. It was a beautiful house and we did extensive remodeling. But before that, we hired a historian to do a history of the house."

He pulls out a large album with a green cover and 700 DEVONSHIRE STREET embossed in gold letters on the front. It's an elegant object, like the house.

"Much of the history is about your family," Gay says. "We sold the house a couple of years ago and moved into a condominium. You can borrow the album if you want and make copies and mail it back to us. We've decided to leave the album to you in our will."

My mind races. They are talking about Nana's house. I can barely manage a 'Thank you' as I pull up a chair, open the album, and begin flipping through the pages. I come upon a photograph that makes my heart leap. It shows a decorated Christmas tree hanging upside down in the stairwell of Nana's house.

When I first contacted different members of the family to see if anyone knew Helen's last name or where she came from, I spoke on the telephone with my cousin Alice Sexton. Alice was living near Chicago at the time and, although she had no memory of Helen, we did talk about Nana. Being the only granddaughter, I suspected Alice had had a difficult time with Nana, and Alice confirmed this. But she also told me a story that cast this formidable woman, the iron-willed child of Patrick McGraw, in a different light.

Nana was always a huge fan of Christmas. She delighted in crafting all manner of Christmasy things and sending them to us in Paterson. But as Christmas drew nigh in 1944, Nana was beside herself with worry because the world was at war and her only son, my father, was overseas fighting the Nazis. So instead of celebrating Christmas in the usual way, Alice told me, Nana decided to hang the Christmas tree upside down.

"She did it because she felt her world had been turned upside down by the war," Alice said.

As I pondered this story later, I began to see how unusual my grandmother's decision was. I would think that if your country and someone you dearly love were in grave peril, if the future is full of uncertainty, even madness, then you would cling to those familiar rituals that in days past provided joy and reassurance. Instead, Nana seemed to be saying to both God and fate, "If this is what you want, then *bring it on*. I have the strength and determination to deal with whatever comes my way." She was strong and was already acquainted with the specter of tragedy having earlier in her life dealt with the untimely deaths of two precious daughters.

Since my own relationship with Nana was not close, I was moved by this story. It helped humanize her for me in a fundamental way. And now here I am looking at a photograph of the upside-down Christmas tree. I can think of no other photograph from 700 Devonshire that would have meant as much to me.

"Where did you get this picture?" I ask the Reigels.

"We wrote to your aunt and uncle in Chicago and asked if they had any information about the house and its history," Don explains. "Your uncle sent the photograph along with other information."

I find something else that is quite special in the album pertaining to the house on Devonshire Street: a single page from a book titled *Unmasked* that was written by a woman named Martha Edith Bannister Moore in 1964.

Gay Reigel explains that Ms. Moore was an African-American woman who was so light-skinned that she could pass for white, and therefore had a unique perspective on race relations in Pittsburgh during the mid-twentieth century. The book is a memoir in which she recounts her experiences working for different families. The reason the Reigels added the page to the album was because Ms. Moore talks about my family in her book. She writes:

*"St. Paul's Cathedral on Fifth Avenue, Oakland, is one of the loveliest Catholic Churches I have ever visited. One of the most beautiful weddings ever held there was that of Nancy McHugh, the daughter of the Edward C. McHughs, of Devonshire Street, former employers of mine. Mrs. McHugh's father founded P. McGraw Wool Company, which is located on the North Side, Pittsburgh. Mr. McGraw died at the age of eighty-six, leaving nine sons and one daughter, Mrs. McHugh. It was because of Mrs. McHugh and her family that I had an opportunity to travel to Quebec, Canada, and to spend an entire summer on Lake Chautauqua, Jamestown, New York. Mrs. McHugh taught me the art of knitting and the value of the imported wools from London, Australia, and Scotland, used in the family business. And, through the generosity of this family, I was acquainted with the musical series for which Chautauqua Institute is famous.*

*"Mrs. McHugh had two other children, Edward Junior, before his death a law student at Notre Dame University, Indiana, and a younger daughter, Mary Ann."*

Fr. Garvey attended the presentation and afterward he comes over and I introduce him to the Reigels and show him the album.

"I have so many fond memories of that house," I tell the Reigels. "As kids, we had the entire third floor to ourselves; it was filled with toys."

"That used to be the linen room," Gay says. "Remember all the cedar cabinets? They even had a mangle up there."

"What's a mangle?"

"It's a big drum for pressing the sheets and tablecloths. It was heated with gas. When we bought the house, the mangle was in the basement."

I try to recall seeing this large object, but can't, even though my cousin Ed and I spent hours pedaling our tricycles madly around the basement whenever the weather was bad.

"We put our daughter up on the third floor," Gay continues. "There was a bedroom at the end, if you remember."

"I used to sleep in that bedroom when I didn't sleep in my grandfather's room," I tell her. "I'd wake up to the sounds of the trolley cars going past on Ellsworth Avenue. The electricity would make a sharp snap as it arced from the overhead wires to the pole on the trolley."

"Well, our daughter kept complaining that she could smell gas up on the third floor. Then, for some reason, we had men in to do work, and they discovered that the gas pipe that fed the mangle hadn't been capped and gas was just spewing into the room. Our gas bill for the first month was $700."

"We had to move out of the house for some time," Don says, "and they covered the windows and worked to get all the gas out."

"Our daughter was a teenager," Gay recalls, "and she was sneaking cigarettes. It's a miracle she didn't blow the house up."

Another woman approaches and introduces herself. Her name is Connie and she tells me we are related.

"I read about you in the newspaper. We're cousins on the McHugh side. Your grandfather and my grandmother were brother and sister."

I know next to nothing about Papa's side of the family other than they came from Connellsville, Pennsylvania. The only family stories we heard growing up were about Patrick McGraw, Nana's father, who came to Pittsburgh from Ireland and started the wool company. Papa never mentioned his childhood. It was a complete mystery to me.

"My grandmother was Mary McHugh and she married a Barnes," Connie tells me. "I have an older brother in Florida who remembers your father. His name is Bert Barnes. You should get in touch with him."

We exchange contact information as the librarian prepares to close up. I gather up my fiddle and the album and head for the door. Fr. Garvey asks if I am hungry and offers to take me to a good Italian restaurant in a neighborhood called Bloomfield. Fifteen minutes later, we are sitting at a table inside Del's Restaurant, looking over the menu.

Fr. Garvey is seventy-one years old and yet he retains a youthful enthusiasm. I attribute this to his love of history. My mother was that way. It was her deep love of history that kept her forever interested in the world and its people.

We are the last diners of the night and I can hear the kitchen staff washing up their pots. The owner comes over, a short pleasant woman with a thick Italian accent, and asks if we would like dessert.

"You don't pay," she says and, before we can answer, she turns and motions to the waiter to bring the dessert tray to our table. She then brings us each a cup of coffee.

Nibbling our cannoli, we talk about how Pittsburgh has changed over the years. We also discuss the nature of religious faith in the modern age. Eventually we say goodnight, and I head back to my hotel. As I do, I recall an interview program I once heard on public radio. The guest was a noted orchestral composer who explained why he chose to premier one of his symphonies in Pittsburgh. Along with the city's three major rivers, he said, there was a subterranean river flowing directly beneath the city. In India there is also a city with three surface rivers and a fourth that flows underneath and, because of this, the Indians consider the city a sacred place.

I like the idea that the city of my birth is somehow special, sacred even, that a hidden river courses beneath buildings and parks in the way a mythic story might flow just below the surface of our everyday consciousness, shaping our destinies in unexpected ways.

# CHAPTER 21

## THE EIGHT-POINTED STAR

My journey began three years ago with a visit to Hell's Kitchen. But as I work to set down my experiences and discoveries on paper, I realize that there are details I have not gathered. Dr. Reigel, for instance, told me he was a retired pediatric neurosurgeon, but I know nothing about the career of his wife Gay.

So I call Gay and she tells me that she was a nurse for many years and that is how she met her husband. We talk about the house on Devonshire Street and she mentions that they did not purchase the house directly from my grandmother, which is what I assumed, but from a family named von Eckartsberg.

"A couple named Evans bought the house from your grandmother, but they got divorced within a year and sold it to the Eckartsbergs," Gay tells me. "The Eckartsbergs were from Germany I think, and the husband was a psychology professor at Duquesne University. They owned the house for seven years. I believe they were good friends with Timothy Leary. He often came to visit them and stayed at the house. When we bought it, there was a huge poster of the Maharishi on the living room wall."

I burst out laughing. Timothy Leary, one of the founders of the psychedelic consciousness movement, slept under Nana's roof? It is beyond imagining.

I thank Gay for the information and we say our goodbyes.

The next morning I call the psychology department at Duquesne University and talk with Dr. Eva Simms. She is the director of the graduate psychology program. Her primary field of study, coincidentally, is early brain development.

"His first name was Rolf, and he died in 1993," she informs me. "I believe Dr. von Eckartsberg came from nobility in Germany, and he was Timothy Leary's graduate assistant at Harvard. His wife's name is Elsa. I'm pretty sure she's still alive."

"Do you know anything about Timothy Leary coming to their house?"

She laughs. "Oh yes. The Devonshire Street house was the party house. Lots of people went to their parties."

"Does Elsa live in Pittsburgh?"

"Yes, I think so. Of the two, she was more the free spirit, if you know what I mean."

Dr. Simms then offers to see if she can find Elsa's contact information.

She calls back the next day with Elsa's email address and I send a note to Elsa asking her to call me if she is willing.

Several days pass and Elsa calls. I explain my connection to the house on Devonshire Street.

"My father grew up in that house but he died in 1951, when I was quite young," I tell her. "My brother and I used to visit my grandparents there. It was a magical place for us. I'd like to email you the prologue to the book I'm writing so you'll understand what I'm doing."

"We loved that house," Elsa says. "We had such good times there. I also had a psychic experience in that house. Maybe I'll tell you about it after I read your prologue."

I am curious to know what she means by "psychic experience," but I think it best not to press her. Instead, we schedule an appointment in a week when we can talk again and I can record our conversation.

In the meantime, I peruse a history of the psychology department at Duquesne University that Dr. Simms emailed to me. It is titled *Fearfully and Wonderfully Made*. The title's reference comes from Psalm 139: "I give you thanks that I am fearfully, wonderfully made; wonderful are your works."

Dr. Simms emailed it to me because it contains a brief biography of Dr. Rolf von Eckartsberg, which, along with describing his work earning a doctorate at Harvard, includes this passage: "His vision and understanding of the essence of human destiny is the call to love the other."

An Internet search directs me to several of his published essays. In one, he describes his experiences ingesting magic mushrooms (psilocybin). The essay is part of a collection titled *The Ecstatic Adventure, Reports of Chemical Explorations of the Inner World.* His particular contribution is introduced with the passage:

"The writer of the following report is a European-trained psychologist who was getting his Harvard Ph.D. in clinical psychology at the time when Timothy Leary and Richard Alpert were disturbing the sleep of the university administrators by experiments with psilocybin."

(I became acquainted with the writings of Richard Alpert in the early 1970s after he changed his name to Ram Dass. I was living on the farm in West Virginia and was much taken with his illustrated book *Be Here Now* that sought to comprehend the psychedelic experience through the precepts of the ancient religion of Hinduism.)

I come across another essay that piques my interest. It is titled "Social and Electronic Immortality" and was given as a lecture by Dr. von Eckartsberg in Pittsburgh in 1988. The first two paragraphs of the essay read:

"How can we overcome the death barrier? Existentialism claims that we cannot. Our life is characterized by finitude, which has death as its limit condition. But the sting of death—mortality—and our acknowledgement of this reality makes us wake up to life and be resolute for our projects of self-realization. Yet we die alone!

"But what if this existential conviction is based on shaky ground? Are we not born into family-community and do we not die within a community of extended family and friends within the social body of our 'existential ensemble,' (von Eckartsberg, 1979) which we have co-created by our living? This cast of characters of our existence survives our death. The survival community is launched at the funeral of the deceased. While the dead person is lowered into the ground, the person's spirit is raised in the speech and imagination of the survivors. A spiritual rebirth occurs. To the deceased person a new state of being, a new life: social immortality is bestowed in and through our collective commemoration. It exists as a circulation in image-consciousness and speech. This is the point of view of co-existentialism. Personal immortality for oneself may well be impossible, but social immortality, continued life in the consciousness and speaking of others is not."

It is at this moment that I realize that I am conducting a ritual of commemoration in researching and writing this book.

As I work on the manuscript my thoughts stray repeatedly to thoughts of my younger self and my own psychedelic experiences. This can be troubled territory for people my age, especially for those who partook of these remarkable and dangerous substances. The period of the late 1960s and early 1970s have been so worked over by the media that the cultural landscape they describe is quite removed from the one I remember. Even the word "hippie" gives me pause for it was a word I seldom, if ever, used to describe who I was back then, despite my shoulder-length hair, Army surplus clothing, and sensation-inspired lingo. We called ourselves "freaks" and "heads," but not hippies. In my case, psychedelics, such as LSD and mescaline, played a crucial role in altering the course of my life. Jimi Hendrix—*Are You Experienced?*, the Moody Blues—*In Search of the Lost Chord*, Carlos Castaneda—*The Teachings of Don Juan*, Aldous Huxley—*The Doors of Perception*, and, as mentioned, Ram Dass—*Be Here Now*, had it not been for psychoactive plants and chemicals and these musicians and philosophers, I imagine I would have completed my college degree and found some proper professional position assuring me a comfortable and reliable living, like my brother and cousins, instead of the artist's path that I now follow.

When I interviewed Dr. Siegel, he referred to my early drug use as possible self-medication. I disagree. I had no interest in drugs such as heroin or cocaine. Nor, as far as I know, was I trying to assuage my feelings of loss. Instead, I was drawn to chemicals that promised to expand my experience of the world. To be truthful, many of those experiences were far from being fun. A few were dreadful, terrifying even.

The mythologist Joseph Campbell wrote a fascinating book titled *The Hero With a Thousand Faces*, in which he deconstructs the pattern for the hero's quest in folktales from cultures around the world. The first phase of the quest, according to these tales, is a descent into a subterranean world, a realm of demons and specters, a pit in which we encounter our darkest fears and anxieties. Whether I was hero or youthful fool, Campbell describes pretty much what I remember. But there were also rare moments when I experienced the sublime, when I peered like a child through the gates of heaven to behold the glorious wedding banquet of joy to which all souls have been invited.

I stopped taking psychedelics in my early twenties when I was living on the farm. All the same, those early experiences exerted a powerful influence on everything I have done or attempted to do since. They also put me at odds with my family. In their eyes, I allowed myself to be taken in by a motley assortment of tin-plated gurus and good-for-nothing con artists. As I have said before, this wasn't necessarily my mother's assessment of my condition, although she was deeply confused by what was going on with her youngest son. But other family members, particularly those on my father's side of the family, regarded me—to borrow a phrase from the *I-Ching*, another book that helped shape my philosophy of life as a young man—as "a pig covered with dirt, as a wagon full of devils."

So there is a weird, bittersweet quality to this revelation that the heart of the consciousness expansion movement in Pittsburgh was the house at 700 Devonshire Street. In fact, the last time I visited Nana's house was during the summer of 1967. I was seventeen years old, between my junior and senior year in high school, and already diverging radically from the traditional mores of my society and class. I was hitchhiking through Pittsburgh with a friend and Nana put us up for the night. It must have been extremely awkward for my grandparents. I was the son of their only son who died suddenly and tragically sixteen years before, and I was a long-haired hobo in shabby clothes who spouted incomprehensible words and phrases. Given their ultra-conservative take on the world, my friend and I might as well have been visitors from another planet.

A week later I call Elsa and she begins by telling me what it was like being a teenager in Germany during World War II.

"I was born in 1930 before Hitler came to power, so I went through the whole thing and almost was annihilated in Dresden. In fact, I wrote a memoir for my children called *A Memoir of Miracles*, because I lived by one miracle after another. It was total chance. We once left our home in Bremen because the Russians were coming, and we had just arrived at the railroad station in Dresden when suddenly my father, who was a Lutheran minister, said, 'Oh, I remember my cousin has a birthday today.' She lived in the suburbs and so we left everything, all our luggage at the railroad station, and went to her place, and that's how we survived the bombing of Dresden. Yes. We saw it all from the distance.

"That is one of those horror stories one goes through in life. But it was a pure miracle because my mother must have been so despairing of my father, you know, because he would leave everything at the railroad station. But he felt he should visit his cousin." Elsa laughs at the memory. "Life is just infinitely fascinating, any life practically."

"When did you first start having psychic experiences?" I am thinking about what she told me the first time we talked.

"During the last part of the war, which was so terrible, so absolutely insane in Germany. Bremen was totally destroyed, and that's where I grew up as a teenager. The destruction, that is very rough for a teenager. So where could I go other than into my mind; there was just nothing for a teenager to enjoy on this earth anymore.

"That's when I became a writer, and I had lots of psychic experiences."

"I read a biography of your husband that said he was born in California," I mention.

"That was by chance. All life is so magical that you cannot even believe it. His family was from one of the most ancient German nobility going back to the ninth century, but they lost everything in the European inflation. They had the biggest house in Frankfurt. They were very well-to-do, but then they lost it all after the First World War. Nobody was expecting this kind of inflation to come. So Rolf's father married this businesswoman just to survive. I don't know how they got [the] money, but they took a trip to California because they wanted to see it. And that's where he was born, in Hollywood. Then they had to go back to Germany, and he grew up there during the war. But later he remembered that he was an American citizen, and he went into the American Army because he didn't want to be a businessman. Later, he came to America and went to Harvard."

Elsa tells me about attending Harvard at the same time and earning her Ph.D. in German and French literature. They moved to Pittsburgh when Rolf was offered a job at Duquesne University.

"Why did you buy the Devonshire Street house?"

"At that time, my husband just made a little inheritance from some businessmen of his family, and so he found the Devonshire Street house and we moved right in. We thought it was an ideal place. I was fascinated with the entrance hall and the shape of the living room, which is octagonal. There were also fabulous stained-glass windows in the dining room and on the stairs going up to the second floor. One was of an eight-pointed star that pointed to Venus. I was totally fascinated with Venus then, and that's mainly what attracted us, and naturally the European style [of the house], since we both came from Europe."

"What can you tell me about the psychedelic movement?"

"A book came out last year about the early psychedelic culture at Harvard and both my husband and I are in it."

"Did you do LSD when you lived in the Devonshire Street house?"

"I don't want to go into that. My husband was a close friend with Timothy Leary to his end. So when Timothy was here in Pittsburgh, they were always big buddies and giving lectures together for thousands of people. But we were not into that anymore in the Devonshire house. I mean, not physically, but mentally I could say. We were behaving very proper. I cannot believe that the neighbors had any inkling of it."

"How would you describe who you were then? Would you call yourselves hippies?"

"I never liked the hippies. We were never run down or looked weird or anything. We were always very proper. I don't know what we were. We were known to all the top people. Ram Dass, who was Richard Alpert, came to our home. And Ralph Metzner, all the leaders."

"What about Alan Watts?"

"Yes, Alan Watts, and the great American poet, the one from Paterson."

She pauses trying to remember the name and I say, "Allen Ginsberg?"

"Yes, that's him," she says. "And G. Gordon Liddy, he came to our house, too. We were never ostentatious. My husband came from a very proper business and the baronial thing, his background, so he was always elegantly dressed and I was always elegantly dressed. We had fancy food. We also loved to dance, for which we also liked the octagonal room. We had a grand piano in the front room and we had dance parties there. Always had fabulous pianists. I loved to dance; I was mainly dancing. We just had a great life."

"Why did you sell the house?" I ask.

Elsa laughs, a merry laugh with no hint of bitterness. "We ran out of money. My husband had a small inheritance from his family in Germany and it was all very expensive. We lived there for exactly seven years, from 1976 to 1983. I wrote it down. It was almost the longest time we stayed anywhere."

"Did you sell the house because you couldn't pay the mortgage or was it the taxes and insurance?" I ask.

"I don't know. I've no idea. I wasn't into money at all. I let my husband do all this. But the kids had to go to the high school there and we had to pay for that. It's just that reality is different from psychedelic ecstasy. Eventually we had to come down to earth and see realities, so then we moved to Squirrel Hill and that wasn't that bad either. We just rented. So that's how it is." Again she laughs. I find her lack of regret and self-consciousness exceptional.

"How did your husband die?" I ask.

"He died in 1993 from some very, very rare cancer. We always thought he had something wrong with his kidneys. But it wasn't the kidneys; it was the adrenaline gland that got cancer. A very rare cancer. That's how he died, much too early. I didn't remarry. Not interested, not in the least."

"You mentioned that you had a psychic experience when you lived in the Devonshire Street house," I remind her.

"Yes, but I don't think it is connected to your family."

"But you said you thought it was."

"I read what you sent me and you wrote that your father died in the Fox Chapel house. So I don't know if what I experienced has anything to do with your father."

I can sense she is ready to finish our interview, but when I interviewed my mother and asked her to tell me about my father's death in detail—that is when I first heard the story of the black opal ring—she made a point of telling me that because my father died of polio, and because the authorities greatly feared spreading the epidemic, they would not allow my father's body to be transported across the river from Pittsburgh to Fox Chapel. So my father was "buried from his parents house on Devonshire Street," as she put it.

I explain this to Elsa and there is silence on her end of the line. I can almost hear her deciding whether or not to tell me about her experience.

"One day I was alone in the house," she replies at last. "The kids were all gone, and my husband wasn't there. It was in the early afternoon and I sat down in a chair in the octagonal room and was looking up at my windows, which I so loved so much, at the eight-pointed star. Somehow I had a piece of paper in front of me and I go into this very mysterious trance. Maybe because I was suddenly alone, you know, and I was totally—this would freak you out, it freaked me out—I started crying. Very immediately, as I recall, and I went into this, that I was at a funeral. So I must have picked up these vibrations. But you said your father died somewhere else so then I thought, that's not it, but now you tell me he was there."

"My grandparents thought the sun rose and set with my father," I tell Elsa. "His death was an enormous loss for them, as it was for my mother. Because he died, they had to sell the family business. His death was a huge tragedy for the family. I can't imagine the depth of grieving that went on."

"There were incredible vibrations left behind in the building, and I picked them up psychically," Elsa says without hesitation. "I went into tears. That came first. I picked up an enormous sadness suddenly, which we never had since we always danced there and all of this. So I was totally astonished. I said, why would I go into tears here? And looking up the stairs to this stained-glass window, I wrote down a series of poems on the spot. I called them *Funeral Songs*. Can you imagine that? And since I didn't know your family, I referred it to myself. I thought it must be my own death or something I'm going through—a premonition that I was going to die. I even told my kids in case I died to read them over me. It's very, very strange, but the poetry is absolutely divine, not depressive at all."

"Do you still have the poems?" I inquire.

"Yes, and I'm still here, eighty years old, and my husband is gone and my children are all grown up. So I never knew what that was all about. I didn't know your grandparents or anybody who lived there before."

"Did you write the poems in German?"

"No, in English. If you want, I can send them to you."

I tell Elsa I would love to have a copy of the poems, and several days later an envelope shows up in my mailbox. Here is the first poem in the series.

*Embalm me not*
  *in tears, in terror*
*when I am gone*

*my face only more*
  *a distant*
*smile, undecipherable—*

*put a wedding-gown*
  *over my cold body,*

*shimmering white,*
  *shot through*
*with threads of silver,*

*—if I smile*
  *in death—*

*for then you know*
  *that I am wedded*

*to space,*
  *to flight*
*through universes*

*without gravity*

*in unearthly*
  *freedom-bliss,*

*finally loved*
  *in my freedom*

*—if I smile*
  *in death—*

*by the greatest*
  *lover whose undiminished*

*existence has bonded me*
  *to the limitless,*

*has branded my brow*
  *with the seal*
*of infinity*

After saying goodbye to Elsa I go looking for a copy of my father's obituary in the newspaper. My mother said my father was "burying from" the Devonshire Street house, but does that mean the funeral was held there? Is it not more likely the funeral was held at a church or the Freyvogel Funeral Home, which was owned by a relative?

Going through the family papers I find the obituary, yellowed with time, and there in the last chapter is proof that what my mother said was true.

"Funeral services were held this morning, from the parents' home, 700 Devonshire Street, Pittsburgh, with High Mass of Requiem in St. Paul's Cathedral at 11 o'clock."

In the days and weeks that follow, I cannot stop thinking how my father's death affected the family. Nana's love for my father was legendary. My Uncle Mack liked to tell about dating my Aunt Nancy and how everyone in her family referred to my father as "the son." They seldom said Ed; it was always "the son." When Mack finally met my father on the train platform in Pittsburgh upon my father's return from the war, Mack went up to him and said, "So, you must be the son."

He said my father wasn't all that amused, but despite this rough start, he and Mack became bosom buddies in the years that followed.

I also recall a conversation I once had with my Aunt Mary Ann during which she expressed deep resentment over how much Nana favored boys over girls. Boys were the future. They deserved to get the best. Girls were supposed to get married and support their husbands. Even my cousin, Alice Sexton, was hurt and angered by Nana's favoritism. Nana made no effort to conceal it.

I can't imagine the depths of Nana's despair when my father died suddenly. I cannot help but wonder whether or not it is possible for strong emotions to imprint themselves on a person's physical environment, such as a house. At some level, many of us believe this is possible, otherwise people would not so readily visit the Gettysburg Battlefield or go on a pilgrimage to the place where John Lennon was gunned down. We believe a kind of soul energy lingers in such places. Is that what Elsa von Eckartsberg tuned in to—the vibrations of Nana's riven heart? And what about Papa's grief? My father was incredibly close to this older man. He even asked Papa to be his best man. They bowled together nearly every week and played golf at the Field Club together. Papa had groomed his son to take over the wool company. The death must have shaken him to his core.

Of course, Elsa didn't know any of this. She just felt *something*.

I first went to Pittsburgh to try and get to know my father's world better. Hitherto, the journey has been more about my mother and Helen. I did attempt to visit where my father was stationed at Fort McClellan, but I arrived too late in the day to get in. So I sat in the car and looked at the camp and recalled the one war story I have from him before resuming my journey.

Now my connection to the man I never knew has deepened. I won't say I feel his presence, but he is somehow more real to me now, and I feel sympathy for him. All that pressure: go to college and get top grades, join the Army and survive the intensive training, get shot at by snipers as you slog your way through one war-ravaged village after another, drive over a mine in a Jeep and get blown up, and then come home to deal with bankruptcy, a young wife who is chronically homesick for her family and who is pregnant much of the time, and conspire to go into business with your best friend even though there is a good chance the whole enterprise will fail. His mother and father worshiped the ground he walked on, and his friends regarded him as war hero with a drawer full of medals to prove it. Only he couldn't get enough sleep because he kept having war nightmares, and he was constantly hopping on airplanes to fly half way around the world—no wonder the polio virus kicked his ass.

But then I think, you did complete the mission at the church, Dad, so, according to your faith, you were right with God when you died. And you left me here. And what did I do? When I turned seventeen I turned my back on the very institutions that defined your existence and to which you pledged your allegiance: the academy, the military, the industrial corporation, and the Catholic Church—even the Field Club and Pittsburgh Athletic Association. Instead, I became a wanderer, a farmer, a leather craftsman, a folk musician, and an oral storyteller, what the Irish call, a seanachie. Different strokes for different folks, I guess, but I will always wonder how my father and I would have gotten along, had he survived.

Have I learned anything? Maybe. I know that spiritual renewal does not come from our relationships with the rich and powerful, but from our relationships with the lowly. And I have learned that true joy is more valuable than money, and that we are all part of a much larger story than any of us imagine. It is like being in one of those grand Cecil B. DeMille films with a cast of thousands, a big story, and a long one, that stretches far beyond the feeble starts and stops of our own biological lives, a living thread of souls working out the nature of love and redemption.

# CHAPTER 22

## A SUSPICIOUS DEATH

Something that preys on my mind is the fact that Helen's grave has no headstone. I have only a general idea of where she is buried in the St. Mary cemetery, but I feel she deserves some physical marker to commemorate her life. George Scott told me that, in years past, a man named Francis Allen who was a builder, and also a fiddler, used poured concrete to make grave markers for the families on Shady Lane. He used a wooden cross-shaped mold and pressed the name of the deceased into wet concrete with a set of letter stamps. Sadly, however, he failed to include any metal reinforcement, mesh or rebar, and so the crosses crumbled as the years wore on.

I learned later that some time during the 1980s, the pastor of St. Mary, Fr. Peter Hiltz, took charge of all the cemeteries owned and operated by the Archdiocese of Baltimore. Unfortunately, Fr. Hiltz regarded the decaying concrete crosses sprinkled across his own cemetery as eyesores, so he ordered the cemetery custodian to dispose of them, which the custodian did by simply throwing them over the fence. The church made no attempt to replace the crosses with markers of any kind, nor was a written record kept to identify who was buried where. Estella told me she didn't know where her own father was buried because his cross was thrown away along with the others.

When I was living on the farm in West Virginia an elderly neighbor named Lynn Springston asked me to help dig a grave at the cemetery next to his church. Three of us dug the grave together, two men in their mid-seventies and me, a twenty-four-year-old rebel trying to fit in. I had youthful vitality; they had wisdom. The church was an old-fashioned white clapboard affair set atop a knoll overlooking Leading Creek, a lazy out-of-the-way watercourse that served as the local swimming hole. It was late summer and as we toiled, time seemed to stretch out in both directions, drawing together the generations of families who tended, and would tend, the farms roundabout. I don't remember the name of the deceased, it wasn't anyone I knew well, nor do I think the elders were in great need of my brawn—I am certain there were other local men just as willing to lend a hand—but grave-digging was a ritual of long standing and I suspect it was Lynn's way of weaving me more tightly into the fabric of the community. Looking back at the youth I was then, I readily admit I needed that kind of weaving.

For most of the afternoon we took turns digging and exchanging rumors and jokes, and I can still recall the serene blueness of the sky overhead, the pungent scent of the earth, the scrape of the shovel as it struck rock here and there, and the pleasant ripple of Leading Creek as it flowed under the branches of the ancient sycamore from which the stout swinging rope dangled, a board tied to the end for the swimmers' feet.

There is a strong tendency to romanticize rural life, and I am as guilty of this as anyone. But forty years later, I continue to cherish those few hours I spent digging a grave with Lynn and his friend. Opening up our Mother so she could receive back into herself one of her own.

Besides Helen's unmarked grave, I find myself frequently contemplating the strange and wonderful role serendipity has played in my quest: the fact that there were two Shady Lanes and two families who searched for coins in the ashes after a devastating fire, a high school student who became a historian because the young teacher who was my mother showed an interest in his discovery of old photographic plates, a newspaper editor who decided to lead with a story about a plague of fires across his state, a Jewish storeowner who documented the life of a small rural community of black people with photographs and then gave the photographs to a man who, on an autumn afternoon years later, decided to rake the leaves in front of his house. Then there was the couple who loved a house so much they commissioned a historian to write a history about it that includes a photograph of an upside-down Christmas tree.

These special coincidences are as close to real magic as anything I have known in my life. Kismet, synchronicity, Providence, the hidden hand of fate, luck, divine will, happy chance, fortune, predestination—our language is rich with words and phases to describe this phenomena. Perhaps serendipity is one of the reasons I am drawn to folktales.

Jack becomes lost in the enchanted forest and fears he will fail in his efforts to find the castle where evil giants hold the King's daughter a prisoner. Suddenly, a small gray pony appears and tells Jack to climb up upon her back, and she carries Jack to the castle and whispers the secret of how to defeat the giants and win the girl's freedom. Or the Cherokee tale of Spearfinger, a terrible witch who slays people with bone finger as sharp as a knife and then eats them and whose skin is as hard and impenetrable as granite, and who, in her fury, is about to destroy an entire village because they dared oppose her. But out of the dark sky a tiny bird appears, the sacred Chickadee, and alights for the briefest moment on the witch's clenched fist, the fist from which protrudes the spear-like finger. A warrior taking this for a sign shoots his arrow through her hand, whereupon she gives a great cry and falls dead upon the ground, her fist falling open to reveal her vulnerable heart, pierced through by the arrow. Then there is the hobbit Bilbo who fled in complete darkness down a tunnel under the Misty Mountains, when he puts his hand down to find...

I struggle every day to make sense of the modern world. Wars that never end, the wanton destruction of the environment, ever-expanding economic inequality, school shootings, overcrowded prisons, political corruption; everywhere I look it seems to me that the things I cherish most are being torn down and thrown away. Evangelical Christians and students of the Mayan calendar assure us we are in the End Times and that the toil and fierce determination of our ancestors to leave something for posterity has been for naught. But then, for just a brief moment, the veil is pulled aside, and I see that everything is connected—the past, the present, and the future, the worlds of matter and spirit. And gurgling and spilling through this glorious Reality, like the creek beside the church where we worked to dig a grave in solidarity, is love. In those moments when I fear I am stumbling blindly through life, I realize we are not alone. There is a helping hand, a faithful guide.

And just when I think I have come to the end of my quest, I discover more. I email Bert Barnes, my newfound cousin, whose sister I met at the Homewood Library presentation in Pittsburgh. We exchange a flurry of messages, attaching photographs and sketches of evolving family trees, and ultimately set up a time to talk on the phone. I learn from Bert that my great-grandfather Albert Bernard McHugh who lived in Connellsville, Pennsylvania, died tragically as a young man. Bert isn't sure of the details—his family was reluctant to talk about it—but he thinks it was the result of some kind of industrial accident in Pittsburgh.

Some weeks pass and Bert calls me back with new information about our great-grandfather's death. Bert has been going through old newspaper accounts and court records, and we wonder if it is possible that Albert McHugh was murdered. The records and accounts and a book titled *The Laws of Innkeepers* provided a fairly detailed sketch of what happened.

In 1892, Albert McHugh sold a hotel in Latrobe, Pennsylvania, for which he was paid in cash. He then went to Pittsburgh allegedly to buy another business, perhaps another hotel. He checked into the Schlosser Hotel on January 30th and paid for lodging for a single night. The next day, he complained of being ill and spent the next two days mostly in bed. He requested a physician and one came to the hotel, examined him, and prescribed him medicine.

Albert also ordered several drinks, and later, according to the court testimony of the hotel owner John Schlosser, an empty liquor bottle was found in his room. By Monday morning, Albert appeared bewildered, and he began wandering up and down the hallway on the floor where he was staying. Around noon a housekeeper found him sitting half-dressed on the edge of a bed in someone else's room. Schlosser became angry and accused Albert of being drunk. He told Albert that he couldn't stay in the hotel any longer, and, according to Schlosser, my great-grandfather replied, "I'll git!"

The hotel porter named Mr. Powers, following Schlosser's orders, took Albert down the freight elevator and pushed him out into the alley that ran behind the hotel. Rain was falling and the day was cold, a stream of water and melting snow running down the alley. According to the police report, Albert was without "overshoes, overcoat, or wraps of any description. His coat was open, he had no vest, and his shoes were untied." The porter attempted to guide Albert down the alley toward Penn Avenue, but Albert collapsed on the pavement. A woman passing by noticed what was going on and went to find a policeman. The policeman, an Officer White, asked the porter what was the matter and he told the policeman that Albert was drunk. The policeman then asked my great-grandfather what was going on and he said, "Officer, I'm not drunk, I'm sick. I wish you would get me an ambulance and have me taken to the hospital."

The policeman went to the patrol box and called for an ambulance, but it took the ambulance more than thirty minutes to get there. All that time, Albert lay on his back on the pavement outside the hotel in the snow and rain. Eventually, he was lifted onto a stretcher and placed in the ambulance and carried off, first to police headquarters, and then to the hospital. However, "all signs of life had disappeared when he was laid on the hospital floor." The post-mortem examination determined that the cause of death was "valvular disease of the heart." Albert McHugh was only thirty-eight years old.

My great-grandmother, Mary McHugh, was devastated when the news reached her of her husband's death back in Connellsville. The money Albert had on him from the sale of the Latrobe hotel was never found, and she suspected foul play. Had someone drugged her husband? All the same, what could she do?

The hotel owner, John Schlosser, maintained that her husband was a drunkard and he denied any knowledge of missing funds. The only recourse left to Mary was to sue the hotel owner, arguing that Schlosser's decision to eject her husband from the hotel when he was sick, not drunk, thus subjecting him to inclement weather had caused his death. She won the case in a lower court along with an award in $6,175 for damages, but John Schlosser appealed the ruling and the case eventually worked its way up to the Pennsylvania Supreme Court where it was decided again in Mary McHugh's favor. The court, however, vacated the $6,175 award, judging that Mr. McHugh's precarious health made his earning potential in the future uncertain, so Mary got nothing. On the bright side, the case, *McHugh v Schlosser*, was a precedent-setting case that to this day prescribes the responsibilities innkeepers, restaurant owners, and railroads have for their customers, especially when there is evidence that a customer is ill.

Beside the bizarre nature of the story, several details stand out for me. One is that my grandfather Edward was born in 1888 and his father Albert died at the beginning of 1891, which meant Papa was between two and three years old at the time of the tragedy, not much older than I was when my father died. And like my own mother, his mother Mary McHugh never remarried. I imagine the sorrow and stress she had to cope with in the aftermath of Albert's death were at times overwhelming, not to mention the cost of legal proceedings for a family that had lost its primary breadwinner.

As I have said, Papa was one of the gentlest and kindest men I have ever known, a man devoid of bitterness or ill humor. I would give much to know what support structure there was for him when he was a vulnerable young child in the weeks and months following his father's death. Did other family members step in to help, or perhaps neighbors? I also think about his situation years later, when he was an adult and a father, and was forced to endure the loss of two young daughters to spinal meningitis and a grown son to polio. It only adds to the admiration I have for the man.

As the weeks pass, a speculation begins to meander its way through the back alleys of my mind. Is there, perhaps, a connection of sorts between my mother's story about my father's death, Gail Lee's story about her father's death, and this last tale of woe concerning the death of my great-grandfather Albert McHugh? Each death was tragic, a young man with a wife and children cut down unexpectedly in the prime of life. There are philosophers and religious mystics who tell us that each human being has an immortal soul and it is the soul that decides when and where a person will be born. The choice is made because there is some essential task or wisdom to be learned in that particular time and place that is essential to the soul's journey through eternity. Reincarnation is a variation of this belief. And so it must follow, if the soul decides when it will enter this world, it must play a part in deciding when it leaves this world.

Much has been written about the stages of loss and grief. After denial and isolation comes anger. The person left behind is angry because the spouse, child, parent, or sweetheart has "chosen" to depart and has abandoned those who linger in the world of the living with the hurt of promises unfulfilled and dreams unrealized. Of cours, this surge of anger is not a rational reaction to death, and yet anger often dominates the emotions following such a tragedy. If not dealt with in some way, this witch's brew of hostility and resentment eats its way like an acid into the spiritual tissue of the survivor's heart and mind. And the more untimely the death, the more seemingly senseless the loss, the more the anger is amplified. The words of our pastor or rabbi telling us that this is the will of God and it is not for us to question that will provide cold comfort. We ache for something more, a story at least that can absolve the deceased of blame, remove the decision to die, as it were, out of his or her hands.

In my mother's case, it wasn't just polio that caused my father to die. Had he wanted to live enough, he would have fought the virus. Others did. But no, there was a curse. They both had dismissed as childish the folk superstition that black opals bring bad luck but, in the end, it was the opal that tipped the scales against my father surviving the onslaught of polio. Gail Lee's father did not die in the fire because he was afraid to jump from a three-story window. Someone had tied him to the bed. And because of this story, Dorothy and her two children, Gail Lee and Buddy, became estranged from Helen's family. When I asked how to contact Gail Lee, no one in Helen's family could tell me. And Albert McHugh wasn't a derelict husband who died because he went on a bender and was justifiably thrown out of his hotel. No, someone slipped him a mickey and, while he stumbled about in a drugged, delirious state, someone stole his money.

I have spent years recording family stories and I am always fascinated by this human need to turn an apparently chance event into part of a deeper mythic story. This process is at the heart of all good literature and why good literature speaks to us the way it does. If absent-minded Uncle Billy doesn't lose the bank payment, then George Bailey won't meet Clarence and learn that it is, after all, a wonderful life.

700 Devonshire Street

Father and Aunt Nancy
dressed for costume
party

Patrick McGraw Wool Company mill

McHugh Family visiting Ireland in the 1930s
My father, Papa, Nana, Maryann, & Nancy

Helen in Pittsburgh

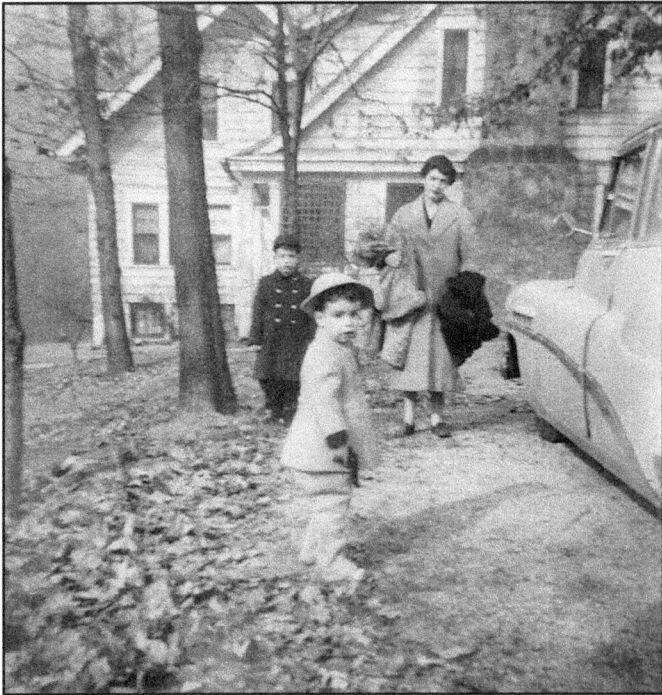
Ted, Joe, and Mom at Shady Lane house

# CHAPTER 23

## ST. MARY CHURCH

Several weeks after my last conversation with my cousin Bert, I receive a phone call from Robin Bowers, a librarian at the Brunswick Public Library. I talked to Robin a few months back when I was looking for information on Meir Kaplon.

"I came across an article in the Frederick newspaper I thought you might be interested in," she tells me with the tone of an intelligence agent sharing classified material with a fellow operative. "It's about a woman named Connie Koenig. She's a local historian and she wrote and published a history of St. Mary parish in Petersville. Isn't that where your Helen is buried?"

I tell her it is.

"I'll send you a link to the article. Maybe you can get in touch with her. She might have some information for your book."

I find Connie, who lives in Brunswick, and we talk for some time on the telephone. She tells me she is a close friend of Estella Belt, and that they meet monthly at a restaurant for lunch.

"Estella was a great help with my book," Connie tells me.

"I'll be in Virginia next month, giving a talk," I reply. "Perhaps I could drive up to Maryland and meet you. I'd like to interview you about the history of St. Mary and anything else you can tell me about Shady Lane."

A month later I am sitting in Connie's kitchen. Paula is with me, and Connie's husband Al, a retired engineer, has joined us as well. Connie shows us her book. On the cover is a photograph taken in 1916 of a young black woman wearing a high-collared white uniform, sitting on a bench next to a small white child in a dress and bonnet. The title is: *As It Was in the Beginning, Is Now, and Can Be*, which Connie explains comes from the *Gloria Patri* of the Catholic Mass, an expression of praise sung to the Holy Trinity.

"I want to propose a trade," Connie says. "I'll give you a signed copy of my book if you promise to give me a signed copy of your book when it gets published."

I can't decide if Connie is a woman of faith or a gambler, but I happily agree to the trade and begin our interview.

"What got you interested in local history?" I ask.

"The Brunswick Railroad Museum downtown hired me to be their director, and we started establishing a history of the town, and it became very important to me, being a farmer's daughter, that the common people would be recognized in that history. The common people of the museum were the Civil War picket guards, the C & O canalers, the laborers who built the railroad, and the locomotive engineers."

"Were you born and raised in Frederick County?"

"No, my husband and I are both from Nebraska. We moved here in 1972 and joined St. Mary. It's an old church. The original building dates back to 1826, and I just love its history and its beauty. It was designed by Jesuit missionaries who came to this area. The founder was Governor Thomas Sim Lee, who was the first governor of Maryland after the Articles of Confederation. Lee was a Catholic, and he founded the church for his family and his slaves. By the early 1800s, he owned as many as two hundred slaves. In fact, he was the largest slaveholder in Frederick County. And being Catholic, I was always fascinated by the fact that he was Catholic and also owned slaves. This didn't compute for me. But I didn't have time to do the research because we were raising a family and I was working, and then later I went back to graduate school."

"So what finally got you to write a history of the church?"

"After I retired, the deacon of St. Mary said the church needed a new history. He just wanted me to write up a one-page history, you know, how the church came to be, that kind of thing. So I asked him for any histories that were written on the church in the past and newspaper articles and so on, and I started reading these things. And it didn't sit well with me. Something wasn't quite right. There were rumors and other stories passed on orally that didn't fit with the written record. So I decided to put everything aside and start from scratch, do my own research. Little did I know how much work that was going to be."

"Where did you start?"

"The most credible place is the land records office at the county, but then I found information written in Latin and some in German in the archives of the Maryland Society of Jesus at Georgetown University. It turns out our priest today cannot translate Latin, so some of the letters I found remain untranslated. The only one I was able to get translated was a German one."

"What role did the slaves play in the church?"

"There were free blacks, the slaves, and the aristocrats who owned the slaves. The early histories, however, only talked about the aristocrats, would say in passing, 'by the way, there were slaves who built the church.' You know, just one sentence. So I wanted to flesh out that history. I wanted to know more about the people who built the church and those who descended from them.

"Fortunately, a member of the Lee family has done extensive research on her family and she helped me with both the aristocrats and the slaves. Also, as I told you, I've been good friends with Estella Belt from the early days when I was the museum director and she was a docent."

I describe my first meeting with Estella and how gracious she was.

"Estella's a remarkable person," Connie agrees, "a very spiritual person, and quite special. She's always been interested in her own history and very willingly shares what she knows. It's mostly oral history. So between the two of us—my ability to research the documents and her ability to remember the oral stories—and her trusting me to do a good job, and then her introducing me to other black people who could tell me these stories, we got the book done. It was a process. You have to establish a trust before people will actually tell you their stories, and tell you the real stories, not just the one you want to hear. It's a process and it's not simple."

Connie laughs. "It's very convoluted sometimes, and I am also a believer in being inspired by the Holy Spirit. Some things just work that way. There's no other explanation, except that this information somehow comes and one little piece is just what you need, and it had to be that way."

"Can you give me an example of what you're talking about?" I ask Connie, thinking about my own moments of serendipity.

"I was looking for an old history written by a man named Stanton, and I was trying to find a copy of his book on the Internet. Of course, this is something Estella can't do, but I can, and I found a copy at a university in Canada. It was a situation where you can look at the book online and flip the pages. So I was flipping through the pages, and it was all about the early churches in Frederick County. Then I came to St. Mary in Petersville, and there were all kinds of handwritten notes in the margins that I was able to zoom in on, and it was all this information I did not know, and would never have known if this person had not written it in the margins. It turns out he was working for the archdiocese in the early 1900s, and he had knowledge of all of these priests and all of these churches. He knew when they were built, and who built them—all of this stuff that wasn't actually in the book. It was like he was editing the book. He'd cross out a date and write another date in the margin and say, 'This is the right date.' It was just a wealth of information. How this book ended up in a university in Canada, and how I found it, is just a miracle to me."

Again Connie laughs.

"And if I hadn't done the research on this book, I wouldn't have known about Estella's grandmother and her great-grandfather Othello."

Connie goes on to explain that Frederick County recently built a new park, and they asked local historians to propose a name for the park.

"I wanted the park named after a slave named Othello who, from everything I read, was a remarkable person. Even though he was a slave, he was educated and did a lot for the community. So I wrote the historical brief and submitted it—twenty other people submitted their names—and eventually Othello was chosen. Then we started this project, and Estella had no idea that Othello was her great-grandfather until we put this intermediate history together from the Lee family, which said that Othello was Julia's father, and Estella knew that Julia was her grandmother. So we put two and two together and we got back that far. With black families, it's especially difficult to trace their roots."

"What was so special about Othello?" I love the name.

"I came across the wills of the aristocrats—I'm calling them aristocrats; to name them, the Lee family is who they were—and each of their wills would list their slaves by first name only, because they were considered property. So you could count the number of slaves in the will, and Othello was singled out as being special because he was sold to William Lee's daughter for $400. Mr. Lee made a special effort to make sure that Othello would stay in the family, and so she [Mr. Lee's daughter] bought him. I really believe Othello was his son. That happened also. Estella's not sure and you can't really tell unless you do a DNA test. But oftentimes in these wills, when a black slave was singled out and taken into the household as a house slave or given special training, or, in Othello's case, made sure that the daughter took care of him, they were actually descendants of the slaveholder. I suspect Othello was too, but we don't know that for sure."

"So why do you think Helen was Catholic?" I ask, remembering that Estella is a Catholic as well.

"In this county there were two main slaveholders. There was Governor Thomas Sim Lee and Charles Carrol of Carrolton and both those gentlemen were Catholics. The slaveholder would bring up his slaves in the same religion he was. It didn't matter what the slaves' former culture was, or if they had a religion, or were brought over from Africa; they were trained in the religion of their slaveholder just as a parent would teach their children the religion they were. It was very much a parental kind of relationship between the slaveholders and the slave because the slaveholders believed that black people were not capable of taking care of themselves."

Connie tells me about a Jesuit priest named Father John Gaffney who was born in County Langford, Ireland, in 1827 and came to Frederick County as a young man. He served as pastor for many of the churches in the area, riding from one parish to another on a pony named Harry, the priest's long legs nearly touching the ground. One of these churches was St. Mary in Petersville. When the Civil War ended, Fr. Gaffney became concerned with the plight of the newly emancipated slaves. He believed they needed help acquiring land to build homes and raise gardens. He also wanted to create a community of black Catholics.

In 1872, he took five acres of the church's property, previously part of the Lee plantation, and subdivided it into ten half-acre plots. He called this strip of land "Church Alley," but over time it became known as Shady Lane. The next year, Fr. Gaffney opened a school for black children next to St. Mary. A hundred children attended this school, one of the first black schools in Frederick County, and it continued in operation until 1912, after which it is no longer mentioned in church records. In all likelihood, there are two reasons the school was shuttered. One is that the Jesuit missionaries turned over their churches to the Archdiocese of

Baltimore before leaving the county in 1902 to move to their new headquarters in Poughkeepsie, New York.

At the same time, the Ku Klux Klan gained strength in western Maryland. Connie believes the combination of anti-Catholic and anti-black sentiment proved too much for church leaders, and they gave up on the school. After that, the black members of St. Mary were relegated to second-class status. At Mass, they were prohibited from sitting in the front and center pews, and were forced to sit to the sides and rear of the church. They were graciously permitted to work the church picnics, but were not allowed to attend them as equals. This atrocious state of affairs continued well into the 1960s.

After the interview, Al Koenig invites us out to dinner. Connie calls Estella and she agrees to join us. Over our meal, Estella tells us more stories about Helen and about the months she worked for my grandparents in Pittsburgh. It is clear that Connie and Estella share a genuine friendship, having found a way to overcome a legacy of racial separation, discrimination, and suspicion that was passed down from one generation to the next since the founding of our nation.

# CHAPTER 24

*SAYING FAREWELL*

The idea that Helen's grave needs a headstone grows stronger as time wears on. Each time I think fate has revealed the final serendipitous connection between two women and a child, I am startled by some new discovery.

My brother then comes to visit us. To celebrate his retirement from the New Jersey Bar, he has spent the previous week sailing the San Juan Islands with his buddies. As he gets ready to leave, he asks if I am still thinking about purchasing a headstone for Helen's grave.

"Yes. Paula and I would like to do that and the sooner the better," I tell him.

"Well, I'm happy to help with the cost. I'd also like to be there when you have it placed."

I call Connie Koenig and ask if she can recommend a local monument company. I call the owner and we discuss varieties of stone and how monuments are shaped and graded. I tell him that we would like to include an oval portrait of Helen on the headstone, and he tells me about a company that fires photographs into porcelain and that, if I order one, he will carve a relief into the stone and use a special epoxy to secure it there.

However, there is a problem with dates. Estella told me that Helen died in the early 1960s, but she wasn't sure exactly when. As for Helen's birth, the year varied according to which census records I consulted. According to the 1900 census documents,

Helen was four years old at the dawn of the twentieth century. Thus she was born in 1896. But in the 1910 census, she is listed as being fifteen years old, which would make her birth-year 1895. The 1920 census agrees with the record from 1910 and lists Helen's age as twenty-five. I really want the stone-carved date on Helen's monument to be correct. More digging, and I locate Helen's official Social Security death record. But here I make another discovery: Helen's birthdate is August 8, 1894. August 8 is my youngest daughter Clara's birthday. This means that my three daughters were born on the three birthdays of the three women who are most significant to my quest. My oldest daughter, Anna, was born on Gail Lee's birthday, Emily, my middle daughter, was born on my mother's birthday, and now I have learned that Clara, my youngest, was born on Helen's birthday.

The unlikelihood of this coincidence takes possession of most my thinking in the following days with images of Jimmy the Greek hunched over his desk in Los Vegas clutching a number 2 pencil and feverishly scribbling equations on a yellow legal pad, so he can offer odds on a bet involving six women from two families sharing the same birthdates. I go so far as to call a friend of mine who teaches physics at the University of Virginia. His name is Dr. Louis Bloomfield and he was my chief advisor on a novel I wrote about the energy industry and the physics of time titled *Kilowatt*. He also hosted a television series on the Discovery Channel called *How Things Work* and taught my daughter Anna physics classes when she was in college.

"I can give you the probability at the most basic level," he says in his perpetually chipper and amused tone. "The math is pretty straightforward. Of course, you are not taking into account how significant the individuals are to each other or to your story. That would increase the odds considerably. Let me get back to you."

Two hours later, Lou sends me this email:

*"Imagine you go into a casino and the house first chooses three different dates, D, E, and F at random from among the 365 dates in a normal year. You then choose three different dates—A, B, and C— at random, using a set of three enormous dice, each with 365 faces for each day of the year. To ensure that all three dates are different, you must re-roll any die that duplicates another die.*

*To win, A, B, and C must match D, E, and F in any order. For example, if A=D, B=E, and C=F, you win. Or if A=E, B=F, and C=D, you also win.*

*The Odds: 6 in 48,228,180 or 1 in 8,038,030.*

*Explanation: For simplicity, let's have you roll your dice one at a time. It makes no difference how you roll your dice, but it helps the explanation. First you roll die A. It randomly chooses one date from among 365 possibilities. Second you roll die B. It also randomly chooses one date from among 365 possibilities, but you must re-roll it if it duplicates A. So it really only chooses one date from among 364 possibilities (all the dates that are not A). Third you roll die C. It chooses 1 date from among 363 possibilities (all the dates that are not A or B).*

*The number of possible arrangements of A, B, and C together is thus 365 x 364 x 363 = 48,228,180.*

*Now it's time to see if you have won. You compare A to D, E, and F. If A matches any one of those three dates, you win. Next you compare B, to the remaining two dates (A already matched one of the house's dates). If B matches any one of those two dates, you win. Lastly, you compare C to the remaining date (A and B have already matched two of the house's dates). If C matches that last date, you win.*

*So there are actually 3 x 2 x 1 = 6 arrangements of A, B, and C that are winners.*

*Thus, of the 48,228,180 different possible arrangements of A, B, and C, there are six winning arrangements. So the odds of winning are: 6 in 48,228,180 or 1 in 8,038,030.*

*Those are seriously long odds, even if you are cherry picking in a vast land of possible coincidences. A lifetime is something like 30,000 days, so you'd have to "roll the dice" about 130 times a day every day of your life to have about a 50% chance of winning this game just once. You'd have to look around you for a crazy coincidence every 5 or 10 minutes just to have a 50:50 shot at winning once in your lifetime. The odds are so long that, even if you "play" frequently, you're still not likely to win.*

*It's similar to winning a state lottery—they have odds somewhere in the 1 in 10 million range so even people who play regularly (several tickets a week) are still extremely unlikely to win in their lifetime."*

I met a woman while giving a talk in California who has been after me for nearly a year to record the stories of her parents. The parents live in Pittsburgh, and they are well into their nineties. So a plan takes shape: Paula and I will fly to Pittsburgh, record the interviews, and then drive down to Petersville, Maryland, for a ceremony to place a headstone on Helen's grave. I contact Estella and several of Helen's grandchildren to make sure they have no objections to us providing Helen with a headstone. On the contrary, they appreciate the gesture. Given the distance between Olympia and Petersville, and my lack of knowledge about such matters, I call Connie Koenig and she offers to serve as the local contact for the monument company and to work with St. Mary Church to locate, if possible, where Helen is buried. She tells me that she plans to ask Estella to walk the grounds, because Estella said that she is pretty sure she remembers where Helen was buried.

The stop in Pittsburgh will also allow Paula and me to visit my old house on Shady Lane and my grandparents' house on Devonshire Street. The owners of both houses have generously agreed to give us tours, and I am particularly keen to check out the pair of matching stained-glass windows inside the Devonshire House.

Paula and I visit the house on Devonshire Street and find the windows with their eight-pointed stars, but I cannot return to the magical wonderland of my childhood that existed on the third floor because it no longer exists. The Reigels traded the space for a cathedral ceiling for the master bedroom when they renovated the house.

Our visit to the Shady Lane house in Fox Chapel brings its own child's parade of memories. The owner Liz tells me that a whacked-out drug dealer during the 1980s barricaded himself inside the house during an armed standoff with the police. She says there is a bullet hole in the ceiling to prove it.

As Liz tells me this macabre tale, I recall the film footage my Uncle George took outside the Shady Lane house shortly after my father's death. I am a rambunctious three-year-old armed with a pair of chrome six-shooters, blasting away at everything in sight: my brother, my grandparents, even the guy behind the camera. Come and get me, coppers!

It is Saturday, October 5th, 2013. We check into the Best Western in Frederick, and a few minutes later my brother arrives from New Jersey. My two youngest daughters cannot be with us: Emily is doing a college semester abroad studying Spanish and politics in Chile, and our youngest, Clara, is at home in Olympia finishing up her last year of high school. However, Kathy, a dear friend and Clara's godmother, has driven down from Connecticut to join us, as has my daughter Anna, my son Patrick, and his wife Rebecca, who drove up together from North Carolina. Rebecca is seven months pregnant with what will be my first grandchild. They have come to honor Helen, and tomorrow we will gather at the cemetery at St. Mary Church in Petersville to dedicate a headstone for Helen's grave.

We stop in Brunswick on our way to Frederick to take in their annual railroad festival. I learn that the downtown firehouse where my search for Helen's family began in Brunswick has closed. I also discover, much to my dismay, that the helpful fireman, Ronnie Lowe, has passed away. This news shocks me, because he was not an old man. I find myself reflecting on the nature of time, something I did when I first visited Brunswick four years ago, about how our stories are like boats in which we float down the river of time and, even after our hearts stop and our brains go still, our stories continue their journey down to the sea we call God.

Sunday dawns warm and sunny. By the time we pull into the church parking lot, the heat is stifling. Connie and Al Koenig stand beneath the shade of a stately maple at the edge of the cemetery to greet us and then take us to a house next to the church. The building was once the rectory, but now it serves as the parish hall. This is where people gather, and Paula lays out a table with refreshments. Soon other people begin to arrive.

The monument company placed the headstone earlier in the week, but no one has seen it yet. It is a bevel-style marker of light gray granite engraved with the year Helen was born and the year she died. There is also an oval ceramic photograph of Helen made from the photograph Estella showed me the first time we met. In the photograph, Helen is wearing a broad straw hat and is beaming a smile. The inscription next to the photograph reads: A MOTHER TO MANY, KNOW YOU ARE REMEMBERED AND LOVED.

One of the first to show up at St. Mary is Timmy Jackson. He is wearing a short-sleeved shirt, and his arms are covered in scars from burns he received on the night the house in Brunswick caught fire back in 1952, when he was forced to jump from a third-story window to save himself. He is accompanied by his daughter, Vivian Jackson. She lives in nearby Harper's Ferry and works for the U.S. Department of Energy. She is also an ordained minister.

Next, Estella arrives, as well as a woman named Vanessa Williams. Vanessa lives in Shady Lane, which is just on the other side of the cemetery. Several more people also show up. There are introductions and people share their stories. Before we go to Helen's grave, I show a home movie that features a few seconds of Helen Spriggs. One scene was filmed outside our house in Shady Lane in Pittsburgh and another shows Helen serving a magnificent Thanksgiving Day turkey to my family at my aunt and uncle's house in Paterson. This sparks a lively conversation about Helen, with several people commenting on the size of the turkey, which, now that they mention it, is enormous.

At last we brave the heat and humidity and gather at the gravesite where Helen's headstone has been placed. Connie walked the grounds of the cemetery with Estella and the current cemetery custodian earlier in the week, and she is confident that the stone is placed very near, if not on, the spot where Helen is buried. Connie also produces two-dozen red roses and hands a rose to each person as we leave the chapter house so we can place them on the grave. There are two young boys in the group: Helen's great-great-nephews, and one of them wants to keep the rose. Who can blame him? The roses are beautiful.

As we approach the grave, I find myself thinking about the home movie. I have watched it numerous times and never considered the fact that, even though Helen is smiling for the camera—everyone is smiling for the camera, come to that—after she serves the turkey and dressing and mashed potatoes and cranberry sauce, she will go back into the kitchen and eat her Thanksgiving Day meal alone, by herself, at the kitchen table. Her own children and grandchildren were hundreds of miles away. It was that way for all the holidays, because that is when we needed her services the most. I wonder how much loneliness and longing she suffered because she couldn't be with her own family.

Gathered at the gravesite, Estella speaks about Miss Helen.

"She was my mother-in-law. People don't say much about your mother-in-law, you know, but she was a *good* mother-in-law. She was a hard worker, taking care of her children."

"And everyone else's children," someone adds.

"Well, that's true," Estella says. "And she would do things that surprised me. When I'd come home from work sometimes, they'd all been there doing things, and she changed my bedroom around once." This makes Estella laugh. "I didn't really appreciate it, but that was okay. That was Miss Helen. It was her house so you did what you were supposed to do to keep her happy. But she really was a wonderful, wonderful woman. And we'd go places together. One time James got a little too much to drink and we were over the mountain to John Brown's Farm at a dance and he couldn't drive and she said to me, 'Get in there, baby, and drive." And I said, 'I can't drive.' But she said, 'If you run out of gas, pull over on the side of the road until he wakes up. Serves him right." Estella and everyone laughs. "But we went on down through Frederick and come around and finally found home. But she was a good woman. I meant to bring a little bottle of holy water but some day I'll get up here and sprinkle it over her grave."

Then my brother says a few words about Helen and her importance to both of us.

"I did the math this morning, and Helen joined us in 1949. I was born in 1947, so I was a toddler at that point. And she returned to Maryland in 1956 or 1957. So she was with us, or we were with her is probably the more likely scenario, for less than ten years, and yet we're here now, fifty-six years later, and we're here because of our memory of her. And the memory survived of that short period of time she was with us, that relatively short period of time, still her memory, at least I know for myself and for Joe and obviously for her family here, is a testimony to how good a woman she was. And we should live lives that have people remember us that many years later. And she certainly deserved that.

"Now in our situation, we remember her essentially as the great woman she was, but also as a mother, a surrogate mother, because it is my understanding from what Joe has told me, that before she came to Pittsburgh and started to work for us, she had had tragedy in her own life. In fact I understand she had been widowed more than once."

"Three times," Estella adds.

"So here she arrives in this young family," Ted continues, "and if you saw the film that was being shown, it's my mother and my father, my younger brother Joe, and myself a little bit older, and a baby on the way, Patrick. And we had the world on a string. And I'm sure Helen must have thought, 'How are they so lucky? I haven't been so lucky.'

"But there was never any resentment or anything of that sort. Then what should happen, in the middle of that, is this double tragedy: my father's death and then shortly thereafter, our young brother's death. And my recollection is that my mother went into mourning and we were very vulnerable at that time. And Helen stood right in the breach, her experience, her understanding being of what mourning was, how it could affect you, she became a surrogate mother for us for at least several months. She was always—and I don't want to use the term a maid—but she was always a maid, and in that period of time when we were probably the most vulnerable, she stepped in and she did it calmly. I remember there was no sense of terror in the household. She filled in that gap."

Estella, who is standing next to me, leans close and says, "She told me she rocked your mother in her arms as your mother cried and cried."

Meanwhile, Ted continues. "And we got through it, and we got through it because Helen was there. After my mother got through her mourning, my mother and Helen continued on. They became best friends. We were in Pittsburgh and then Helen came with us to New Jersey. Then she had to return home. I guess we heard from Estella that she had some medical problems."

"She had a sore on her side," Estella points to her side just under her right arm, "and they took her to John Hopkins and opened the sore, but it never healed."

"Well, what that deprived Joe and myself, and we were little boys at that time, and also my mother I think, and that's probably more important, was the opportunity to say, 'Thank you' to her. To tell her to her face what an important person she was in our lives, how she held us up in a moment of real tragedy. And then beyond, becoming a mother in a certain sense to our cousins and all other family members during parties and things of that sort. So we didn't have that opportunity. And yet through Joe's efforts, we've not only found where she lies, we found her relatives and it gives us the opportunity, this fifty-six years later, to say, 'Thank you.'

"And you mentioned she was very religious and I remember when we were in Pittsburgh, we lived out in the suburbs, so she couldn't get to church, at least I don't think she could, I don't think she drove, and where we were in Pittsburgh I don't think there were the churches she would have gone to. But there was the radio, and they used to have the Sunday services and I remember as a little boy listening to the services, listening to the preacher who was, let's say, chewing the crowd out. And then came the music and you could hear the gospel singers and you'd hear Helen singing. She could sing. And so I'm confident she believed in everlasting life and that she has gone to her reward and is here with us today. And I hope that she appreciates that, while we delayed our thanks and appreciation, we now have the opportunity to say, 'Thank you Helen, Helen Spriggs, for what you've done for Joe and myself, for our family, and for your family.'"

I have my violin and I follow Ted's remarks by playing a solo fiddle tune for Helen that comes from an old shape-note hymn from the Appalachian Mountains. It is a hauntingly beautiful melody titled "Queen of the Earth, Child of the Skies." When I finish, Vivian Jackson, Timmy Jackson's daughter, leads us in a short prayer. She then asks us to join hands, and she leads us in singing "Amazing Grace."

Time passes. People begin to depart in groups of twos and threes. During the ceremony, a refreshing breeze began to blow, strong enough to shake the branches of the proud old oak that stands in the middle of the cemetery, a descendant of the oaks hewed for the church's pillars in days past. The temperature cooled as well, allowing us to enjoy the pleasant autumn afternoon and the leaves delight our eyes with splashes of red and gold.

Paula takes some group photographs of our family and one of Ted and me kneeling next to Helen's grave. Anna, Patrick, and Rebecca are driving back to Raleigh and my brother is heading down to Florida to help his son, young Ted, move into a new apartment.

Everyone says goodbye and, after they leave, Paula and I spend a few moments with Estella. She mentions she is having trouble with her vision and her doctor thinks it has something to do with her brain. Connie is driving her down to Georgetown University Hospital in Washington, DC, in a few days so the doctors can run some tests.

I can tell Estella is worried but she continues to make little jokes and tell us how much Helen would have appreciated the headstone and everyone being there.

Considering Estella's age and health challenges, I recall a recent conversation I had with a friend. Her mother was dying of cancer and the local hospice organization sent a woman to the house to help care for her. The woman's name, if I remember correctly, was Selena and she was from Jamaica. My friend described Selena as "an angel of compassion." She said the family was grateful beyond measure for the kindly way Selena cared for her mother during those last, trying days of her life.

How many other families, I wonder, have had a similar experience, a woman appears in their midst to help with the passing of a loved one? She might be African-American or a recent immigrant from the Caribbean or African, the Philippines or Guatemala. She does the jobs no one else wants to do, or that are too emotionally painful to do: she changes diapers, administers morphine, washes bed sores, cuts hoary toenails. But more than that, she emanates a kind of gentle soul energy that the suffering person and the distressed family can draw upon for comfort and spiritual strength. I am enough of a realist to know this is not always the case, but I suspect it happens far more often than most people realize.

Life is a house with two doors: we come in the front door and go out the back. Helen was there to greet me when I came in the front door, a lump of vulnerable need, and she changed my diapers and washed my infected feet and fed me pureed sweet peas. She sang to me and tried to make me smile. And there are women like Helen who stand near the back door doing much the same kind of sacred work, helping our parents and then us as we get ready to leave this life, vulnerable and needy again. These women are far more than hired help; they are angels sent to us by God and we are in their debt.

Meanwhile, Connie and Al and their daughter have straightened up and locked the parish house, and they join us as we say our goodbyes to Estella on the walkway leading up to the church. Paula and I have a four-hour drive to Pittsburgh in front of us. From there, we will fly home to Olympia.

The memory of my grandfather, Poppy, and Joe Walls comes to mind. When the fun of the evening was over at Aunt Kate's or at some other family gathering, and friends and family members were putting on their hats and coats and getting ready to leave, Poppy would sing a certain song. It was a sentimental song titled "For All We Know," and Joe would accompany him on the piano. It made us sad, but we loved that song and everyone would stay until Poppy was finished, some of us, like my mother and Aunt Ruth, joining in for the last lines.

Here are the words as I remember them.

> *"For all we know, we may never meet again,*
> *Before you go, make this moment sweet again.*
> *We won't say goodbye, until the last minute,*
> *I'll hold out my hand, and my heart will be in it.*

*For all we know, this may only be a dream,*
*We come and go, like the ripples on a stream.*
*So kiss me tonight, tomorrow was meant for some,*
*Tomorrow may never come,*
*For all we know."*

Gathering of friends and family for dedication of Helen's headstone
St. Mary Catholic Church in Peterville, MD. - October 6, 2013
Front row L to R: Michael Williams, Gladys Weedon, Claritha Jackson,
Estella Belt, and James (Timmy) Jackson
Middle row: Clarice Henderson, Vanessa Williams, Anna McHugh, Kathy Peck,
Rebecca Bossen McHugh, Connie Koenig, Vivian Jackson, and Frances Moddy
Back row: Joe McHugh, Paula McHugh, Ed (Ted) McHugh,
Patrick McHugh, and Al Koenig

McHugh family at Helen's grave

HELEN SPRIGGS
1894 — 1964
A caring mother to many,
know you are loved
and remembered.

# ABOUT THE AUTHOR

Joe McHugh is a traditional storyteller, musician, and award-winning public radio journalist. In 1970, he purchased an eighty-acre farm in Gilmer County, West Virginia, where he raised goats, chickens, and draft horses. He also fell in love with the traditional music and storytelling of the southern Appalachian mountains. He has served as a consultant for numerous government agencies and non-profit organizations including the United States Justice Department, California Department of Education, National Council of Family Court and Juvenile Judges, and California School Library Association. His radio work has been featured on numerous public radio stations around the country as well as *Morning Edition, Inside Appalachia*, and *Voice of America*.

He is married to Paula Blasius-McHugh who is a musician and artist. They have performed together at libraries, schools, festivals, and colleges throughout the United States and in England, Scotland, and Ireland.

To learn more about their work, please visit:
www.americanfamilystories.org
www.joemchugh.info
www.timetravelers.info

## BOOKS BY JOE MCHUGH
www.callingcrane.com

SLAYING THE GORGON:
*The Rise of the Storytelling Industrial Complex*

KILOWATT
A novel about the energy industry, global warming, and our troubled relationship with time.

PHANTOM FIDDLER
*and Other Notable Tales*

THE FLYING SANTA:
*A True Story*

RUFF TALES:
*High Octane Stories from the Ruff Creek General Store*

BETTER THAN MONEY:
*Tales to Treasure for a Lifetime*

www.ingramcontent.com/pod-product-compliance
Lightning Source LLC
Chambersburg PA
CBHW021045090426
42738CB00006B/195